DEMCO 38-296

DIAGNOSIS AND TREATMENT OF THE YOUNG MALE VICTIM OF SEXUAL ABUSE

ABOUT THE AUTHOR

William Breer is a Licensed Clinical Social Worker
and Marriage Family and Child Counselor. He is in full
time private practice specializing in male victims of
molestation, adolescent molesters, and male identity
issues. He is board certified in clinical social work,
a member of the American Group Psychotherapy Association, and a Fellow of the Society for Clinical Social
Work. Mr. Breer has previously worked as a probation
officer, a child protective services worker, and as a
therapist for a community mental health clinic.

His undergraduate work and some of his graduate
work was in anthropology with special emphasis on
Latin America. This remains a strong secondary interest.
Mr. Breer is fluent in Spanish and does some therapy in
that language.

DIAGNOSIS AND TREATMENT OF THE YOUNG MALE VICTIM OF SEXUAL ABUSE

By

WILLIAM BREER, MSW

CHARLES C THOMAS • PUBLISHER
Springfield • Illinois • U.S.A.

d Throughout the World by

OMAS • PUBLISHER
2600 South First Street
Springfield, Illinois 62794-9265

© *1992 by* CHARLES C THOMAS • PUBLISHER

ISBN 0-398-05816-4

Library of Congress Catalog Card Number: 92-527

With THOMAS BOOKS *careful attention is given to all details of manufacturing
and design. It is the Publisher's desire to present books that are satisfactory as to
their physical qualities and artistic possibilities and appropriate for their particular
use.* THOMAS BOOKS *will be true to those laws of quality that assure a good
name and good will.*

Printed in the United States of America
SC-R-3

Library of Congress Cataloging-in-Publication Data

Breer, William.
   Diagnosis and treatment of the young male victims of sexual abuse
   / by William Breer.
      p.   cm.
   Includes bibliographical references and index.
   ISBN 0-398-05816-4
   1. Boys—Abuse of.   2. Sexually abused children—Mental health.
3. Sexually abused teenagers—Mental health.   4. Sexually abused
children—Rehabilitation.   5. Sexually abused teenagers—
Rehabilitation.   6. Masculinity (Psychology)   I. Title.
   [DNLM: 1. Child Abuse, Sexual—diagnosis.   2. Child Abuse, Sexual—
therapy.   3. Culture.   4. Gender Identity.   5.   Men—psychology.
6. Psychotherapy—methods.   WA 320 B8315d]
RJ507.S49B74   1992
618.92′8583—dc20
DNLM/DLC
for Library of Congress   92-527
                                                                      CIP

ACKNOWLEDGMENTS

Many people have contributed significantly to the production of this book. Without their help and support, it could not have been written. Perhaps I owe the most to Frits Bruinsma, M. D. It was his invitation to attend the International Congress of Sexology in Amsterdam in 1991 that overcame my resistance to writing this book. I had sworn that I would never attempt another book while engaged in active private practice. Dr. Bruinsma's hospitality and introduction to many people in the active field of sexology and the treatment of sexual abuse overcame my reservations and led, ultimately, to my determination to write about young male victims.

Additionally, Dr. Bruinsma reviewed the entire manuscript and thoughtfully commented on it as it was being prepared. Frits and I have not always agreed, but he has repeatedly drawn my attention to important issues and controversies surrounding the basic concepts within this book. It was he who many years ago got me to thinking about the pivotal role played by the father in the lives of adolescent molesters a concept easily adapted to understanding the male victim.

I also owe a great debt to Loes Knutson and Julie Mason of the I.D.E.A.S. program at the University of California at Riverside. This is a data retrieval service which allowed me to access literature which otherwise would be unavailable to someone operating outside of academia. These two individuals took great interest in the project and were of invaluable assistance in obtaining relavent literature.

Other individuals reviewed specific chapters to offer a "second opinion" from within specialized disciplines or other cultures. The chapter on culture was reviewed by Francisco Montes, a Mexican-American professional in mental health. Vance Norum, M.D. has also been of great assistance. He reviewed the chapter on theory with particular attention to the section on neurobiology and critical periods.

David Glidden, a philosopher at the University of California at Riverside also reviewed the chapter on theory, with particular reference to theory construction, cogency, and the interaction between theory, reality, and practice. My wife, Barbara, helped in myriad ways ranging from reading, reviewing, and reflecting on the material with me to emotional support on a project which at times felt utterly overwhelming.

Although I acknowledge a great debt to everyone who has helped in this project, I must accept responsibility for its final form. Any errors and defects of this work must be attributed to me and not those who helped so generously.

FOREWORD

Perpetrators of sexual violence are not all men, and the victims not always women or girls. Though this is known, sexual violence by men and sexual abuse of women remains at the center of attention. That boys are not the group that first come to mind as victims of sexual violence is probably due to the common notion that boys are well able to overcome or to deny their negative experiences. It is for that reason that boys who have been abused do not speak openly about their secret.

In most Western countries, stereotypes exist concerning the role of the two sexes. Such attitudes can lead to a hostile approach towards minorities such as homosexuals. But confrontation with male vulnerability, such as is the case with sexually abused boys can also be threatening.

It appears from legal reports and from the treatment of sexual delinquents that many of these offenders have themselves been sexually assaulted earlier in life. It is precisely because boys have not learned to talk about what has been done to them that this becomes an important factor in the development from victim to perpetrator.

Boys are much less likely to have a confidant to whom they can talk freely than are girls. That is why they are generally less able to put themselves in the place of another than are females. In particular, sex delinquents have not experienced the empathy for others which might have prevented them from using their power (or lack of it) to create victims.

The victims of sexual violence deserve our full empathy. That is the best place to break the cycle of sexual abuse. It is also an opportunity to grow from victim, to "survivor," to worthy human being. Traumatic experiences can be integrated into the development of personality without their having to lead, once more, to "learned helplessness" or "acting-out" behavior.

In Europe, more attention is generally given to the client's personality than to what has actually been done to him or her. The consequence of this has been that, until recently, we in Europe have not been aware of the full impact of sexual abuse. And until very recently, particularly unaware of this regarding boys.

In the United States, on the contrary, sexual violence has long been at the center of attention. This has led to there being several treatment programs for perpetrators, both adult and adolescent, as well as for victims of all ages and their families. This, however, sometimes blots out the attention to detail which is often necessary for the special person who committed an offence or was the victim of specific abuse.

During one of my visits to the United States, in 1989, I was invited by William Breer from San Bernardino, to be present at a group therapy session for adolescent sex offenders. It struck me how empathetic and modest he was. The youths were surprised when I told them about his first book *The Adolescent Molester.*

Since then I have found my contacts with Bill to be very stimulating. In his psychoanalytic approach, he puts his fatherly empathy into practice. Transference or therapeutically-effective countertransference? His approach to sexually abused boys, as depicted in this book, can certainly contribute to breaking their silence. His involvement can help the victims and the families in their ever ambivalent motivation towards the healing process.

Bill Breer links the cognitive behavior therapy programs in the United States and the more psychodynamicly-oriented approach in Europe. In both continents the goal is the same: reducing the amount of sexual violence as well as the traumatic consequences thereof. As a result of his theoretical base and practically-oriented approach, Bill Breer provides a good insight into the diagnosis and treatment of the young male victim of sexual abuse.

FRITS BRUINSMA, M.D.
Utrecht, The Netherlands

CONTENTS

DIAGNOSIS AND TREATMENT OF THE YOUNG MALE VICTIM OF SEXUAL ABUSE

Chapter 1

INTRODUCTION

This book is written largely for a professional and/or academic audience whose work requires an understanding of the dynamics and treatment of young male victims of sexual abuse in particular and damaged maleness in general. It will probably be of interest to case managers in social service and law enforcement agencies. Many hypotheses rooted in the literature and clinical experience are offered here. It is hoped that they will be of interest to academics and researchers in the fields of sexology and sexual abuse who may use them in designing future research. What I hope any reader will get from this book is a better understanding of how and why being molested affects young males. For practicing clinicians a methodology for repairing the psychic damage done by sexual victimization is offered. Finally, I believe this book will be of interest to any intellectual who is interested in how maleness develops, how it is cultivated, and how male identity is both damaged and repaired.

A uniqueness of this book is the diversity of disciplines from which data is gathered and focused on the specific issues of sexual assault of young males. This is not standard in the field of sex abuse. It may put off some readers. Such lectors are urged to consider the entire work and evaluate carefully information drawn from disciplines such as anthropology and neurology. Input from these disciplines is rarely found in this type of work. Since I am writing outside of my own discipline in these cases, I have asked other professionals to review these chapters (see acknowledgments). I must accept, however, ultimate responsibility for any errors since the content of the final draft was my decision alone. In these sections, I have also followed very closely the content of the sources cited to assure as little as possible loss in translations between disciplines.

In order to write this book, it was necessary to ask very basic questions about the nature of masculinity. The origins of maleness and the vicissitudes of male development became important questions. This inevitably led to issues like: What part of maleness is culturally determined? To what extent is it biologically determined? This led inexorably into the examination of data from anthropology, embryology, neurology, psycho-dynamic psychology, and social learning theory.

Culture is examined a great deal here. If we are to really understand maleness and develop techniques to repair it when it is damaged, it is necessary to look at how it is expressed and nurtured in other cultures. For historical reasons to be explained later, some of the best cultural data comes from the Highlands of New Guinea. The reader will be taken on an armchair tour of that remote area. This material is often hard to believe yet it comes from the most reputable of anthropologists and psychoanalysts.

This Melanesian data is here because it brings into focus issues about maleness in the West. These cultures seems to present in the most pointed possible way the same issues that many men in the West must wrestle with. It implies that some of our deeply held ideas about how masculinity develops and changes are wrong. We will also look at cul-tural variables in the treatment of members of other cultures and subcul-tures living within the borders of modern America. To treat participants of other cultures, clinicians must understand what maleness and its violation mean in the victim's own cultural context. That, too, is explored here.

The reader may be startled by the conclusions and implications of this work as well as the diverse sources from which these conclusions are drawn. I make no secret about relying heavily on my clinical experience with this population. The work also looks extensively into the literature on this population. First this literature is surveyed to see what is known about this population statistically and clinically.

This is accomplished in the literature review proper. Elsewhere other literature particularly from self psychology and neurobiology is woven into later chapters. Neurobiology has offered a theory of why is so terribly difficult to change sexual pathology in *Homo Sapiens,* but also offers insights about how change can be fostered. Self psychology inte-grates well with neurobiology and offers some important suggestions about how and why maleness develops. It also helps with the puzzling problem of how some males survive childhood molestation relatively intact, something recent research suggests is more common than the older literature would have predicted.

The analytic writings of Peter Blos and Phyllis Tyson offer sugges-tions that led me to formulate the central hypothesis of this book: There is a male developmental line with predictable and identifyable stages from infancy to mature manhood. When molestation damages males it does so by knocking them off the main branch of this developmental line and forcing them onto its deviant branches. Such a development usually leads the male victim into behaviors and feelings that are either personally or socially maladaptive. Successful treatment consists of returning the damaged boy to the path leading to a maleness acceptable to him and those he cares most about.

A derivative of this central hypothesis is that older men have a vital role to play in helping younger men develop or restore their maleness. In my judgment the role of the father is vastly underestimated in male development. A male therapist also needs to play a key role in repairing the damage done by those of us who molest.

In preparing this work, I realized that my own caseload is large enough to be a research sample as well as a clinical sample (N = 45). So I did a lot of counting up of basic facts about the group of boys I was treating at the time I began to write this book. This data is presented in several places in this book partly for the data it offers on a particular question and partly to be sure the reader is aware of the exact nature of the caseload from which my conclusions are drawn.

The focus of this book is on boys who have been molested prior to their eighteenth birthday. The victims discussed in this work were molested anywhere between infancy and middle adolescence. Most have been molested prior to twelve years of age. At this point it is necessary to raise briefly the question of definition. This will be dealt with in detail in the chapter on assessment. Here it is sufficient to say that in spite of a raging controversy about where to draw boundaries on what is defined as sexual abuse, I am writing throughout this work only of boys who have been victimized by hands on offenses such as fondling, oral copulation, and sodomy. The research literature most often requires a five year age difference between participants to call a sexual encounter molestation. My clinical definition in my caseload sample and throughout this work requires two to three years of age difference with exceptions for specific circumstances detailed later. Most of the boys I treat have been molested by males more than five years older than they are.

REASONS FOR CONCERN

Since the 1970s there has been an increasing concern with the male victim. This problem seems to have been uncovered as a byproduct of the women's movement's focus upon the sexual abuse and exploitation of young females. Once society began to look into the sexual abuse of young females, it led to the question of what was going on with young males. We began to discover that boys were also being abused in great numbers. A recent review of the literature (Urquiza and Keating, 1990) presents a table of studies giving the incidence of the sexual abuse of males in the American population. The rates range from two and one-half percent to seventeen and three-tenths percent. If these figures are accurate, it can be expected that there are somewhere between three and twenty-one million male victims in the American population (based on a U.S. male population of roughly 121 million males). Whichever figure we accept, it is clear that the sexual victimization of young males is a problem of massive, epidemiological scale.

Along with the discovery the existence of the male victim, society has also discovered that males are damaged by sexual assault. The dominant culture's earlier position had been a sort of "boys will be boys" approach. This analysis assumed that boys were more sexual, had more sexual experiences as children, and that these were not necessarily a problem. If sexual abuse set off conflict in the male victim, the manly thing to do was to be quiet about it and get on with one's life.

Recent changes in the American culture have permitted men to be more introspective and expressive. Males who, in another generation, would have suffered in silence, now speak about their victimization and seek help to overcome its consequences. Parents have become aware of the damage done to boys by molestation and are bringing their sons to treatment in greater numbers than ever before.

The popular literature and media are making it known to the American public that there are life-long consequences of sexual abuse for men. These are known to include sexual dysfunction, depression, low self-esteem, and addiction. At least the educated public is becoming aware that there is a greater incidence of perpetration of sexual assaults by men who have been molested. All of these reasons have caused greater concern and a greater willingness by parents to seek treatment for their molested sons.

As might be expected there is an increasing literature on the problem of the young male victim. In 1980, there was very little in print about this population. The number of research studies addressing the young male has exploded since then, as can be seen from the bibliography of this work which does not encompass everything in print.

METHODOLOGY

This is not primarily a research study but some comments about how the clinical data presented here will help the reader to evaluate this information. I was initially trained in anthropology, and was saturated in the old tradition of the field study and participant-observer research. In the type of study, the investigator lives among the people he/she wishes to study. The anthropologist talks with his subjects, collects their myths, songs, poems, dreams, and artifacts, Finally, all this material is synthe- sized into an interpretative work. This kind of study offers some unique opportunities. A modification of this technique is an excellent way to learn how victims think, feel, and react to treatment. It also allows for the collection and presentation of projective material for examination and analysis. No statistical study yields this kind and depth of information.

Those of us who are concerned with understanding and helping must become involved in this kind of undertaking. This in no way demeans the collection of statistics or the production of rigorous research. That kind of study provides a solid, empirical basis to integrate with the data that emerges from intense and empathic interaction with our fellow human beings. The only other alternative would be to retreat to completely statistic and empirical work and abandon any attempt toward an intui- tive and subjective understanding of the mental state of our patients. This would be terribly unfair to our patients and to society.

In recent decades, there has developed a giant gap between academic researchers and practicing clinicians. This is unfortunate, since each has much to offer the other. The practicing clinician is in a position to gather extensive data, which could be used to generate hypotheses for empirical studies. Statistical and empirical studies can provide an anchor to base the clinician in reality. When clinical conclusions are supported by empirical studies, it is easier to get a professional consensus about what needs to be done, what works and what does not. Clinical energy can then be confidently directed to areas where it will most benefit patients and society. It is, in my judgment, through the blending of knowledge gathered clinically and intuitively with that gathered in methodologically elegant research that everyone involved can best understand and treat the young male victim of sexual abuse.

In using clinical material throughout this book I have been acutely aware of the issue of confidentiality. Case studies have been somewhat modified to protect the identities of the patients. Where such modifications have been necessary, they have been made to preserve the validity of the interpretation, while protecting the patient's privacy. Many of the individuals presented here are composites of several individuals. All of the tabulated data, however, refers to an actual clinical population in treatment with the author at the time of the preparation of this work.

THE CLINICAL SAMPLE

Since 1984, I have treated approximately 135 young male victims of sexual abuse. The average duration of treatment is one to one and one-half years. Every therapist knows that a certain percentage of patients come, stay for a few sessions and leave. These have not been included in the 135. Some patients have been with me for as long as six years. Typically, they are seen both individually and in group, and sometimes with their families. I also have the opportunity to work with a colleague who provides a parent group for some of this population.

The actual sample on which some statistical data will be offered is a group of forty-five boys currently in treatment (November 1991). The age range on this population is from six to eighteen years of age. Of the forty-five boys in treatment, twenty-four are victims only. Twenty-one have both been victimized and become involved in for the most part minor acts of perpetration against still younger children.

It is important to note here a clinical distinction between boys fourteen years of age and older and those under fourteen. Most clinicians are aware of the relative rarity of adolescent male victims in treatment. When they come to treatment it is often after they have also developed into perpetrators. This is the pattern of this sample. Of the forty-five boys, twenty-six are less than fourteen years of age, and nineteen are over fourteen years if age. Among the population under fourteen years of age, twenty-four percent are perpetrators as well as victims. For the population over fourteen years of age, seventy percent are also perpetrators. The dynamics behind these figures, I suspect, are the unfortunate tendency for male victims to turn into perpetrators with the passage of time, as well as a tendency for parents to delay treatment until the boy has perpetrated.

Regarding the gender of the perpetrator, thirty-nine of the boys experienced molestation at the hands of another male. This is eighty-five percent of the sample. Ten (twenty-two percent) were molested by females. The total exceeds 100 percent because some boys were molested by both males and females. Among the boys molested by males, forty-four percent were assaulted by unrelated, older males. Fifteen percent were assaulted by a mother's boyfriend or stepfather. Twenty-four percent were assaulted by their own fathers. Brothers were responsible for 10 percent of the assaults, and an extended family member for five percent.

Among those victimized by females, (n = 10), four, were assaulted by unrelated females, five by their own mother, and one by a female in the extended family. Regarding the number and nature of the assaults, almost all of this sample have been sexually assaulted on multiple occasions, some over a period of years. Most were assaulted several times in a relatively brief period before it came to the attention of authorities.

These victims have been exposed to multiple forms of sexual assault. Most of them have been victims of several specific types of assault, such as oral copulation and sodomy. In this counting, only the most serious incident happening to the victim is tabulated, since it is impossible to keep track of everything that has happened to each of these young males. Of the sample molested by males (n = 39), sixty-seven percent have been sodomized. Thirty-one percent have been involved in oral copulation (Most of those sodomized also have been involved in oral copulation). Two percent experienced fondling by older males. Of the ten boys who were molested by females, five were involved in oral copulation and/or intercourse with their mothers. The remaining five were involved in fondling and oral copulation with older, unrelated females, usually baby-sitters.

The details of this sample are presented here because it offers some countable information about a group of young male victims of significant size who are well known clinically to me over a relatively long period of time. These boys have offered me a window to their psyches which would be available to few others, unless they are involved in a similar clinical practice. It is from them that most of the clinical material presented in this work has been drawn. From a research standpoint, this sample suffers from being in being a population in treatment which almost certainly biases it in the direction of greater pathology than many of the populations studied by researchers. It is likely that this sample is representative of a clinical population, but not of research populations where data from non-patients is collected. It is also an outpatient sample and therefore should reflect less pathology than boys being treated in inpatient facilities.

SUMMARY

This book is an attempt to integrate a wide variety of material, to provide a comprehensive view of the psychodynamics and treatment of the young male victim of molestation. The information presented here is gathered from a long and intensive interaction with a clinical population of sexually abused boys. This information is to be integrated with material drawn from research literature in the field of sexual abuse and other disciplines such as material that has emerged from prolonged interchange with colleagues involved in similar undertakings. The material is aimed at clinicians, and its goal is to help them to treat a difficult and disturbed population, about which little is known, psychodynamically.

Chapter 2

THE LITERATURE

To review the literature on young males who have been sexually abused at first seems like a seductively simple task. It is a cliche in the field that little is known about the sexually abused boy, that the molestation of boys is under-reported and little researched. The task is reminiscent of a geologist who walks up to a cliff full of fascinating stratigraphy and spots an important fossil. Upon reaching out to grab it he discovers that it is embedded in a matrix that ties in with everything else in the geologic formation. It cannot be easily be separated from the remains of other organisms and the environmental milieu in which it lived and died and which now locks it into a greater unity.

The problem with reviewing the literature on the sexually abused boy is to set limits on what literature is to be searched. To examine the literature on boys under 18 who have been sexually assaulted is manageable. Examining the huge volume of literature which touch upon this topic is not. A full review would not look simply at books and journal articles discussing this narrow topic, but at the broader literature on the sexual abuse of children. Also relevant would be the extensive literature on adult survivors of sexual assault. The incest literature and the literature on the perpetrators of sex offenses would also shed light on the problem of the molested boy.

Since young male victims are imbedded in a family matrix, family theory as it relates to sexual acting out should also be reviewed. The literature on male identity, the men's movement and homosexuality could also be profitably reviewed, as could literature on adolescent acting out and the stages of child development since each child molestation occurs in the context of his developmental stage. Needless to say, all of this relevant but voluminous research cannot been reviewed here. Some of this more extended literature will be brought to bear in specific later chapters to shed light on problems under discussion there.

In this chapter we will look at the literature relating specifically to males under 18 years of age who have been sexually assaulted. This search began at the University of California at Riverside with a computer search assisted by professional library staff. The staff searched for all periodical and book length literature on the topics, males, (eighteen or under, victims of sexual abuse). This database yielded ninety-two entries. A search of a broader database covering adult sexual abuse victims yielded 173 entries. Examination of the bibliographies of the works that turned up in the computer search showed scores of additional articles which did not emerge from the search itself. To review all of this literature in detail would be a book length work in itself. Of necessity, some selectivity and judgment has been exercised in the selection of works to be reviewed.

The intent of this review is limited to the discovery of what is empirically known about the juvenile male victim, as well as to examine the nature of informed sepculation about these young males. It is also the author's hope find whatever consensus there is in the research. In doing so, it is hoped to avoid any conclusions which fly in the face of what is already known and agreed upon and to rest the conclusions of this work on any solid empirical facts which are available regarding this population. The literature surveyed falls into nine rough categories with some overlaps. Many of the journal articles and all of the books cover two or more of these categories within their pages. The author has attempted to categorize them according to the principal thrust of their conclusions and concerns.

General Surveys

General surveys are usually book length treatments of the population under study. There is only one book length treatment dedicated exclusively to the treatment of the young male victim of sexual assault (Porter 1986). Hunters' 1990 work, *Abused Boys,* contains valuable material on this population. Much of the text, however, is the retrospective descriptions of abuse and impact by adult male survivors. Although not limited to child and adolescent victims, Hunters' 1990 work, *The Sexually Abused Male,* contains many contributions by many individual authors dealing with various aspects of the identification, assessment, and treatment of the young male victim. Many of these chapters will be reviewed separately.

Outside of works which specifically deal with the sexually abused male, there are a number of general treatments of sexually abused children of both sexes (Friedrich 1990), (Sgroi 1982), (Goldman and Wheeler 1986), (DeVine 1980), (Geiser 1979), (Finkelhor 1979), (Schultz 1981).

Descriptive and Quantitative Studies

The literature contains numerous descriptive and quantitative studies which attempt to count numbers and percentages of victims and the situations in which they find themselves. This literature contains bedrock statistical information necessary for any meaningful treatment of the problem at hand.

Dube (1988) sampled 511 children under twelve years of age who had been sexually assaulted. Eighty-five percent of the sample were female, 45 percent were male. Dube concludes that males are more likely to be assaulted longer and to suffer more severe abuse. Kercher and McShane (1984) studied 619 molested children. They found most of the victims to be female, most perpetrators male, and male victims most often victimized by unrelated males.

VanderMay (1988) also found males more often abused by non-family members. She also found risk factors including those factors for abuse outside the home. These included a history of neglect, a mother headed household and a child who had previous homosexual contact. Predisposing factors for children molested in their own home are the presence of other siblings who have been abused and a father who has been victimized sexually himself. VanderMay concludes that the effects of childhood sexual abuse are serious and long lasting.

Rogers and Thomas (1984) studied 402 children ranging from three months to 18 years. Again, they found a predominance of female victims (seventy-five percent) male offenders (ninety-seven percent). They also found males less likely to be abused by a parent. Mian et. al. (1984) studied 125 children six years of age and under. Females outnumbered male victims three and three tenths to one. Cupoll and Sewell (1988) undertook a study of 1059 children who had been sexually abused. This study was done in an emergency room. Forty-two percent of the victims were under seven years of age, eighty-nine percent were female and ninety-seven percent of the perpetrators were male. This study found blacks over-represented as compared to the general population and Hispanics under-represented. Whites were present in the statistically expected percentage for the general population.

Rinehart (1987) studied 189 children representing all suspected child abuse cases referred to a University of California Medical Center in the Sacramento area in a two-year period. He found the racial composition of the sample representative of the general population of the area. Showers et. al. (1983) studied 81 victims with a mean age of 7.89 years. Sixty-three percent were white and thirty-three percent black.

DeJong and Hervada (1982) also found girls to far outnumber boys and found males to be significantly younger than females, with median ages of seven and ten. Male victims were also found to experience more violence in the course of abuse.

Johnson and Shrier (1987) studied twenty-four males culled from a large general pediatric population. They found eleven of these boys were molested by a female and fourteen by a male. With this small but provocative sample, they challenged the assumption that the overwhelming percentage of boys are molested by other males. This sample is interesting because it is not a mental health or juvenile court population. Resin and Koss (1987) studied 2,972 children in a national sample. They found seven and three-tenths percent of the males surveyed acknowledged being molested prior to age fourteen. They also found that eighty-one and two-tenths percent of these boys had not previously disclosed their victimization. This suggested a very high percentage of unreported victimizations in the general male population.

The most recent available quantitative and descriptive study is published in Hunter (1990). This work is entitled "The prevalence of Sexual Victimization of Males" by Urquiza and Keating. They review a number of previous studies of the incidence of victimization of young males. The studies show prevalence rates ranging from two and one-half percent through seventeen and three-tenths percent obtained by one of the authors in a separate study. The authors argue that the higher incidence figures are more likely and that male victimization is usually under-reported. Several writers have commented on the reluctance of males to report their own victimization (Peake 1989), (Finkelhor 1984), (Nielsen 1983). Kersher and McShane (1984) also found that male victims were most often victimized by unrelated males.

Johnson and Shrier (1987) note that their own study as well as that by Fritz et. al. (1981) report much higher incidences of victimization of boys by older females. Finkelhor (1984), Bell and Weinberg (1981) and Gebhard, Gagon, Pomery, et. al (1965), report significantly lower numbers ranging from 15 to 27 percent. Johnson and Shrier and Fritz et. al. suggest incidences in the forty to sixty percent range.

Finally within the descriptive studies are two which attempt to describe the previctimization characteristics of the young molested male. David Baker (1980) examined records from the Los Angeles Police Department and concluded that the typical boy victim is age seventeen years of age, has parents who are physically or psychologically absent, has a previous history of homosexual contact and is an underachiever. Another study of this nature is more clinical, Rossman (1980). This writer is mostly concerned with the perpetrators rather than the victim, but does note that boys targeted for victimization come from the lower social class, from multiproblem families, were hungry for affection, and have previous homosexual experience. Fisher and Howell come to similar conclusions in a 1970 study.

Literature Reviews

The most extensive of the overviews of the literature on the young male victim is by VanderMay (1987). VanderMay reviews a large number of existing studies. She concludes that, excepting works by Finkelhor and Pierce and Pierce, most of the research has serious problems. Some of the samples are too limited. Others are simply conveniently available to the researchers. Much of the data comes from after the fact reports by victims. There is an excessive focus on the victimization of females or a focus on only one type of abuse such as incest, paedophilia or rape. VanderMay also notes a lack of replication. VanderMay does draw conclusions from the literature in spite of the problems cited. She feels the literature supports the fact that boys do indeed suffer personality damage as a result of molestation. She also feels that the literature supports that there are both differences and similarities in the risk situations for males and females as well as in the way males and females respond to sexual victimization.

VanderMay feels there is a need for further explanation of the exact nature of young males responses to victimization and the duration of the damage. She feels that both differences and similarities between males and females in their responses to abuse need to be further explored and clarified.

VanderMay stresses that there is a need to more clearly define the various types of victimization experienced by male children in order to assure the reliability of research. Without consensus on what is abuse and a typology of abuse, meaningful comparisons are hard to make. She also stresses the need for longitudinal studies to explore the possibility of victims turning into adult perpetrators.

Another much more limited research study, Pierce (1987) explores the available literature on father-son incest. Williams (1988) also reviews the literature on father-son incest. He concludes that where fathers molest their son, the father's history and personality are critical variables. Whereas if the daughter is the victim, it is more likely to emerge from dysfunctional family dynamics.

Psychological Impact

A number of studies discuss the psychological impact of molestation on young males. In general the sources are consistent in their reporting of the sequelae. Several sources record a complex of feelings surrounding homosexuality. A high percentage of sexually abused boys develop a homosexual orientation in adult life or develop serious doubts and conflicts about their sexual orientation as a result of molestation (Finkelhor 1984), (Brown and Finkelhor 1986), (Dimock, 1990), (Johnson and Shrier 1985), (Shrier 1988). A related but more generalized sexualization of the young victim are reported by Friedrich et. al. (1988) and Hewitt (1990).

Shrier and Johnson produce some very interesting data on an admittedly small sample. In their 1985 study these researchers culled out forty adolescent males reporting sexual victimization from a large general hospital population. This study group reportedly identified themselves as currently homosexual at seven times the rate of such identification in a control group and bisexual at nearly six times the rate for a control group. Nasjleti (1980) notes a tendency to deny any traumatic impact if the perpetrator is female.

In addition to issues of sexualization and conflicts about gender identity and orientation, the literature reports a number of less specifically sexual symptoms which seem to result from the molestation of males. Several writers refer to a cluster of feelings involving depressions, suicidal impulses, low self-esteem and a sense of loss of control over one's life. Nasjleti (1980), Froning and Mayman (1990) and Hewitt (1990). Shrier stresses in a 1988 article that low self esteem and depression are the most important long term effects of childhood sexual abuse. Boisso (1989) notes depression, a sense of lost control and inability to trust others.

Harrison et. al. (1990) note a connection to substance abuse. Also mentioned in the literature are chronic anger and fire setting. Dean and Woods (1985) report difficulties in the area of sexual dysfunction, sexual identity conflicts, sexual compulsiveness and at least fantasies about molesting younger children.

Victim/Offender Transition

It is a truism in the sex abuse field that male victims are at risk of becoming perpetrators. There is no study which details what percentage of male victims develop into adult perpetrators. This author explored this issue in an earlier work (1987). It has also been explored by O'Brien (1989). In this work O'Brien develops the argument that the gender of the abuser will in turn influence the male victims selection of his own future victims. A male molested by a male will in turn decide to molest males because of the dynamics of his victimization. Similar issues have been explored by Freund, Watson, and Dickey (1988) and by Hindman (1988). Gerber has most recently addressed this issue (1990) in the anthology assembled by Hunter. In this work he lists a number of variables which facilitate the transition from victim to perpetrator.

Identification of Male Victims

There is also a body of literature focusing on the question how do we discover the fact that a male has been sexually molested. Boys' shame and secretiveness in this matter is widely known to therapists. This literature acknowledges that it is much more difficult to detect sexual abuse in males than in females (Hunter, Kilstrom and Lota 1985), (Whitmore, 1990), (Gerber 1990) Clark and Bingham (1984) and Siebold (1987) discuss specific techniques for eliciting information about abuse from male victims.

Treatment

Literature directly discussing the treatment of male victims of abuse less than eighteen years of age is rare. This is dealt with by Porter in a 1986 work as well as by Friedrich and others cited as authors of general works on the treatment of children of both sexes who have been molested. Hewitt (1990) has most recently addressed this issue. Her target population is specifically preschool boys. She breaks even this population into a series of subgroups depending upon developmental age and developmental need. Froning and Mayman (1990) take up the issue of treating somewhat older boys in the same volume. They advocate and exploration of homophobic concerns targeting sexualized behaviors, and management of rage.

Turning to adult men who had survived childhood abuse, there is a more extensive literature which can only be touched on here. Dimock (1990) suggests a therapy focused on the clarification of sexual confusion, positive identification with the masculine gender and the development of the ability to sustain intimate relationships. These generalized goals would certainly seem relevant in the treatment of young males who have been abused.

Dimock also advocates treatment in all male groups with a male therapist. He recommends individual treatment only at the beginning of the process. He also suggests referral to sexual addiction groups as necessary. Bolton et. al. deal with the treatment of the adult survivor in their 1989 work *Males At Risk*. The approach is behavioral cognitive. The literature contains a number of anecdotal case studies: (Kolko and Stauffer 1991), (Halpern 1987), (Barton, Buell and Marshall 1986).

Closely related to the issue of treatment is the small body of literature dealing with young male victims who deal with victimization in a surprisingly healthy manner. Gilgun (1990) has prepared a paper exploring the issue of mediation of the effect of abuse. She concludes that the mediators are actually more important than the actual fact of abuse itself. She places particular weight on the presence of trusted and supportive individuals in the child's life with whom the child can discuss the problem. Similar conclusions are being reached by Martha Erickson in work that has only been briefly reviewed in print (1991).

Differential Impact Male and Female

This topic has been of considerable concern in the literature. This is probably due to the fact that the very discovery of the prevalence of the male victim has been due to the earlier attention focused on the young female victim of sexual abuse. Much more is known about the female victim. The similarities and differences in responses to sexual victimization in male and female children is of great practical and theoretical interest. No literature addresses the impact of the same sex perpetrator versus an opposite sex perpetrator, which in the author's opinion may have as much significance as the sex of the victim. The literature does not have a firm consensus whether and how much differential impact actually exists. This may be due to the high number of variables that co-exist with the sex of the victims, things such as age, nature, extent of the abuse, sex of the perpetrator, et cetera.

Most of the existing studies simply look at the demographic differences between male and female victims. Pierce and Pierce (1985) find differences between male and female victims in family composition, the sex of the perpetrator, factors that contribute to a continuation of the abuse, and the type of services offered to the victim. Bolton et. al. (1989) also address this issue. Faller (1989) finds male victims more often to be abused by someone outside the family as well as by a perpetrator with multiple victims.

Studies looking for differences in symptoms and behavior of victims disagree in their conclusions. Briere et. al. (1987) studied a population of forty male and forty female crisis center clients who are victims of childhood sexual abuse. Briere et. al. conclude that there are no differences between the males and females based on the variables they studied. They note that in spite of their findings they still have not thoroughly explored the possibility that males victims may act out violently toward others whereas females are more prone to turn their trauma inward. Two other studies support that conclusion. McCormack, Janus, and Burgess (1986) study 144 victims of sexual abuse, both male and female. They find the males more likely to report bodily symptoms and fear of older men, whereas the females are more likely to be confused about sex and become involved in antisocial activities. Carmen, Reiker and Mills (1984) study 188 psychiatric patients with histories of molestation. They found the female victims more likely to take their rage out in self destructive ways, while the males will direct their anger at others.

CONCLUSIONS

What based on this review and discussion of the literature can we solidly conclude about the male victims? Little, if anything, is established beyond doubt. There is widespread agreement that male victimization has been under-reported for largely sociological reasons. Probably the best study available gives an incidence approaching twenty percent of the male population. The lowest figures are less than three percent.

There is an increasing suspicion that the higher numbers are more accurate and that the incidence of male victimization may eventually prove to be close in number to that for females. The latter conclusion has yet, however, to be supported by rigorous and replicated studies.

Most males appear to be molested by males. Although, again, the incidence of victimization at the hands of females seems to be either increasing or more frequently discovered as attention is focused on the male victim. The more recent research, however, seems to tend toward greater percentages of female perpetrators particularly in non-clinical samples. It may be that molestation of males by other males causes more trauma and symptomatology and therefore leads to an overrepresentation of males molested by males in clinical settings. A higher percentage of boys appear to be molested by perpetrators outside of their immediate family. The more clinical literature suggests that there are risk factors predisposing some boys to become victims. These include neglect, households headed by females, and previous homosexual experience.

The very thin data available suggests that major racial groups are equally represented among male victims in proportion to their percentage of the general population. There is some indication that males may be more severely abused by females, although the literature is in conflict on this question. It is certain that males are more reluctant to report.

Regarding the impact of molestation on males, there is a consensus that it is traumatic. Many researchers emphasize that molestation at the hands of another male sets off conflicts about sexual identity and sexual orientation. A few writers, particularly those heavily involved in treatment, stressed the generation of homophobia as a response to molestation. There is little doubt that most males tend to deny the traumatic impact of molestation by females. The literature on male victims, and particularly that on sex offenders is unanimous that there is an increased tendency for male victims of sexual abuse to become perpetrators of sexual offenses in later life. It is also clear that a large percentage of male victims never do become perpetrators. Very recently the phenomena of the male victim who does not become a perpetrator has begun to be explored, although the literature says nothing conclusive about this issue at this time.

The literature also emphasizes that young males are sexualized by molestation. Obsessive masturbation and precocious sexual interest are common after-effects mentioned in the literature. Sexualization is probably also involved in the increased tendency to perpetrate against others.

Most writers agree that a number of less specific psychiatric sequelae arise in the aftermath of molestation. Most significant of these appear to be a complex centering around depression and low self-esteem. Also mentioned are chronic anger, a tendency toward substance abuse, anxiety, guilt, impairment of the ability to trust, and issues centering around helplessness and loss of control. These are soft findings, but few clinicians seem to dispute them. The limited literature suggests that the male victim is difficult to both interview and to identify. This is connected with cultural homophobia as well as the victim's sense of shame. Our cultural attitude that boys are expected to have more sexual experience, and that it is not supposed to be traumatic to them is probably also involved.

The literature on treatment remains largely clinical. There appears to be a consensus on the type of thing that needs to be done. But there are few, if any, studies reviewing the effectiveness of such treatment. The most radical idea in the treatment field is probably that proposed by Dimock proposing that males be treated by male therapists in all male groups. This may or may not apply to the treatment of children, since his treatment program is targeted at adult survivors.

At this time little is known about the differential impact of sexual abuse on males and females. The data is very limited but what is so far available suggests that females act out in self destructive ways, while males become aggressive toward others.

Chapter 3

THEORIES

A meaningful discussion of issues of diagnosis and treatment of the young male victim of molestation requires an examination of the major theories applied to the understanding of these problems. Attempts to understand and change human behavior and personality must rest in some kind of theory. Theoretical assumptions of some kind underlie all professional understanding in any discipline. Theories are the cognitive structures which shape our conceptualization of any phenomena we wish to understand.

For both clinicians and academics, this can be a controversial and emotional arena. Theories are not just abstract entities without connections to everyday life. There is some connection between the theories one finds acceptable or helpful, and one's broader view of the world including ideology and politics. The door is thus opened to great divisiveness. This problem can be particularly acute for individuals who have devised their own theories and feel a proprietary interest in them. The manifold conflicts among early psychoanalysts are a case in point.

Before proceeding, we need to look at what is meant by theory in the discipline of psychotherapy. What is being discussed here is a system of coherent hypotheses or explanatory statements, proven or unproven, which explain or attempt to explain the meaning of behavior, social relationships, and/or fantasies. These propositions explore and make statements about intrapsychic realities (or, in some cases, deny the existence of such intrapsychic realities).

An adequate theory allows for the development of explanations of human behavior and social relationships. It offers a way to understand complex behaviors and interactions which might otherwise seem random or meaningless. A theory allows inferences regarding what can be changed in human behavior, fantasy, and feeling. It can be used to hypothesize about what cannot be changed. It can also address the issue of how to produce change where it is possible.

The operation of the human mind is, in my judgment, such that none of us can act without basing these actions on some kind of theory, stated or unstated. The theory may be as simple as, "It is impossible to know what really goes on in the human psyche, therefore we should concern ourselves only with behavior." A good theory is a system of thought which has propositions that are much like equations. They can be manipulated to generate new explanations and treatment strategies when we come to an impasse in treatment. Such impasses are frequent in dealing with the young male victim of molestation. Anything that can help us through these difficult spots is a valuable adjunct to practice.

The literature review has already turned up a number of key questions which need answers if one is to understand and treat young male victims. This list is intended to illustrate the possibilities rather than to exhaust them. For example, the literature indicates that some boys are more likely than others to become victims. What about the boys or their social context underlies this observed phenomena? Only some kind of theoretical system can offer an answer.

We also know that victimization is much more devastating to some young males than to others. This, of course, begs the question of preexisting personality and the role of family and cultural support systems. All of these questions must be addressed in some kind of theoretical framework if they are to be meaningfully answered. For those of us who are therapists, the most vital question is, "What can be changed in the realm of human sexual behavior and feeling, and what cannot?" Again, any answer must be embedded in the context of a theory which explains it.

More questions to pose for the theories. If a behavior cannot be changed, why is this the case? How and why is this immutability connected with other problems which can or cannot be changed? To attempt to understand and to practice without some kind of theoretical road map poses the same difficulties as trying to drive in a strange city without a map. Eventually you may stumble upon the route from one point to the other, but far less efficiently than can be done with theoretical map in hand.

So far, this discussion has been abstract, whereas this book is concerned with some very concrete problems. Exactly what kind of theory do we need to examine in order to better understand the impact of victimization on young males and the proper therapeutic response to this victimization? The theories that are most relevant to this undertaking are those about how sexual feeling and behavior are developed in human beings.

The reason for concentrating in this area is that the existing research suggests that the greatest trauma for the young male victim is specifically in the area of sexuality and sexual development. A high percentage of male victims complain of lifelong sexual conflict and dysfunction. These often include an ego-dystonic homosexuality, homosexual panic, tendencies toward pedophilia, and profound guilt and shame about sex. Also on the list of unfortunate sequelae are such things as low self-esteem, depression, and substance abuse. These can probably be interpreted as derivatives of the trauma in the sexual area.

The most traumatic damage from molestation is in intervention by the perpetrator in the child's process of sexual development. We do know that some children recover well from this, but others are devastated. In some cases, the changes induced by the perpetrator are in a direction that is highly distressing to the young victim, particularly as the logical consequences of molestation unfold in the child's inner life. In order to understand the impact of molestation, we need to look at some of the theories of sexual development, and then compare them with what we see in the consulting room and the social environment.

The best explored byway of human sexuality is the etiology of homosexuality. The literature seems to support the view that most homosexuality is not the result of molestation. It appears to be a multiply-caused phenomenon, with strong partisans for various conflicting views. After heterosexuality and homosexuality, probably the next-best studied behavior is pedophilia. Finally, there has been some work on the perversions, such as transvestitism and fetishism.

SOCIAL LEARNING THEORY

A bit of shorthand is used here. Under this rubric are included a group of related behavioral and cognitive theories of human development in general and human sexuality in particular. The only one particularly focused upon here is the social learning theory developed by Bandura in the course of many years of research and writing. This is probably the most popular theory among academic researchers and among clinicians for a variety of reasons. This focus on social learning theory considerably oversimplifies the complex discipline of learning theory which is itself rent with theoretical divisions (see Hilgard 1975). It is a practical necessity since many learning theories do not address sexual learning *per se.* A general review of the manifold learning theories would take us well beyond the scope of this book.

Bandura (1963) notes that, "for the preceding half century, learning theory approaches to personality development, deviant behavior, and psychotherapy have been favored by the majority of research-oriented psychotherapists." Academic researchers have been generally uninterested in or unsatisfied with the elaborate but untestable hypotheses of psychoanalysts. Bandura also objects to the "uncontrolled trial and error experiences of practicing clinicians." The research community needs clearly identifiable and measurable behaviors in order to design statistical studies meeting the standards of their discipline. The behavioral-cognitive group of theories, and social learning theory in particular, have filled this need for most of this century.

Social learning theory and related theories have helped in the formulation of research hypotheses in the field of sexology and, more particularly, in the understanding and treatment of sex offenders. Out of this body of theory and its world view have come many of the recommendations for treatment of perpetrators. There is a tendency in this same direction in the treatment of male victims (see Bolton 1989).

Social learning theory assumes that the unconscious of the Freudians is either nonexistent or irrelevant. It also strongly objects to the concept of unfolding periods of development, determined by some kind of biological timetable. Bandura (1963) draws from Skinner the concept of the human being as totally plastic material in the hands of its social environment. Biological limitations and imperatives seem to have little or no role in this framework. The closest Bandura can come to accepting critical stages in development is the concept that certain tasks must be mastered cognitively before the individual can be trained in other tasks. This is simply because the initial tasks are prerequisite to the accomplishment of the later tasks.

The major component of behavioral shaping in Bandura's system is the cognitive processing of rewards, punishments, and imitation. Rewards and punishments are most effective when administered by someone in high status in relationship to the subject. Translating this into child-rearing, parents would be potent shapers of behavior for their children. One gets the impression that, in the earliest stages of development, reward and punishment play a larger role. As the child develops, imitation becomes an increasingly important process. Bandura states, that "children develop a generalized habit of matching their responses to successful models." It seems that these role models, plus differential reinforcement add up to the process by which personality is shaped. Whether a behavior will endure or die out depends on how the social environment and particularly key prestigious individuals in that environment react to the behavior.

Turning to the sexual area, Bandura gives some illustrations. One is of the development of a transvestite. He cites the case of a boy, five, who is dressed in his mother's clothing and jewelry by a cooperative and enthusiastic mother who also suggested a girl's name for him. The boy took on an increasingly female role, which the mother rewarded with demonstrations of affection and verbal approval. Grandma and neighbors joined in to furnish an abundant supply of women's clothing.

Bandura's interpretation is that these reinforcers, in the form of approval and support from key figures, stamped in a habit of cross dressing which, presumably, became one of long duration. Social learning theory would further assume that this pattern could be modified at a later stage in life by reinforcement processes in the opposite direction. Since Bandura does not believe in critical stages, he would see any of these processes in the area of sexual or other development as reversible.

A second example further illustrates sexual development in the social learning theory model. Here Bandura discusses a boy, seventeen, with a problem of exhibitionism. Bandura attributes the problem to showers with the mother, during which she exhibited herself to the boy, examined his nude body, and demonstrated affection for the boy during these interactions. As a result, the boy was sculpted into an exhibitionist. Bandura notes that these cases "pair positive reinforcement, in the form of close physical intimacy, with sexual responses that are inappropriate for the age and sex of the child" (1963).

It would be easy for any clinician working with young male victims of molestation to furnish examples of how sexual orientation and deviation has been sculpted in these children by pedophiles who gained prestige and influence in their lives. Feldman and MacCulloch (1971) develop a similar line of reasoning for the origins of homosexuality. In this paradigm, intense erotic homosexual experiences at puberty are reinforced by orgasm. This experience is combined with unpleasant heterosexual experiences to create a homosexual orientation. Storms offers a similar theory (1981).

Bandura's work deals more with process than content, and there is very little specific elaboration of details of how any specific personality configuration emerges. One gets the impression that personality is a complex aggregation of learned stimulus/response hierarchies, and that each individual is probably unique and complex. The general disinterest in psychodynamics characteristic of social learning theory results in lack of much further detail.

Bandura is antagonistic toward psychoanalytic interpretations. He makes a specific point of showing that the phenomena described by psychoanalysis at the time of his writing (1963) can be explained by principles of social learning theory. For example, he feels regression can be explained in terms of intermittent reinforcement, fixation by principals relating to scheduling of reinforcements. He also devotes much space to rebutting and reinterpreting the analytic notion that development unfolds according to a developmental timetable with such stages as the oral, anal, and phallic. My hunch is that social learning theory might not be as uncongenial to a critical development or stage theory rooted in biology. It is currently popular to understand many of the problems of the male victim as a form of addiction, specifically a sex addiction. This theoretical matrix seems to me to be most closely related to the learning theory model and, for purposes of this work, is classified here.

PSYCHOANALYSIS

After social learning theory, psychoanalysis has probably been the most influential theory represented in the literature on sexual development. This is particularly true of the clinical and anecdotal literature. In sheer volume there is probably more psychoanalytic literature on sexual development than on all other theories combined, but much of the material is repetitive. These remarks apply only to general psychoanalytic literature on sexual development. Psychoanalysts have rarely, if ever, turned their attention to the young male victim of molestation. If analysts treat victims of sexual abuse, they rarely write about it. The outstanding exception is Levine (1990). This work, however, deals with treating victims of childhood abuse when they are adults. One possible reason is that purely analytic techniques are very poorly suited to children and adolescents. Another may be that the teachings of the classic analytic schools are anathema to feminists and, for that reason, are unpopular in the sex abuse field where the feminist position is well represented.

The term psychoanalysis is like learning theory. It represents a variety of somewhat similar approaches with much internal differentiation. Non-analysts tend to think only of Freud and the classical school which many contemporary analysts would regard as obsolete. Currently the most influential of these analytically derived schools is probably self-psychology. This discipline lacks some of the defects of classical analysis and, in my judgment, has much to offer in the field of understanding and treating male victims.

The currently immensely popular writings of Robert Bly are also an offshoot of psychoanalysis, although in its aberrant Jungian form. Bly's writings seem to express the tremendous yearning of contemporary American males for information about masculinity and methods for strengthening their sense of male identity.

Probably the single most dominant model for treatment of victims of sexual abuse is the trauma recovery model, which is regarded here as a derivative of psychoanalysis, or at least of its foster child psychodynamic psychiatry. The most commonly used diagnosis for victims made by clinicians of this school would be post traumatic stress disorder. This diagnosis itself implies an underlying theory and treatment approach. Emphasis is to be placed on reliving, reworking, and reintegrating the abuse experience. There is be particular concern with repressed or denied victimizations and the recovery memory.

FAMILY SYSTEMS THEORY

Surprisingly, this immensely popular theory has had little theoretical application within sexology and victimology. Swan (1985) uses this theoretical framework to argue against individual treatment for child victims of incest. Many authors (Garrett and Wright 1975), (Vander Mey and Neff 1986), (Walker 1984) have noted that the non-offending parent plays an important role in setting up an abusive environment. The Parents United Program seems to use family systems theory as one of its key theoretical underpinnings to run a nationwide program for the treatment of incestuous families.

Years ago, Adelaide Johnson (reprinted in Esman 1975) published a classic paper in which she outlined the way in which parents act out their own pathologies through their children. If the parents' pathology is sexual, the parents are likely to act out aspects of this pathology through their children. Family dynamics loom particularly large in the literature about female incest victims. Presumably, they loom equally large in the situations of the poorly known male victims of incest.

Turning to my own practice, I have identified situations where I believe that parents have created psychodramas to act out via transference their own victimization. In this way they seem to hope to address their own traumatic issues about being victims. Fathers filled with rage as the result of violent and sexual abuse by their own male parents will turn with the same fury on their sons in an apparent attempt to destroy them. Women who have been sexually victimized will often unconsciously seek out molesters as spouses or companions, placing their children in high-risk situations.

In both cases, the parent seems to be attempting to place a child in exactly the situation they were placed in, i.e. sexual molestation. They can then act out what they see their own recovery needs in a more controllable context. Obviously, this offers no real healing to the parent and often destroys the child. I suspect a kind of projective identification here in which the victim parent acts out their own self-blaming and self-hatred upon a child who is a self symbol. The child may also be a symbol of a hated molester against whom pent up rage can now be safely vented. This may explain why the male victim is the family member who would be most likely to be identified as the scapegoat by family system oriented therapists.

FEMINIST SOCIOLOGY

Feminists have been perhaps the key group in developing and sustaining the current concern with identifying and treating victims of sexual abuse. Traditional American culture considered females to be the property of men to be used as they saw fit. Sexual abuse was denied and ignored. The feminist movement militantly brought this situation to public attention. At first the focus was solely on the female victim. But if women are the property of patriarchal men, so are children, including male children. Hence a focus on the male victim. This same revolution in consciousness has generated increased focus on male perpetrators of sexual abuse.

One of the earliest feminist contributions was an insistence that victims allegations be taken seriously and that victims be believed, supported and protected. Feminist sociology identified the American system as one in which males were assigned near absolute power over females. Power and control issues became dominant factors in male sexual expression as opposed to loving and sharing. Men participated in this system because of the power and dominance rewards, but lost much else in the process. Feminist sociology got American therapists to look at how male socialization turned many men into rapists and child molesters. This same socialization complicated immensely the treatment of males once they became victims.

The power and control elements of male sexuality in America facilitate the process by which male victims became perpetrators. Traditional American values encourage men to feel good by wielding power over others sexually and in other key aspects of life. In the area of treatment, feminist sociology has emphasized the role of empowerment as an essential to victim recovery. This perspective has now transcended the boundaries of its feminist origins and is almost universally accepted as a part of the healing process for victims of both sexes. In the case of the male victim, feminist sociology would suggest a resocialization and abandonment of culturally traditional male roles as part of the curative process. One result would be greater male respect for the boundaries of others. Such respect would vastly reduce the incidence of sexual abuse in this country.

Looking at sexual abuse in the context of patriarchy is a relatively recent concern in the literature on the sexual abuse of males (Strube, 1991). This is an area where there will probably be growing interest and publication. Strube urges that clinicians target the social conditions that allow for the abuse of men, and also that interfere with their ability to use treatment, largely by encouraging them in a process of denial. His perspective suggests that the long-term "cure" for sexual abuse is a social reorganization in which men and women occupy a more equal status. When men give up their need to dominate and focus on loving and sharing, the problem of the sexual abuse of both girls and boys will be reduced.

Much of the feminist approach is aimed at preventing sexual abuse by facilitating social change. There is no doubt this needs to be done. Therapists working with male victims will do well to implement its implications for direct treatment such as empowerment of the victim, and helping the male victim to de-emphasize the culturally prescribed pursuit of power and control over others. The massive social changes advocated by feminism will more likely have to be carried out in the political arena rather than in the consulting room.

BIOLOGICAL THEORIES

Biological theories divide into two categories: those that argue that sexual development follows a genetically programmed course, and those that argue that it involves a complex interaction between genetic and constitutional factors on the one hand, and environmental factors on the other. Some of the most interesting theories involve critical periods during which the brain is particularly responsive to programming along key developmental lines.

Genetic studies have focused specifically on the etiology of homosexuality. A well-known study by Simon LeVey has received national attention, even in the popular media (1991). This study suggests that there are structural differences in the brains of homosexual and non-homosexual men. The differences are specifically concentrated in the hypothalmic area which controls, among other things, sexual responsivity.

Further research will probably modify the implications of this study. Major criticisms involve the nature of the sample—its small size, and one afflicted with AIDS. The research design also implies a rigid dichotomy of men into homosexual and heterosexual.

In reflecting on LeVey's data, Thomas Schoenfeld of Clark University (1991) objects to his creation of bipolar categories of homosexual and heterosexual. The existence of self-identified bisexuals, which is easily confirmed by any clinician, implies that there is no unity of sexual behavior among men who have sex with men. We are dealing with a heterogeneous category, not a polarity. Schoenfeld urges greater caution in interpretation of this type of data.

Bell, Weinberg, and Hammersmith (1981) argue obliquely for genetic determinance of homosexuality. They examine the major hypotheses about the development of homosexuality that have arisen out of psycho-dynamic models. They then test these hypotheses with a complex and difficult statistical model. They conclude that none of these environmental factors can be supported statistically as involved involved in the etiology of homosexuality. They therefore assume that there is a genetic cause for homosexuality. I have two problems with the study. One, it relies heavily on self-report and questionnaire and two the absence of any identifiable cause does not prove the presence of an unstudied cause (genetic) just by the supposed absence of environmental factors.

Whitham and Mathy take a similar position based on other data. They examine twin studies, studies of children reared against their genetic sex, meaning children who were misidentified at birth and reared as a sex opposite their biological sex and, finally, children reared in what they call "atypical families," meaning children of gay or lesbian parents. The twin studies that they cite indicate a high concordance among identical twins for homosexuality. They do note, however, that the correlation is not 100%, therefore meaning that homosexuality is not likely to be completely genetic. They quote Diamond (1982): "Nature sets limits to sexual identity and partner preference, and it is within these limits that societal force interact and gender roles are formulated."

Regarding children raised against their biological sex, they note that these children generally identify according to their biology rather than their social history. Finally, they note that children raised in homosexual families do not become homosexual at any greater rate than children raised in non-homosexual families. Whitham and Mathy also note that there is an apparently world-wide pattern for boys whom they describe as pre-homosexual. These boys, regardless of cultural context, can be identified early by their preference for cross-dressing, playing with girls' toys, and other activities typical of the opposite sex. All of these arguments are summed together by Whitham and Mathy to conclude that the preponderance of evidence supports a very strong genetic component in homosexuality.

Critical Periods

A biologically rooted but much more complex argument is developed by Winson, a neurobiologist at Rockefeller University who specializes in the study of the hippocampus and related brain structures. His work (1984) is a synthesis of the efforts of a number of previous writers, as well as his own research. In addition to neurobiology, Winson is interested in the adaptive and evolutionary function of various brain structures. He looks particularly at critical periods of development, which he defines as genetically encoded periods of time, in which the brain of a developing young animal can be neurally programmed to develop lifelong behavioral repertoires in several different areas. Information on this process is more available for animals than for human beings. Winson brings to bear what data there is for human beings, particularly in the area of language development.

His argument begins with the observation that mammals are born with small brains. All neurons are present at birth. No new brain cells will ever be added. Yet there is a tremendous brain growth involving the extension and patterning of the axons and dendrites of the neurons as the young mammal grows toward maturity. He points out that the average human infant is born with a brain of 330 grams which develops to 1350 grams by age twelve, and 1380 grams by age fourteen (1984). Since the total number of brain cells is given, most of this growth involves the lengthening and branching of dendrites and axons.

This sounds very reminiscent of recent developments in neural computing. Instead of computing at a central chip, neural computers compute at many small stations located within the networks linking larger computing centers. Most of the processing takes place in the interconnecting networks (I beg the indulgence of any computer analysts for oversimplifications). Neural computing sounds very much like the brain model Winson is describing.

Winson further notes that the growth curve for the human brain ascends steeply with the most dramatic growth occurring in the earliest years, and a rapid drop in growth of brain size following this early explosive development. Most of the growth occurs in the first two years of life. It would appear that whatever is being programed into the neural system of the brain in these periods is laid down very early in life. As time passes, less and less is added to this "neural hardware." Around puberty, this process stops completely.

Winson reviews the development of hunting behavior in cats. This involves complex learning including the integrating of visual and motor skills. As part of this experience, the mother cat must bring live prey on which the kittens can practice during a critical period between their sixth and twentieth weeks. If this does not happen in that period, the kittens later either do not kill, or they can only do so in a slow and laborious way.

To illustrate the neurological underpinnings for critical period learning, Winson looks at experiments by Hubel and Wiesel on young kittens. They have a critical period for the neuronal development of vision, ending at twelve weeks. If kittens between four and twelve weeks are deprived of sight in one eye, even for a brief period, the kittens behaved as though they were blind in the eye that had been deprived of visual input. Beyond the age of twelve weeks, depriving one eye of input had no effect on its vision. Closing an adult cat's eye for over a year resulted in no change in the brain organization of the visual system or in its behavior.

Winson's data indicate that in lower mammals there are extremely important critical periods in which neuronal pathways determining behavior are laid down, and which are modified later only with difficulty. Winson feels that this is an adaptive advantage for mammals in their struggle for evolutionary survival. The optimal adjust ment to the environment is realized in a species that can be born with certain genetic programming which then can be enriched during a critical period by the animal's post-birth environment. This allows each individual animal to be fine-tuned to its environment for optimal functioning. The evolution ary advantages incurred by this mechanism result in natural selection of animals who possess this adaptive advantage. In order to obtain this evolutionary benefit the neural mechanism which underlies critical periods must be at first plastic, and then set.

Winson speculates about the neuronal basis of this process. His best guess is that there are inter-neuronal connections formed within the neocortex and between the hypothalamus and the neocortex which are influenced by environmental stimuli during critical periods, and then become permanent. Winson believes that most strategies for behavior are located in the prefrontal cortex of the brain. Less is known about this area than is known about the visual areas, although Winson suspects that the process is similar.

The hypothalmus and hippocampus are evolutionarily very old structures. We share a common evolutionary heritage with the lower mammals. I see no reason *homo sapiens* should be exempt from this process. We should reap the same benefits from it as do the lower mammals. As with the rest of our brains we may have elaborated and specialized, but the presence of the basic process is likely.

Winson does offer one example of critical periods in human development. This involves language. In reviewing the data on human development of language, he cites studies which suggest that below age two, the human neocortex is not sufficiently developed to sustain the organization of language, and that beyond twelve, any new learning of language is based on different neural mechanisms. A language learned in the critical period is programed into the neural hardware. Language can be learned after the critical period is closed, but the process will be more laborious and less complete. For example, the sound system will probably never be fully mastered. A person learning a new language outside of the developmental stage will probably never learn to speak without detectable accent.

Winson does not say it, but there is no reason to suspect that sexual behaviors would not be subject to the same processes. Much of our sexual behavior seems to be determined in the interaction of the hypothalamus with the higher centers of the brain in the neocortex. It is a realistic hypothesis that during a human critical period, connections are made between the hypothalamus and the prefrontal cortex. As with vision or hunting behavior, these connections become a kind of neural hard wiring that contain patterns for behavior that are from that time forward deeply ingrained in the human psyche. Sexual behavior is just as adaptive as vision and hunting. There is no reason to believe that they are not included in this neuronal patterning process. Programed behaviors probably include sexual preference, sexual orientation, sexual feeling, and sexual expression.

Reasoning from very different data, John Money (1957, 1965) came to similar conclusions about critical periods many years before Winson's work was published. Money, being a sexologist, did address the issue of critical periods in sexual development as a specific issue. Money had been looking at work involving children born with the sexual characteristic of both sexes (hermaphrodites). In the course of treating such children it became necessary to assign them to one sex or the other. In reflecting on this process Money made the following remarks (1965):

> The acquisition of a native language is a human counterpart to imprinting in animals. So also is the acquisition of a gender role and psychosexual identity. The critical period in establishing psychosocial identity appears to be approximately simultaneous with the establishment of native language.

Money regards efforts to assign gender to hermaphrodite children as a natural experiment in the issue of critical periods of human development. In this "field experiment" he concludes (1965):

> Psychosexual differentiation follows in agreement with a sex reassignment made in the neonatal period or up to a year or 18 months of age, provided the parents negotiate the change successfully. Thereafter, adjustment difficulties and the likelihood of residual psychopathology increase with the child's memory of life-history experiences and appreciation of gender concepts.

For some reason few researchers are following up on the lead provided by Money and Winson. A computerized literature search of the topic "Critical Periods in Human Development" done for this work by the

---

*Excerpt from *Sex Research: New Developments* by John Money, copyright © 1965 by Holt, Rinehart and Winston, Inc., reprinted by permission of the publisher.

University of California at Riverside, turned up nothing that could be used here, other than an additional article on the development of language. In a January 1992 phone conversation, Winson indicated that there had been no significant research in the field of critical periods in human postpartum neurological development since the publication of his work. It is curious that material of such potential import has not been followed up upon.

It is probably premature to make these conclusions, but the area of postpartum critical periods in sexual development is of such import that some hypotheses will at least be suggested here. The weight of the scanty evidence is that we share a critical period kind of learning process with our mammalian kin. Psychosexual development is most likely one of the areas in which these processes are active. Once the critical period is closed down, this marvelous opportunity for flexible and plastic learning is no longer available.

Any therapist who has attempted to help disturbed patients make basic changes in personality organization will recognize the type of paradigm just described. To follow Winson's analogy, once we are out of a critical period, we must learn a kind of override function to change many dysfunctional behaviors including those in the sexual area. If the analogy is valid, the override function is more tedious and less efficient than the original program. To use the language metaphor, the earliest language of sexual expression is the one which will always come most easily to us. To learn something different will take a lot of therapy, of whatever sort. We will probably never be able to speak the new sexual language without an accent.

Differences: Resolvable and Irresolvable

The material presented here is complex, contradictory, and confusing. The reader might be tempted to select the theory that they prefer, disregard the others, and get on with their practice or research. This would seem both unnecessary and unwise. Virtually every theory presented here is backed by extensive research and/or clinical practice. Each of these theories have involved lifetimes of work by bright and talented clinicians and researchers. There is no justification for assuming that any of them are without merit. The task of anyone wishing to understand the psyche of the young male victim and to help him cope with and overcome the damage done by molestation is to select the best and most useful from each theory and put it to maximum use.

Much of the apparent contradiction is a matter of issues of professional turf and temperament. When actual differences are distilled to their essence, they are not as great as would seem at first glance. Some of these theoretical systems deal with different levels of organization and, therefore, are not contradictory, but complementary. If the family is appreciated as the vehicle by which most non-genetic learning is transmitted to the child, family system theory could allow families to translate patterns of behavior and feeling to their offspring following either the social learning model or the psychoanalytic model. Feminist sociology also targets the broader social system as it interfaces with the individual. It would be at least theoretically possible for one to adhere to all of the belief systems of classical analysis and, at the same, accept the feminist analysis that we live in a patriarchal and unjust culture. (The actual coexistence of these two beliefs in the same individual is unlikely.)

The greatest contradictions probably exist between psychoanalysis and social learning theory, although even these are not totally irreconcilable. It would be possible to render any of the competing psychoanalytic theories into a learning theory paradigm. Hilgard illustrates this in a chapter of his classic text, *Theories of Learning* (1956 edition). Critical periods and unfolding developmental stages pose the main obstacle to integration with social learning theory. Integration might involve special reinforcers which are particularly appropriate in certain developmental stages. Social learning theory says little about content and much about process. Psychoanalysis says a great deal about content and not so much about process. This leaves some obvious room for reconciliation.

The psychoanalytically oriented would deny at their peril that there are conditioning processes which lead to habits and addictions which are dysfunctional and need to be corrected. They would also ignore only at their peril experimental and research data that behavioral techniques can impact and change these behaviorally ingrained processes. If anyone cared to do it, there are a number of areas in which psychoanalysis and social learning theory could be joined together. Both postulate the existence of something like a conscience. To oversimplify the matter, psychoanalysts see it as an internalized and modified parent (or parents). Bandura talks about the existence of "self-generated inhibitory responses which may be relatively independent of situational cues." (1963). Avoidance of these inhibitory responses can be motivated by anticipation of self-punishment. This sounds like a description of what the analytically oriented would call a superego process.

Bandura also describes an internalization of prohibitions, leading to the development of self-control. In this kind of process, the individual learns not to commit certain disapproved acts, even in the presence of a great deal of temptation, and when the external punishing agent is not present. Again, this sounds like a rather precise description of superego functioning. A final example. Bandura states that response patterns in one situation often generalize to others in which they are socially undesirable. This sounds very much like the old psychoanalytic concept of neurosis as reacting to the present as if it were the past.

The major remaining and irresolvable difference between psychoanalysis and social learning theory appears to be in the concept of critical periods. As late as 1977, Bandura was arguing against the existence of critical periods, which he refers to as "stage theories." There is, however, a more basic and possibly unresolvable difference between the psychodynamic and the social learning approach. They do, indeed, seem to involve a difference of world view, a difference of spirit or soul. Social learning theory sees stimulus hierarchies and looks for clearly measurable behavior. It is peripherally, if at all, concerned with what goes on within the black box of the psyche, if, indeed, it believes anything happens there.

The most contemporary and widely accepted theories of psychoanalysis talk of the self and are intensely interested in the reconstruction of thought processes and fantasies which are beyond the reach of any empirical technique. Analytic writers, such as Blos unashamedly refer to such sources of wisdom as Shakespeare, known never to have entered a behavioral laboratory. In spite of the almost overwhelming differences in temperament and world view between the two approaches, each is rich enough to justify the humility involved in learning from the other. A clinician who is not too deeply and dogmatically committed to either can learn from both. A final and major obstacle to complete reconciliation of the two major theories is that the psychoanalytic concept of the self seems to imply that individuals can become impervious to rewards and punishment from the outside. Once an individual has established his sense of self, his value system, his nuclear goals for life, self-psychology at least would say he may indeed not be as manipulatable by his environment as Bandura and his followers would imply.

Critical periods can be integrated with all of the theories that focus on individual development, and should be. This is a cutting-edge area, about which little is known, and may become increasingly important as a vehicle for integrating the already existing theories. The only obstacle to the integration of the new neurobiology and social learning theory is social learning theory's rejection of critical periods. Within the framework of accepting critical periods, it should be quite easy to adopt social learning theory as the method by which individuals learn within critical periods. If affective rewards from key parenting figures were accepted as major reinforcers, that could create a bridge between psychoanalysis, neurobiology, and social learning theory. Social learning theory might need to accept the notion that its principles work best in critical periods and may be ineffective against some behaviors outside of their period of neurological programmability. Psychoanalysis may need to make the humble admission that its treatment techniques cannot reverse what is laid down in the neurological hardware. Both psychoanalysis and social learning might be able to teach individuals override programs, analogous to second languages, by which they can learn better ways to cope with problems than those encoded in their neural wiring.

I would like to leave the reader with a final synthesizing idea. It seems to me that all theories can be reconciled if we accept that there are three kinds of human learning. One is genetic, encoded and unchangeable. Another is neural. It is encoded in what neural computing would call hardware (perhaps technically firmware), and probably impossible, or at best extremely difficult, to change. This hardware is laid down during critical periods of life and not amenable to much tampering afterwards. Finally, there is an override process, probably involving the prefrontal cortex and a type of neural process different from that encoded in the hardware. It is in this last realm that all psychotherapies operate.

Chapter 4

CONTEMPORARY PSYCHOANALYSIS
AND A SEPARATE LINE OF
MALE IDENTITY DEVELOPMENT

This chapter will explore the existence of a separate uniquely male line of sexual development which has separate and distinct stages. I believe there is an equally independent female line of sexual development which will not be discussed here. A separate male developmental line has been implicit in recent psychoanalytic thinking. Blos (1985) touches upon it, but does not outline it. Definitive papers on this topic were finally offered by Tyson (1982, 1986).

The basic theme of this work is that derailment from the male developmental line is the principal damage done by molestation. In order to repair this damage through treatment, a number of other recent developments in psychoanalysis must also be examined with a view to the light they shed on male sexual victimization and the treatment of male victims. This work seems largely unknown or ignored in the field of victimology. In my judgment it has much to offer.

The focus on these concepts does not mean clinicians should not draw, sometimes heavily, from other theoretical matrices. Nor does it mean young male victims are best treated with psychoanalysis. It is the theoretical content of some of the new branches of psychoanalysis that is to be tapped in this work. Treatment plans will be best drawn from eclectic sources. The theories reviewed here offer understanding of process in the development of dysfunction and help conceptualize goals in treatment. Specifically psychoanalytic treatment techniques are, in general, unsuited to the young male victim population.

CLASSICAL PSYCHOANALYSIS

Most non-analytic clinicians will be put off by this undertaking because of the bad name given "psychoanalysis" by the classical school. In general, academicians and therapists in the field of sex abuse are unaware of recent developments within psychoanalysis. It is no longer one discipline, but has fragmented into several related theoretical schools. The greatest problem in the acceptance of psychoanalytic thinking in the field of sex abuse appears to be the perception that old-fashioned classical Freudian psychoanalysis is the only psychoanalysis. Indeed, many research studies dredge up this entity as a kind of straw man to be torn apart. That is easy to do, because the original Freudian theory consisted of a number of propositions which have not withstood the test of time.

Classical analysis, as developed by Freud, emphasized a number of concepts which not only had little empirical validity, but are repugnant to modern socio-political thinking. Freud's formulations about women are demeaning to them. They imply that women are a sort of second-rate male, condemned to work out an identity without the presence of the magical penis, doomed, in a sense, to spend their entire lives compensating for its absence. This author does not subscribe to this classical Freudian formulation.

Central to Freud's thinking about sexual development was the Oedipus complex. Freud considered the period of life between 3 and 6 years of age to be the most basic for formulation of all later personality. He also felt that this complex existed in unmodified form in all cultures. A number of psychoanalytically oriented anthropologists dispersed across the world to gather data and, at times, manipulated it to arrive at the preordained conclusion. Less central, but easily attacked, was Freud's hydraulic model of personality involving dammed-up energies flowing here and there, creating neuroses and other psychopathologies. The classical formulation of id, ego, and superego is also associated with the early Freudians, and has been more recently ignored, if not superseded, by other formulations.

A *bete noire* in the sex abuse field has been what was felt to be Freud's excessive reliance upon insight as a treatment technique. This is particularly true in the area of treatment of sex offenders. Contemporary psychoanalysts have a much more complex notion about how human feelings and behavior are changed. The notion that insight in and of itself is curative is probably an oversimplification of even the classical Freudian position.

The classical Freudians are still around. They are probably the best-known psychoanalysts to those outside the discipline of psychoanalysis and those who follow it closely. Classical analysts do not, however, represent the cutting edge of contemporary psychoanalysis. Since at least the 1960s, this discipline has been increasingly fragmenting and exploring areas only lightly touched upon by Freud. There has been a tremendous emphasis on exploring what happens in the pre-Oedipal period, i.e. the first three years of life, which most developmental theorists would now feel are the most important to human development. Outside of the orthodox analytic institutes, it is my suspicion that most analysts now would say that the events of the pre-Oedipal period are more important to personality development than what takes place in the Oedipal stage itself.

Penis envy has been at least de-emphasized. It seems to have largely been abandoned, except as a pathological aberration, by the self-psychology school, which has grown out of psychoanalysis. Kernberg does not refer to it in the index of his influential book, *Borderline Conditions and Pathological Narcissism* (1985). Without doubt, many analysts still adhere to the notion that penis envy is a key dynamic in female development. Phyllis Tyson still attributes great significance to it in a 1986 article reviewing female development. She cites as her source influential Margaret Mahler (1966, 1975).

Tyson, however, has toned down the classic position:

> Where the mother/child relationship has been poor, penis envy as a developmental metaphor comes to represent a general sense of worthlessness, narcissistic vulnerability, inadequacy, deprivation, and damage" (1982).

Tyson feels that it is the discovery of anatomical differences, rather than penis envy *per se,* that function as a psychic organizer for the developing female. Peter Blos (1985) takes this a step further and states clearly a belief that the developmental lines of the male and female child are each *sui generis,* that is independent with separate milestones leading to separate ends. Another important addition to the classical repertoire has been the discovery that at least some males have considerable envy of females, their anatomy, and sexuality (Bettelheim 1955), (Stoller 1985), (Litz and Litz, 1989) (Herdt 1981).

Another addition to Freud's pioneering work has been the development of the concept of developmental lines. These were first elaborated by Anna Freud (1965), arising out of her extensive work with children. Gertrude and Reuben Blank picked up the idea and elaborated upon it considerably in a 1974 work. The Blanks point out that Freud basically focused on one developmental line, which they call psychosexual maturation. These are the classic phases known to every undergraduate: oral, anal, phallic, and genital. This line implicitly places male and female sexual development on a single line, creating much of the controversy that has surrounded psychoanalysis in the sex abuse field. Blank and Blank argue that development proceeds not along one line, but along a whole series of parallel lines. They list eleven. Anna Freud gives a different list in her 1965 work. Historically, it is the concept of multiple developmental lines which set the stage for the idea that males and females follow separate developmental paths to the development of sexual identity. This, in turn, has immense implications for further understanding in the field of sexual abuse.

Self-Psychology

Self-psychology is explored here not because it is rich in explanatory value regarding victimization, but because for me it offers the most comprehensive and plausible theory to explain the development of human personality in both sexes. It is fundamentally important that maleness develops along its own developmental line. But maleness does not constitute the whole human being. In order to understand and to treat, therapists need a framework to understand the dynamics and functioning of the entire self. Self-psychology offers this.

This discipline seems to be little known in the sex abuse field. It is an offshoot of psychoanalysis developed by Heinz Kohut and subsequently embraced by numerous followers. It represents the cutting edge of current psychoanalytic thinking and is the theoretical underpinning for much current psychoanalytically-oriented publication. Kohut's writings are exceedingly difficult to wade through. This has probably impeded his acceptance outside narrow psychoanalytic circles. For those willing to brave the jungle of jargon, there are treasures here for the clinician working with the young male victim of sexual abuse.

The Nuclear Self and Nuclear Goals

The Nuclear or core self is the central concept of self psychology. Pathology and acting out (including sexual acting out by implication) are ways of shoring up gaps in the nuclear self or preventing its collapse. The structure of the nuclear self can be strong and intact or weak and buried beneath defensive structures. The nuclear self develops very early in life. Most of it is in place within the first two or three years of life. Self-psychology sees the essential nature of the self as bipolar. At one end are the person's key life ambitions and at the other key ideals. The life cycle is viewed as a struggle to attain the nuclear goals implied in the ambition pole and the ideals pole of the self. The person uses their congenital abilities as well as the skills they develop in life to push toward a nuclear program implicit in these ideals and ambitions. Anyone familiar with classical analysis will be struck by the existential nature of the core of self-psychology as opposed to purely hedonistic and sexual nature of the self in Freud's thinking.

The concept of the nuclear self and nuclear goals are important in male victimology for several reasons. By appraising the strength of the core self we can understand the strengths and weaknesses with which we have to deal in treatment. Our treatment goals will be better accomplished if they are tied to the self's nuclear program. More importantly, I believe that goals relating to maleness are a part of the nuclear self and that pushing for the self's optimal maleness is, for most men, an essential part of their nuclear program for their life.

Where the nuclear self is weak, there is a constant danger of fragmentation. Fragmentation to a trained but non-psychoanalytic observer would most likely be reflected in psychosis, delinquency, drug addiction, and/or other severe pathologies. Much of the sexual acting out of victims and perpetrators can be interpreted as a mechanism to avoid fragmentation or repair the damage to sexual identity caused by victimization. A coherent and well-developed sense of self allows for optimal social functioning. Individuals with this kind of self-structure develop healthy relationships, get themselves well through life, and experience minimal danger of fragmentation. The development of such a self provides a goal not for just the treatment of male victims, but for any and all patients who have the inner resources to reach such a high level goal. It is an ideal to be sought whenever possible. Sadly, some patients cannot work at this level and must be helped to develop compensatory structures to cover over structural defects in the self. More will be said of this later.

Selfobjects

Selfobjects are a key concept in Kohut's psychology. The term is clumsy, but if properly understood, is useful in the sex abuse field. I suspect that many of the transactions between victims and perpetrators have a selfobject quality for at least one of the parties. These relation-ships are one of the major vehicles males use to strengthen their sense of masculinity. I believe that sexual identity is part of the nuclear self. When it is damaged by molestation, the victim will seek out selfobjects to help in the repair process. This opens the door for therapy and the person of the therapist who will take on a selfobject role in the course of treatment.

The term selfobject is obscure and technical. In simple terms it means that people from birth to death are presented with and/or seek out other human beings with whom they can interact and, in the course of this interaction, either enhance the growth of the nuclear self or stave off its collapse. Most likely selfobjects will be used to both ends in the course of a lifetime. Selfobjects would include parents, relatives, friends, mentors, and so forth.

The precise and technical meaning of the word, selfobject, reflects the fact that, because of the early developmental stage at which this mecha-nism forms, the ego does not distinguish fully between itself and the selfobject. The selfobject, although a person, functions structurally as a part of the self. This other person is selected as a selfobject because of desirable attributes they possess. In selecting a selfobject we seek to "borrow" or to incorporate into ourselves something we lack and desire or need to bring into our developing self. For males who have been derailed from the line of male development by molestation, a male who has masculine traits desired by the victim will be a most likely choice of selfobject for self-repair.

Another important concept from self-psychology with application in the sex abuse field is erotization. Where the nuclear self is weak and danger of fragmentation high, people will have a great hunger for selfobject relationships. At times, these relationships can become sexualized. In analytic treatment, they are seen in an erotization of the analytic relationship. The patient develops sexual fantasies which on a deeper level are fantasies of merging with the idealized therapist so they can obtain the qualities they need to complete their own damaged self. The implication of this for the treatment of male victims is that they may erotize many of their relationships. This makes them vulnerable to further victimization. For therapy it is both a treatment opportunity and a risk to the capacity to remain in treatment.

Where erotization is present, the emphasis is on merging with the idealized object and thereby developing better internal structures through incorporating those of a stronger self, but the specific technique is sexual. The merging here takes the form of yearning for sexual fusion with the proposed partner. In my own earlier work (1987), I noted that, many times, the adolescent molester seems to be looking for qualities in his victim that he lacks in himself. Very often, these qualities are masculinity and/or the innocence of childhood. Through sexual merger, the adolescent molester is attempting to obtain these qualities for himself. Similarly, some males seem to be especially vulnerable to victimization because they yearn for stronger masculinity and seek to obtain it by sexual fusion with older, stronger males.

SELF-PSYCHOLOGY AND TREATMENT

Self-psychology also offers theories about how human beings can be helped in treatment. A basic premise is that pathology arises out of efforts to maintain the cohesion of the self. Self-psychology outlines a treatment technique for expanding the boundaries of the self and developing structures within the self which will allow the individual to function successfully in the world and to be free of feelings of overwhelming panic, anxiety, and fragmentation.

If therapy takes hold, the patient will create a classic selfobject relationship with the therapist. The formation of this transference allows the patient to reactivate the growth process at the point at which it was stopped. The implications of this for the treatment of male victims are clear. Self-psychology would postulate that, in the course of entering an interaction with an analyst, the two would return to the psychic time in which the wound was inflicted. By a complex and highly technical interaction, including identification, interpretation, and a bond of empathy, the patient is allowed to resume the growth process and to develop the structures in the self necessary to the creation of a healthy adult masculine identity.

Self-psychology makes little use of insight and interpretation as curative mechanisms. Treatment and "cure" are the results of a complex interaction. Kohut (CF Goldberg 1985) argues that the only interpretations that should be offered in the course of treatment involve the relationship between patient and analyst, specifically events which interrupt the selfobject bond between patient and analyst. By offering the patient empathy and understanding, the patient is able to identify with the therapist. Also unleashed in the patient are a series of transmuting internalizations which lead, in turn, to the development of an enlarged and strengthened self.

As noted, the nuclear or core self is believed, by self-psychologists, to develop very early (Shane 1985). If all goes well, the developing human being is able to gather the psychic resources to develop a strong and coherent sense of self. It should be no surprise to a therapist of any school that many individuals do not develop this. Kohut refers to this kind of condition as a "persistent hollowness in the center of the patient's self." He connects this kind of condition to the psychoses and borderline personality configurations (from Strozier 1985).

My experience is that borderline individuals are common among young male victims of sexual abuse. Self-psychology does not believe that this condition can be totally "cured." It offers instead the concept of the development of compensatory psychic structures. These structures provide ways of bridging the gaps in the self to allow the individual to function and realize the self's nuclear program. This nuclear program consists of essential life goals laid down at the very center of the person's self in early life (Detrick, 1985). To be regarded as successful, analytic treatment should also give the patient the ability to make efficient use of selfobjects throughout the rest of their life. These measures allow a "successful" life (successful from the standpoint of nuclear goals and avoiding fragmentation) even in the absence of a strong nuclear self. The inherent deficiencies in the self can thus be prevented from destroying the person's ability to have a successful life even though a strong nuclear self can never be built in the face of certain severe pathologies. This needs to be kept in mind by those treating male victims because there are many with such severe pathologies.

INDIVIDUATION

Moving outside of self-psychology, other branches of modern psycho-analysis also offer useful concepts for understanding and treating male victims. Once such contribution is the concept and process of individua-tion. The word is often associated with Carl Jung, but it is not the Jungian concept that is discussed here. Individuation has been most recently elaborated by developmental theorists within psychoanalysis, particularly Margaret Mahler, Gertrude and Reuben Blank, and Peter Blos. The basic idea is that to develop successfully, the individual needs to separate from the maternal matrix into which they are born. At the earliest stages in life, the individual exists in a mental state of complete fusion with the mother or mothering person, called a symbiosis. Anyone not developing out of this stage is *a priori* psychotic.

All subsequent development centers around separating and distinguishing oneself from the maternal matrix and developing a separate, discreet, and defended sense of identity. At the end of this process, the individual should be able to relate to others as independent and separate objects, rather than as parts of the self. Individuals who get bogged down in the actual separating process, once the original symbiosis has been broken, are *a priori* borderline. Basic individuation is believed to be complete by 36 months of age. Problems arising after 36 months of age are of an Oedipal or neurotic nature.

Individuation has become a very important concept throughout modern psychoanalysis. The concept is particularly important for this work, since males are born of women and pass through the earliest and most critical stages of development in a state of symbiotic fusion with the mother. Males must thus, in essence, reverse their basic identification from female to male in the course of successful development. The material drawn from cultures all over the world suggests that this is a universal male dilemma. Males seem to feel a need everywhere to emphasize and exaggerate their separateness from the female.

Robert Stoller

Robert Stoller, a somewhat maverick psychoanalyst, has put great effort into the study of male sexual identity development. His vehicle for study has been the perversions, particularly transvestitism. Stoller (1985) seems to view perversions in men as a failure in the individuation process as well as in male identity development. Both, of course, are closely related. The poorly individuated male who later develops a perversion has a tremendous fear of being reengulfed by the mother. This fear is aggravated if the mother belittles, humiliates, or degrades the developing boy's sense of masculinity.

Because of the boy's poor ego boundary and fear of reabsorption by the mother, he will have a great fear of intimacy. In Stoller's words:

> The non-perverse person does not powerfully fear intimacy because he or she is not afraid that it will lead to a merging that swallows up identity" (Stoller, 1985).

The most difficult cases seem to arise when a developing boy's sense of maleness is assaulted or humiliated by a female. This assault may take the form of some kind of feminizing behavior, treating the boy as a little girl, reinforcing feminine behaviors, or other such activities repulsive to the developing child's ego.

This kind of situation leads to the perversions which Stoller has studied extensively. A central theme in transvestitism, for example, is to allow oneself to be dressed as a female (assaulted by femaleness) while retaining one's essential sense of masculinity intact. As evidence, Stoller (1985) presents fantasies from transvestite literature in which females forcibly dress males in women's attire, but fail to really feminize the man. Here the central theme is the preservation of male identity in the face of overwhelming attack. Stoller feels that men do not so much fear castration, but that their most basic fear is the loss of the sense of maleness.

Where male identity is poorly formed, the male must engage a number of defense mechanisms to prevent merging with females and thereby, feminization. True intimacy with a woman is threatening. Other perversions protect from the danger of being swallowed up by femaleness in situations of real intimacy by partializing females. For example, erotic interest may shift from the whole woman to an item of clothing in fetishism.

I would add to Stoller's formulations that where issues of fear of merging with females and panic about feminization as a result are prominent, one defense mechanism is to seek an extreme degree of control over the female partner. Control itself is often seen by men as an aspect of masculinity. Hence control becomes a part of the dynamics of perversion, allowing sexual contact without danger to male identity. This can easily be factored in to explain how the young male who is a victim of sexual abuse, in turn, becomes a perpetrator. The role of control as a dynamic in perpetration is well documented (see for example Salter 1988). In many of the eclectic theoretical explanations, it becomes the prominent dynamic (see for example Ryan and Lane 1991). If control of the sex object is understood as a mechanism for defending masculinity, then perpetration can be interpreted as a form of perversion which follows the dynamics outlined by Stoller.

THE MALE LINE OF SEXUAL IDENTITY DEVELOPMENT

What is offered here is a synthesis of the thinking about male development drawn from several sources. For the milestones, I have relied heavily on Tyson (1982, 1986) and Blos (1985). It is known that the male infant emerges from the womb with a strong propensity to be male (Money, 1965). I believe that there is a drive toward maleness in men, which is thwarted at their psychic peril. This drive seems to have its roots in both biology and the kind of nuclear goals of the male self proposed by self-psychology. When this drive is frustrated or blocked, individuals dangerous to themselves and to society often emerge. The male's propensity for aggression in the sexual area is well known. This aggressiveness seems to be heightened when males cannot proceed along their developmental line toward mature gender identity. In the language of self-psychology, rape and child molesting can be interpreted as "compensatory structures" worked out by males who have strayed from the main path of this line. For victims of assault, and molest, this is devastating. For the perpetrator these behaviors are an attempt at self-repair.

A head start on masculine development takes place in the womb. Numerous studies indicate that the testes secrete hormones *in utero* and that these hormones act on the fetal brain to switch on certain circuits that promote male behavior (Money 1965) (Diamond 1965) (Young, Goy and Phoenix 1964). The next milestone is the assignment of gender at birth. In most situations, parents are able to readily recognize the sex of their child, correctly identify it, and begin a socialization process that gives the child a shove in the direction of maleness. Of course, biological abnormalities exist which can complicate this process.

Tyson cites the discovery of the penis, with its genital sensations, and masturbation, as a milestone in the development in the sense of maleness. She also notes the importance of urinating in a standing position in the process of differentiating sexually from the mother and providing an early and visible gender link to the father.

A powerful and pervasive theme throughout the early years of male development is growing out of symbiotic fusion with the mother. If this is not done, core identity will remain female. The logical outcome would be transexualism. A strong impetus is given to the development of maleness when the child recognizes his father or key male figure in his environment and he begins to identify with that figure. If he loves and admires his father, this both strengthens his gender identity and lures him away from symbiotic attachment to the mother.

The mother has important roles to play here. She must permit and encourage the boy's growth out of symbiosis with her. Otherwise the boy will have to choose between giving up her love, approval, and support and being male. If the mother is not supportive in the area of maleness, the boy may opt for a feminine identification or choose to remain a passive, dependent baby (Tyson 1982). If the mother communicates her liking and approval of masculinity, she facilitates the growth of her son's masculinity by providing narcissistic supplies for its development.

Finally, the mother must avoid devaluing the father lest the boy read this a general devaluation of masculinity and a denial of permission by the mother to form a gender bond with the father. The father, of course, has responsibilities to communicate enthusiasm for his son's developing masculinity and to provide an admirable example of masculinity. If he devalues himself or is in chronic conflict with the mother, the father will make it very hard for the mother to provide her necessary input for the boy's developing masculinity.

The parents' work permits the next developmental step, the entry into a dyadic relationship with the father. Blos (1985) cautions here that what he calls "male isogender object relationships" are very poorly known, but he does indeed suggest that the young male forms an intense relationship with a fathering figure if one is available. This is an early, pre-Oedipal phase of idealization and identification with the father. The developing male shares what he perceives as the father's power by imitation of the father and submission to the father. This has an implicit passivity which, for some males, can pose a threat of feminization. If a male becomes stuck in this developmental phase, he will spend his life in an unceasing search for father figures. This will, in turn, ensure an emotional infantilism just as significant as that created by an over-dependency upon maternal figures (Blos, 1985).

Next on the young male's developmental odyssey is the Oedipal phase. Blos describes the boy as beginning to move away from the father, to "play big boy," and develop what he calls an "overbearing turn to noisy motions of self-affirmation" (1985). It is in this age that the boy tests himself against the father. The classical situation of competing with the father for the mother comes into play. Ideally, it is resolved with a rapprochement between father and son in which the son gives up desires for the mother and moves toward other love objects. In ideal situations, this involves a friendly identification with the father. This, in turn, provides a foundation for peer and mentor relationships with other males throughout the rest of life.

The next milestone comes with puberty. Blos feels that at or near puberty there is a resurgence of the old idealization and identification with father. As with the pre-Oedipal situation, submission and passivity in relationship to the father characterize this phase. This often leads to some limited homosexual acting out, and to homosexually-tinged yearnings for the father's love. This stage is followed by a reactivation of the Oedipal themes of competition. Ideally, these issues are again resolved through a relationship of cooperation, friendship, and identification between father and son. This process is not easy for father or son. Even if the process is proceding well, Blos warns of "usual, obligatory conflicts."

The vignette of male development offered here is far from complete. Failure at any point can lead into byways of sexual development some of which have been discussed, others which have not been. Throughout the process the developing male must also strive to attain an integration of sexual and aggressive impulses that is balanced and non-destructive to self and others. If this balance is tipped in favor of the aggressive aspects of male behavior a number of unfortunate outcomes can be expected.

The developmental theory presented here has several implications for understanding the impact of sexual victimization upon young males. There are two stages in which young males are prone to form idealizing passive and submissive relationships with older men. They are the early or immediately pre-Oedipal stage and a relatively brief period on both sides of puberty. The dynamics of these phases offer a potential explanation as to why it is so easy for pedophiles to find male children to molest.

Certain boys at these two stages of development are easy prey. Boys with a developmental vulnerability, such as a father who is absent or psychologically remote or cruel, can be expected to have a hunger for a male selfobject, and might seek one outside safe circles. This developmental need is what is capitalized on by the pedophiles who prey on boys whom they instinctively identify as needing father figures. A boy deprived of a father *imago* in these critical periods is the type of victim most easy to obtain. This would most likely explain why some male victims are so cooperative in their own victimization.

Turning to other aspects of the development of mature male gender identity, we can identify the etiology of some other problems of concern to therapists in the sex abuse field. Sexual acting out of several kinds can be explained as an attempt to defend one's basic sense of masculinity. Male victims of sexual assault act out in a number of ways. Some become involved in a sort of "Don Juan" syndrome, involving hyper- and/or pseudo-masculine behavior of a heterosexual nature. The compensatory function of this is obvious and needs little comment.

Homosexual acting out may seem contradictory as a mechanism to defend masculine identity, but it may not be. The analytic literature is suggestive that males whose sense of masculinity is weak may attempt to attain maleness directly by merger with males whom they regard as masculine ideals. This dynamic could lie behind some of the homosexual acting out of previously non-homosexual victims after they have been victimized. Once their basic sense of masculine identity has been damaged, the young victim may seek to repair it by sexual fusion with men who represent their masculine ideal. My clinical experience is that such idealization is not confined to older males. A younger male may have attributes that an older male desires to fortify his masculinity after it has been weakened by sexual assault. Hence the victim becomes a perpetrator. I was once told by 14 year old perpetrator that he sought out a nine year old victim because he admired the masculinity and male confidence of his nine year old victim.

Where molest has been brutal and humiliating, males may attempt to repair the damage to their masculinity by assuming control, humiliating, and destroying symbols of the man who molested them. This would be an attempt to repair the damage along the traditional lines of the trauma model: recreate the trauma, but in a situation where you are now in control. Whatever the specific dynamics, I would argue that molestation places masculinity under siege. The siege may be brief in duration and minor in impact if the young boy's sense of masculinity is already strong, if he has strong family and cultural support for recovery. On the other hand, if the boy's sense of masculinity is already weak, the results of molestation may be absolutely devastating to his developing sense of masculinity.

Chapter 5

THE CLINICAL PICTURE

So far this work has addressed theoretical and cultural issues as a necessary foundation to the understanding and treatment of the young male victim. In this chapter we will put clinical flesh on theoretical bones. The intent here is to communicate to the reader the kind of raw data from which many of the theoretical conclusions of this work have arisen. This can best be done by giving the reader a feel for what sessions with these boys are actually like. Young male victims of molestation will speak for themselves through play, drawing, and group process. At times, the material is shocking, both in terms of its candor and its violence. There are indeed some vague but provocative analogies to the way Sambia men in New Guinea protect their fragile but fierce masculinity.

A word about how this material was collected. My office is located in a large converted house with the specific intent of creating a relaxed, home-like environment. The room in which group and play sessions are conducted is the old living room, complete with a fireplace. My goal is to facilitate the freest possible flow of clinical information from these young males and, as often as possible, to encourage primary process communication for both diagnostic and treatment purposes.

From the onset of treatment, I make it plain to male victims that no communications are out of bounds. Neither in group nor individual sessions do I put any limits on the kind of language that can be used, nor do I make any attempt to discourage (nor encourage) fantasies involving violence and sadism. As the treatment process unfolds, I may introduce some counterbalances and alternatives to pathological fantasies. But uncensored communication always remains a basic goal. This permits boys to share material that they can express nowhere else except possibly in peer groups where no adults are present. Most of this material comes from boys between the ages of eight and thirteen. Many of the boys contributing material to this chapter were right in the midst of puberty as it was gathered. The groups are all-male. Boys tend to stay in these groups for as long as three years.

The Basic Themes

The clinical material examined here has been separated for purposes of study into a series of basic themes to which young male victims return over and over in talk, play and projective material. In clinical experience the actual data is a complex of interweaving psychodynamic themes. Each fantasy, each verbalization, seems to meet the classic primary process definition of overdetermination, i.e. it means many things at once. In order to make this comprehensible, basic themes have been isolated from what originates as a fast moving swirl of clinical material or chaotic drawings. The basic themes which emerge again and again in the productions and projective materials of this population are: sexualization, ego dystonic homosexuality, homophobia, compensatory hypermasculinity, fear and hatred of females, fear and hatred of males, sadistic fantasies toward both sexes, paranoid fears of renewed assault by perpetrators, tendencies to become perpetrators themselves, generalized rage and aggression, and sexual chaos. In my judgment most or all of these basic issues can be viewed as a reaction to molestation. Some are reactions to the homoerotic feelings stimulated by molestation. Others are an effort to use compensatory mechanisms to repair damaged masculinity.

A Play Session

Perhaps the best way to introduce several of the basic themes in one overdetermined place is to look at a play session with a young victim. The word "play" trivializes the material presented here, but the usage is traditional. Play is regarded by many analysts (see Anna Freud, 1965) as the functional equivalent of free association and dream work in child psychotherapy. This session contains in one form or another most of the basic themes seen in the projections and productions of young male victims. Sam is eight.

> Sam enters the playroom. He was sodomized by his father on several occasions. This was ignored by his mother, although he reported it to her. When this was discovered, he was removed from parental custody. Sam came to therapy a distrustful and secretive child. One can imagine some of the difficulties he might experience in intimacy with a male therapist. This is his first play session. Previous sessions have involved board games, including talk games requiring self-disclosure by both Sam and myself.
>
> The couch in the large playroom is arrayed with a series of stuffed human and animal figures. The largest is a benign-looking gorilla whose trunk and

head total about three feet in height. The animal is much-beloved by other patients. Also on the couch is a much smaller gorilla, a monkey, to whom a penis has been attached, a malignant looking bearded male figure, also phallic, a stuffed animal representing, Tom, a cat in a popular cartoon series, who looks friendly and benign (no genitals), and a mixture of other male and female child figures, some anatomically correct, some not. One is a small rubber baby doll.

Sam identifies the large gorilla immediately as "father." He quickly arranges the girl dolls, Tom, the baby gorilla, and the pleasant-looking phallic monkey around father. He arms the gorilla/father with a foam rubber bat. Spotting the bearded and phallic sinister-looking male figure, Sam labels him as "the molester."

The family now goes to bed with girls and boys in separate rooms. The molester sneaks into the girl's room, fondles and has intercourse with the small female doll. The girl tells father, who promptly punishes the molester.

The molester is unrepentant. He now molests two young male dolls, one of whom is the benign, phallic monkey. Father is again notified, and the molester punished. This time, the smaller gorilla (who was never molested and stays closest to the father) beats up the molester on behalf of the father.

The victim males, father, and the victimized girls now go to beat up the molester, with great emphasis on pummeling his genitals. One of the boys asks for dynamite to blow up the molester. I furnish a cylindrical block from a toy box, which is first fastened to the penis and then inserted into an imagined rectum.

Like a phoenix, the molester emerges from the fragments. Sam now labels him as "grandfather" and says that he is worse than the former molester. Later on in the course of play he slips and refers to the molester as himself. Again, the perpetrator sneaks into the girls' rooms, fondles and has sex with them. Next, he molests a young male figure. Dad is again informed.

The children are now grown up and leave home. The molester comes to assault them, but dad comes to protect. The father/gorilla falls asleep. The molester sneaks up on him, sucks his penis (nonexistent, this is a non-phallic figure), and then inserts his penis into the gorilla's imagined anus. Earlier, the father has taught the monkey doll to offer his penis to the molester and then kick the molester in the face when he accepts the offer.

As Sam is engaged in the play of the molester anally penetrating the father, I comment that he is doing this because he feels small and weak. The father then wakes up and kills the molester.

A week later we are in the same room with the same family configuration. Sam now selects a baby doll as a newborn girl. There is also a girl, age five, the phallic monkey, and Tom, the benign cat figure. A similar scene is repeated with the female doll representing a five year old. Sam shows obvious pleasure in removing the clothing from this anatomically-correct doll.

The five year old girl goes home. She not only does not tell the father what has happened, but also makes up a lie to cover up her whereabouts. The young gorilla son (father's favorite) asks me to go away so I won't see how angry the father is. I pretend to leave the scene. Sam takes what he calls a shotgun. The molester yells for a lawyer. Sam shoots his penis off. I asked Sam what happened to the younger molester. He said he gave molesting up and joined the family. He concludes by telling me that father has died. He is old, and has fallen off a building (apparently a reference to the King Kong movies).

The principal issue in this session is Sam's tremendous conflict about becoming a perpetrator. He clearly has strong sexual attractions to younger children. He has, in fact, acted them out. He is, in many ways, highly sexualized in his behavior. Since the beginning of treatment, his sexual acting out has considerably reduced and, subsequent to the sessions described above, reduced even further. This child, to my clinical surprise, is functioning quite well in his foster home and in his school setting. Clearly, the potential for future severe sexual acting out against younger children is present, but in remission.

Homosexual conflicts are present in this play in the form of pedophilia with homosexual object choice. This manifests itself in the molester's occasional assaults on male children. This child's power needs are so intense, I doubt he would ever be involved with a consenting peer of either sex. Also present in this play is an attempt to reinforce maleness by merging with an older, superior male seen when the small molester figure anally penetrates the large gorilla.

Sam's reaction to molestation seems to be in the direction of molesting younger females. True, his play includes assault on young males, but there are more assaults on young females and they are longer in duration and more consciously erotized. When Sam targets younger victims there is a ruthless, almost psychopathic denial of their feelings and needs. This is a child who has been humiliated, controlled, and dominated, in specifically sexual ways. He seems to be turning all of his erotized rage toward younger females. This seems to be compensatory for being made to feel small, weak, and helpless by his father. In these fantasies he seems to be using sexual assault of young females to preserve his sense of masculinity. By selecting female victims he is avoiding a homosexual outcome which is clearly not part of his nuclear sense of maleness. These fantasies also enhance his feelings of power which I suspect is equated in his nuclear self with masculinity. An identification with a brutal father who also molested young females is another likely dynamic portrayed in this play.

Sam is wrestling with his tendencies to become a perpetrator. They are not ego syntonic. The conflict comes through strongly in his severe punishment of the perpetrator. He is beaten, his penis is blown up, and dynamite is put up his anus. Nor is the issue of future pedophilia with homosexual preference resolved. In spite of a preference for female victims, Sam plays out a lot of molesting of younger boys. The erotic quality of his sexual activity with his father is suggested in the anal assault upon the father. Themes of pansexuality, sexual chaos, and rage against both sexes come through clearly in this play session.

This child's attempt to repair himself through relatedness to other males is also significant. His desire to merge with a strong male to strengthen his maleness has already been commented upon. The father is repeatedly presented as a source of help and as a kind of conscience who punishes the molester. The father's death at the end of the session is not a good prognostic indicator.

A Dream

A six-year-old patient had been molested by an older brother for several years. Molestation took the form of sodomy. About four months into treatment, this patient produced a dream in which he was now sodomizing the adolescent brother. On another occasion, this child's father reported to me that the boy had had an anxiety-ridden dream about being raped by the older brother. On inquiry, when the father was not present, the boy told me the actual dream. The older brother had come up in a vehicle, invited him to get in. He did so, with the specific understanding that they were going to go off and have sex together. Most of this boy's conscious anxiety had to do with the extreme displeasure this dream would invoke in his father if the actual dream were told to him. This boy could experience homosexual feelings only in the form of rape and still be acceptable to his father. His yearning for such contact is obvious in both dreams. This dream illustrates both the sexualization and the ego-dystonic, homoerotic feelings that often come as a result of molestation.

Boys also illustrate sexualization in their drawings. A very pathological example is illustrated in Figure 1. The intense sexualization implied by this drawing needs little commentary. Implicit also is the possibility that this victim continues to wrestle with issues of perpetration since the scene portrays adult-child sex. The scene also implies a sort of pan

Figure 1. This figure reflects the intense sexualization and sexual chaos in a boy molested by a step father. See text for more detailed description.

sexual, anything goes kind of sexual chaos. This boy was molested by his father, and has molested younger children. He was also forced, by the father, to have intercourse with his sister while the father watched. The scene is framed by an erect penis at one boundary and a penis hovering over a vagina at the other. The central scene consists of various sexual acts taking place between an adult female and children of varying ages. On inquiry, this young adolescent stated that the small figure on the left is a little kid coming up to say "no, no, no," suggesting some ego-dystonic quality to the material in the drawing.

Figure 2. This drawing is a mildly humorous presentation of sexualization in a boy molested by his father. His struggle with sexualization succeeded. This boy was successfully treated and is unlikely to perpetrate.

In Figure 2, the drawing again speaks for itself. It is a somewhat humorous presentation of the sad issue of how molestation excessively enlarges the role of sex in the victim's life. The entire figure is reduced to a few simple lines enclosing little more volume than the penis itself. The long and rather fragile-looking arms are engaged in an attempt to hold up the huge member. This is a boy, molested by his father. He made a good recovery in the course of treatment. The rather humorous quality of this drawing seems to me to reflect one of the strengths that allowed this boy to do well in treatment.

Ego-Dystonic Homosexuality

This phenomena among male victims has been discussed extensively elsewhere in this work. Clinically, it is most often manifested in direct statements rather than in projective materials. Perhaps the most poignant of my experiences in this area involve an after-group discussion with an adolescent who was terminating therapy at the insistence of his parents. His parting statement was, "If I could have one wish, it would be to be very masculine, not to be homosexual, and not to have been molested. I want a wife and children."

I have one group which concentrates boys who acknowledge strong homosexual feelings. They are told the nature of the group and no one is forced to join. In spite of this screening virtually every boy arrives in the group protesting that they are not gay, and speaking in the most negative terms about homosexuality. The group is open-ended, so boys are coming and leaving much of the time. After boys have been in this group for a while, they get very tired of this traditional routine with new boys. In a recent session, after hearing the usual protest, an articulate group member spoke up, "I get tired of hearing this from every new boy. We don't care if you are gay or not. That's up to you. Why do you think everyone cares so much about how you feel?"

Another member of this group, aged fourteen, was molested by an adolescent when he was nine. It happened several times, and included sodomy and oral copulation. He had also molested a younger male. I also see this boy individually. He shared a dream with me which he would not tell the group. He dreamed that he was in bed with a male of his own age who fondled him, and he fondled the other male. He was extremely anxious to end this discussion. Highly stressed, he blurted out, "I did not try to stop it." This led into a discussion of his attraction to a boy in the group. This boy is sexually appealing to several group members. This particular patient attributed his attraction to the other boy's tough, masculine appearance. He further volunteered that he had started smoking to imitate the other boy who smoked. The dream shows this boy's guilt over not resisting his homosexual impulses. His attraction to a more traditionally masculine boy seems to be an effort to repair his masculinity or obtain masculinity vicariously through identification with the other group member.

Younger boys are more likely to play out themes of ego-dystonic homosexuality rather than discuss them openly in therapy. This can be clearly seen in the play of an 11-year-old boy. Using the usual play room molester figure, this child plays out a sexual advance on the small gorilla. The setting is at school. The molester rubs up against the younger figure and invites him to the bathroom for a sexual episode. The large gorilla/father figure comes running to the scene and carries his son away, stepping maliciously on the perpetrator on his route home. This child clearly fears his impulses to become involved sexually with older men.

He was molested by a foster father multiple times over a period of many months. This man apparently became a foster father for the purpose of molesting children. This patient slept regularly with the foster father and was regularly sodomized by him. There were other children in the home, and this victim was rewarded with special privileges as a result of his sexual involvement with the father. This victim did not report the abuse but admitted it when someone else disclosed it. He feels very ashamed and corrupted. The corruption and temptation show up clearly in this play scene. His solution is to turn to a father figure for the help he needs with control of homoerotic impulses that are unacceptable to him.

Homophobia and Pseudohypermasculinity

These are frequent reactions to victimization of males by males. They are probably better known to clinicians than the more concealed homoerotic impulses that dominate the clinical picture in other cases. I have an entire adolescent group of such boys who will rarely, if ever, discuss anything dealing with homosexuality. To listen to them talk, you would, at times, assume their lives were nothing but one long heterosexual orgy. Seen individually, they tone this down, will acknowledge attractions to other males, and sometimes rate themselves as three on Kinsey's zero to six heterosexual to homosexual scale.

The defense mechanism here seems to be projecting one's own homoerotic urges onto others and hating them. Mixed with this is a kind of

Figure 3. This drawing represents a compensatory hypermasculinity in a boy who felt profoundly damaged by molestation. See text for details.

strutting, aggressive masculinity designed to cover up any hint of "feminine" interests or homosexuality. Figures 3 and 4 are graphic presentations of hypermasculinity. Figure 3 presents an undisguised symbol of hypermasculinity, a superman. This boy had been molested by an older friend of the family and had, in turn, molested a younger male. He was deeply ashamed of both. He had strong masculinity strivings and, in the course of treatment, was able to orient himself strongly toward females. This drawing was done relatively early in the treatment. I would speculate that the two mutilated figures in the drawing are symbols of aspects of the self. The figure on the left is this boy as he wishes to be seen by others—masculine and powerful. The two damaged figures on the right may represent the vulnerable, nearly-destroyed real self.

Figure 4 was drawn by Jim, whom I consider a treatment failure. He was prematurely returned from foster care to a relative, against my advice. He had been molested for years by an older male, including multiple episodes of sodomy. When he arrived in treatment he was a delicate, feminine, passive child. Puberty and forced termination arrived at roughly the same time. He experienced a tremendous surge in physical growth as well as sexual aggressiveness. He became interested in gang activity. He barely resembled the child who entered the group when he left. This drawing seems to me to reflect the entire spectrum of exaggerated masculinity used defensively. The aggressive nature of this male-

Figure 4. This is another example of hypermasculinity developed in reaction to victimization. Some features suggest a soft, dependent core is surrounded by intensely aggressive symbols. This drawing can be seen as a graphic presentation of the kind of personality produced by culturally prescribed means among the Sambia of New Guinea.

ness is obvious. Also aggressive are the paranoid stare and the fierce, oral-aggressive mouth. The figure thrusts forward toward the viewer in a menacing manner. The only remnant of the passive little boy I met are the buttons lining the chest, usually interpreted as a symbol of dependency yearnings. I would expect this boy to become extremely aggressive in the future. His rage may be directed toward males who represent his molester. I would expect no surface indication of any conflicts surrounding homosexuality, and a homophobia that might be dangerous to any gay person who falls into this individual's orbit.

Jim's buttons suggest that in the core of his psyche there is still a little boy yearning for a mother. To allow that yearning any expression would destroy the defensive, compensatory masculinity he has developed. The little buttons are a kind of soft core, denied contact with the external world by the enraged and aggressive symbols that dominate this drawing. The personality picture here is much like that of a Sambia male from the highlands of New Guinea (see following chapter).

Fear and Hatred of Females

The overwhelming majority of the boys I treat have been treated far worse at the hands of men than of women. In spite of this, they spontaneously manifest a much greater hatred and fear of females than of males. The reasons for this will be touched upon momentarily. This phenomenon is almost universal, at least in my sample. It can probably be best illustrated by some actual group process.

What follows are summaries of exercises done with a group of boys ranging from nine to fourteen years of age. The exercises consist of the presentation of a picture. One boy starts a story, and then hands the picture to the boy next to him, who continues the story. The picture in the first case consists of a cruise ship in the background and a woman in a bathing suit floating on a raft in very shallow water. A uniformed waiter has walked out to her with a serving tray.

Tom starts the story rather simply. The man is giving service to the lady. It moves to Larry, who says, "He wants to take her to bed and hump her." I asked Greg to continue the story, but he refuses. Alton volunteers to go next. "The guy pulls out a gun and he rapes her." Alton continues, "But instead, she kicks the gun in his hand and throws him over her back and grabs the gun and rapes him." Richard takes it from there. "Then another man finds her and they get it on. He starts raping her and chewing her dick—I mean, her pussy—and they start fucking, fucking. And then he goes, 'Ah! Help me!'" Ted now picks up the story. "And then she was raping him because she stuck a toothpick up his ass. After she stuck the toothpick up his ass, then . . ."

Tom now takes over, and the story degenerates into a complete primary process. "And then, after she shoots his balls off; then, like, ten other guys come in, and then they all have sex together. The girl takes one at a time, and they all have sex, and they go around and around forever. The end." Alton is not satisfied. I had told him he could make the ending to the story. He asserts his right and proceeds. "O.K. And after that, she throws them off the edge of the boat, and she goes speeding off after this other guy, and then she takes them out of the boat and knocks them off." Alton seems to be continuing with Tom's primary process material, not following the rules of secondary process logic. Alton, who is probably uncomfortable with the polymorphous sexuality of Tom's presentation, seems to take the entire story in the direction of flight from group sex between males and female hostility to men.

I now invited Greg, who had previously declined to contribute, to put his ending to the story. He continues in or close to primary process. "All right. After she cut off the man's dick, she roasted it and had . . . she smorged it. You roast a dick until it is all brown and crispy. When you roast a dick, you put chocolate on it and some crackers." Somewhat shocked at this addition, I invited other endings. Ted again stepped in. "O.K., and made a sandwich out of it. And then she chopped off his head, and they said, 'Bye-bye, head.' The end, by the boys' group."

This story starts off relatively benignly. Alton turns it to themes of rape, which are recurrent in these stories. In this case, however, the female is more than adequately equipped, protects herself, turns the tables, and rapes the male. Richard changes the theme, brings in a new, presumably stronger man to continue the rape. Curiously, he slips and has the man chewing on the woman's "dick," suggesting a possible displacement of rage with males (perpetrators) onto females. Ted turns it back to a woman raping a man. This woman adds the sadistic injury of sticking a toothpick into the man's rectum. Again, the phallic imagery is suspicious of displacement.

Tom tries to end the story by having it degenerate into a polymorphous perverse sex orgy in which it is not clear whether the men are after each other or the female. Alton has also decompensated and tries to quickly end the story with an illustration of female hostility to men. Ted, a victim of severe molestation by his father, finishes the story by having the female kill the male by chopping off his head (castration?).

Greg is a victim of molestation by his mother at a very young age, and physically and sexually abusive treatment at the hands of his father. His ending was a surprise to me. He is so private that he had previously concealed his intense fear of females from me. This is one of the diagnostic values of the story telling technique. His image of the mother, totally destroying his masculinity needs little comment. During another group, Greg drew a question card: "What is your greatest sexual fear?" His response was that his greatest fear was that his penis would become stuck in a woman's pussy or a man's butt. The theme of destruction of the penis often by devouring or engulfing are recurrent in the stories and question card responses of young male victims. It is among the most primal of the evidences that the basic anxiety of this population relates to loss or destruction of masculinity.

In another group story, Tom reacts to a picture of a male and female adult lying on a bed with a large dog with this narrative: "The man pulls out his dick, and the dog bites it off. And then it's bleeding, and he tells the woman to call the paramedics. And then she takes the dick and uses it for a dildo, and sucks it and puts it in her pussy and jabs it in there. And she can't get it out." This story emphasizes Tom's feeling of women as totally self-centered, pleasure-oriented, and unconcerned with the suffering of men.

Continuing in this same story, Mike introduces the element of the girl sucking on the dog's tail. I ask Jeff to continue the story, with the comment, "Jeff, can you figure out what the guy does when he sees the girl sucking on the dog's tail?" His response, "Slap the bitch. Yeah, I'll, slap her, slap her, and then he forces her to have sex." Here, the precipitant of aggression may be the narcissistic wound of preferring the dog's tail to the man's penis.

The themes of fear of women and violence directed toward women are obvious. The vision of women as powerful, attacking figures is equally obvious. Greg's symbolic comments on the destructiveness of women toward his sexual identity are extreme, but, in more benign form, are shared by a high percentage of male victims. What is to be made of this intense hostility to females? There is no clear answer. Several hypotheses come to mind. These stories contain some internal evidence, suggesting that this is displaced rage with males. Perhaps because they are male themselves, they cannot totally distance themselves from maleness. Perhaps to vent rage while preserving a bond to maleness, they must shift the rage to women. Perhaps, in American culture, it is safer to direct this rage at females. Perhaps they are taking advantage of cultural values which imply that it is masculine to treat females in this way. Perhaps we are dealing with the old psychoanalytic truism that mother gets blamed for everything, including failure of omnipotence in not protecting from molestation. Perhaps because I am a male therapist, it is difficult for these boys to fully vent their rage with males, and they displace it partly out of deference to me or fear of me onto female figures.

The rage and hatred of females seen so often in male victims may also be linked to defending against a yearning for a comforting symbiotic fusion with the mother. Such a fusion would damage both male identity and one's very sense of being a separately existing human being. In terms of psychodynamic theory it would lead the patient into a transient psychotic state, something the ego defends against at almost any cost. Under the stress of molestation, male victims may be tempted to seek comfort in regression into infantile oneness with the mother. This is simultaneously recognized by the ego as a threat to the existence of a separate, male self. Defense against such temptation can be mobilized through hatred and devaluation of women.

I suspect that there may be merit in all of these hypotheses about why damaged men need to hate, fear, and devalue women in many parts of the world. One of the nice things about psychoanalytic reasoning is that several things can be true at the same time, particularly if they operate at different psychic depths.

Rage and Revenge Against Males

This theme is recurrent, if not as obvious as the rage and fear of females. Some boys in group have openly told me that they do not trust me and they fear that, like other males, I will betray them and sexually assault them. Occasionally, I cannot work with a boy because of the intensity of these fears. On one occasion, I invited the boys' group to conduct a trial of a perpetrator, represented by an anatomically correct male doll. The group quickly found him guilty, and sentenced him to castration, a sentence which they carried out with available scissors.

Drawings and fantasies about retaliation against perpetrators typically include castration and genital assault. If these boys fight with each other, they are particularly prone to aim at the genitals. On one occasion, I observed a boy in group grab a large toy alligator and pretend to be inserting it up the rectum of another boy. Figure 5 graphically presents this complex. This was done in group by a boy molested by an adolescent male. He describes it as his punishment of the molester. The perpetrator is represented as hanging upside-down from his testicles, which are attached to a rope, which is, in turn, attached to the gallows.

Paranoid Fear of the Perpetrator

Probably closely related to the rage and revenge complex regarding males, is the truly paranoid fear that many victims hold of the perpetrators. This is almost always a serious issue in early treatment. Terror of the perpetrator and nightmares involving assault and retaliation for telling are *de riguer* in the early treatment process. Rather than being resolved, these fantasies often just go underground and are kept secret by the victim. One boy concealed such fears from me for two years. During this period, he was having tremendous difficulties in foster homes where there was only a single female foster parent. He was eventually placed in a group home because of the failure to adjust to foster placement. In general, I regard group home placement as a disaster for the children I work with. Yet this young man adjusted quickly, was happy, and stated that he had no desire ever to return to a foster home. When I asked him what he liked about the group home, he told me he had been afraid for two years that his mother's boyfriend, who had molested him, would seek him out and get even with him for telling. He described often getting up in the middle of the night and looking out the window to see if the molester was lurking nearby. He was terrified of certain passing cars, assuming that the perpetrator was scouring the neighborhood for him. What he liked about the group home was that there was a full-time staff awake all night. For the first time in years he felt safe in this protective environment.

Male victims tend to hide their fears of the perpetrators. This is an area in which clinicians need to make frequent and careful inquiry. This denial is probably related to the general tendency of males in our society to deny fear of anything. One of the questions typed on a card used in group is, "What is your greatest fear?" The younger boys' most frequent

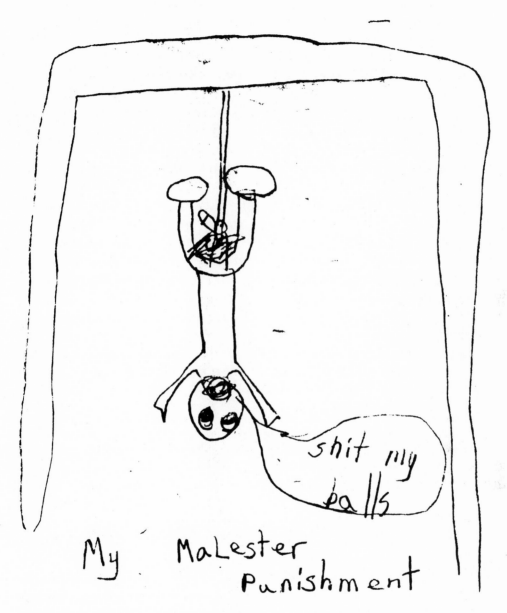

My MaLester Punishment

shit my balls

Figure 5. This drawing presents in undisguised form the rage and revenge fantasies toward perpetrators and often towards men in general which characterize much of the young male victim population.

answer is that they are not afraid of anything. The older boys will typically answer something connected with homosexuality.

Sexual Chaos

This is implicit in much that has already been described, but seems worth some specific elaboration. There is a curious pansexuality to the productions of this population. Once into a realm of free flight of fantasy, every conceivable and prohibited kind of sexual idea seems to emerge out of the boy's individual and collective psyche. The term "sexual chaos was suggested to me by Heinz Kohut's term, "prepsychological chaos." Kohut (1984) uses this to refer to the unstructured and incomprehensible chaos at the center of a damaged self. It is what the defenses of the deeply disturbed wall off to avoid experiencing. Kohut suspects such a chaotic core exists in the borderline conditions and psychoses. My instinctive reaction as a clinician is that the sexual chaos I have illustrated so often in this chapter is the sexual manifestation of the mental state Kohut calls prepsychological chaos. This implies that many young male victims have borderline or pre-psychotic personality patterns, or that they regress with stress to such a state as a result of molestation or other severe trauma.

Sexual chaos is implicit in most of the material presented in this chapter. A brief example illustrates much chaos in one place. This was written by an adolescent boy who is not a perpetrator.

> You are reading a Playboy magazine, and the next day you fuck a girl. And she finds the Playboy, and she says, "You fucking pervert!" So you go and slap her in the face and you grab her and rape her. She tells the police and her parents, and the police come and put you in jail, and you go to court and they say you're not guilty. And you go and rent XXXXX–Rated movies. You also rape another girl, and you rape your mother, and they find you guilty. You go to jail, and they rape you.

One element which stands out markedly here is this boy's inability to control his sexuality and violence in the face of strong sexual stimulation. The stimulation he cannot resist is pornography, something with which this child is obsessed. In the face of it, he starts down a slippery slope into sexual chaos. This process leads him not only into rape, but into incestuous rape of his mother and, finally, to homosexuality. Each new act is more disorganized and pathological for him than the one that precedes it. As he writes the material becomes more chaotic, antisocial, and toxic. For this boy, homosexual assault would be the ultimate degradation and annihilation.

Attempts to Repair the Sense of Maleness

Young male victims are very consistent in their effort to repair damage to their sense of maleness. Freud is quoted as saying, "We can treat neurotics any way we like. They treat themselves with transferences." In a general sense, this statement seems true of male victims also. A more modern statement might be that these boys attempt to treat themselves with selfobject transferences to male figures. The hunger of these boys for affective contact with older males has been illustrated numerous times. The gorilla/father in my playroom is virtually always a benign and helpful figure for the boys. At other times he is a taskmaster, demanding appropriate sexual behavior.

Anyone familiar with psychoanalytic theory is well aware that idealizing transferences have a flip side in the form of negative transference, rage, and hostility. In their effort to reach out for help, male victims generally suppress this side of the transference as long as possible. Only rarely does the father/gorilla come under attack. Only rarely do I come under attack in group, but it does happen to the gorilla, and to me. It is occasionally quite ferocious. This is particularly true of boys molested by father or men to whom they were very close.

A few clinical illustrations are in order. The same late adolescent who told me that his strongest desire was to be masculine and not homosexual added to the conversation that his boyfriend (with whom he was having sex) was very masculine. He stated that just being around him was causing him to pick up the other boy's masculine ways. He had previously lived with an indulgent grandmother, and currently lived with a brusque and demanding grandfather. He stated that he did not go back to the grandmother because there were no men around. He felt this would undermine his efforts to be more masculine.

Another example: In this case, a ten year old became involved in a group drama, with the stuffed human and animal figures. Two boys were busily acting out the usual molest scene. Louis spontaneously picked up the father/gorilla and put the younger gorilla on his lap. He commented that he missed his own father (who had molested him).

Later on, Louis picked up the molester figure and the young phallic monkey. He arranged a sexual scene between these two figures. I simply noted what he was doing. Other boys in the group said he was gay. I commented that, since the sexual scene was between a child figure and adult figure, it was more likely a molest situation involving Louis and his father, and probably connected with Louis's own urges to molest younger boys. At the end of the group, Louis returned the molester and the young monkey to the pile of stuffed figures. He quietly stated to me that he wanted to grow up to be like me, to have a family, and not to molest anyone.

Immaturity

A pervasive characteristic, at least of the boys under fourteen in my sample, is a gross immaturity. A high percentage of boys up to age fourteen function best when placed in groups with boys as young as eight. Most fourteen year olds cannot handle the older boys group, which ranges in age from fourteen to eighteen. I often give the younger boys a choice of game to play in the group as a warm-up activity. Frequently, a group with boys from ages eight to fourteen will select the game "Candy Land" which is designed for children four to six years of age. The projective drawings of these boys also suggest a gross immaturity. I am unclear as to the reasons for the immaturity of this population. It may simply be typical of all samples of children and adolescents in treatment, or it may have to do with developmental arrest caused by the trauma of molestation.

CONCLUSION

In this chapter we have looked in detail at the clinical and consulting-room manifestations of the behavior, fantasy, and projective material of the young male who has been molested. The intent has been to give the reader a kind of visual and verbal insight provided largely by young male victims themselves into how they perceive their victimization and the crisis into which it has thrust them. Clearly this is a clinical population and the material offered here may not be typical of all boys who are molested. It is in my judgment that this is typical of those who do come into treatment when they encounter a climate in which they can give vent to the troubling fantasies that underlie their behavior, expressing their pathologies.

Chapter 6

CULTURE

A central theme of this book is how a boy's developing sense of maleness is often damaged by molestation. One important question is the extent to which this process is influenced by cultural factors. Certain key elements in the development of maleness seem to be pan human and manifest in all cultures. These elements are probably rooted in genetics and in common early life experience such as a universal dependance upon females for care and nurturance in the earliest and most critical stages of life.

Within the boundaries of these intrinsic elements there is a wide latitude for the expression of masculine identity that is developed, shaped, and channeled by culture. In order to understand how molestation effects the developing male in our culture, it will be useful to look at a number of other cultures where males are exposed to what would clearly be called molestation in our society. In these societies this exposure is normative and socially acceptable. Looking at this data will serve several purposes. Most important for the purposes of this book will be to see to what extent cultural variables can mitigate the sense of damaged masculinity that is so commonly the result of molestation of males in our culture.

A broader issue to be examined here is how and why cultures intervene in the development of masculinity. This can tell us much about the nature of masculinity. What is intrinsic to it? What feelings and behaviors are universally consistent with a strong, intact sense of masculine identity? What behaviors and sexual expressions are shaped by nothing more than culturally determined attitudes and institutions? To what extent do these cultural attitudes rather than molestation itself influence the psychic damage done to the male victim? Hopefully the ethnographic and sociocultural literature can broaden our own understanding, improve our diagnostic thinking and offer hypotheses about how to best help boys who have been molested.

It is probable that sexual contact with much older males always has some effect on psychosexual development although not always traumatic.

Indeed, in some cultures, what we would call molestation is deliberately introduced for results that are consciously or unconsciously sought as part of a cultural design, and to meet the needs of a cultural system. These complex ideas will be explored in detail as this chapter progresses.

The focus of the next chapter will be to incorporate insights about culture into the process of working with male victims of diversified cultural backgrounds living within the boundaries of the United States of America and in the context of its dominant culture. Whatever the answers to more abstract questions about culture, it is undeniable that, in treating a patient from a different cultural group, it is essential to take into account the values of that culture regarding sexual behavior and sexual identity.

The Anthropological Record

In looking at the literature available, it is clear that no anthropological or related work surveys sexual behavior of the type we would call pedophilia. No data is available on men in any culture who prefer sexual contact with pre-pubertal children. The literature which touches on this issue generally deals with "homosexuality." If this literature is examined carefully, one finds that literature ostensibly dealing with "homosexuality" describes a great deal of sexual contact between adult men on the one hand and adolescents, and male children on the other. What is usually documented is sexual activity between young adolescents and adult males in the context of complex initiation rituals. There is some literature on institutionalized homosexuality between adult men in some cultures, but this is tangential to the purposes of this chapter and will not be belabored. Examining that anthropological and related literature on what western psychiatry would call pedophilia will make it possible, I believe, to throw some light on the focal questions of this chapter.

The Classical World

Virtually every literate person in our society is aware that "homosexuality" was tolerantly viewed in the Greco-Roman world prior to its domination by Christianity. These societies indeed seemed to have few clear-cut rules on what was acceptable and what was not in the area of sexual expression and behavior. The available information, however, concentrates largely on institutionalized sexuality between adult males and adolescent boys.

In its normative form, this involved a special relationship between a mature man who was supposed to be less than forty years of age and an adolescent or young adult male. It was expected, at the end of this relationship, that the younger male would shift his sexual interest to females, marry, and have children. The older male was expected to abandon these relationships after roughly age forty. How closely these norms were adhered to is not known, although the Roman emperors, Trajan and Hadrian, seemed to have largely ignored the upper age limit (Lambert 1984).

Rhetoric vs. Reality

Most cultures seem to have official rhetoric about how things are to be done and realities about how they are actually done. For example, the anthropologist, Geza Roheim (1974), inquired about the status of masturbation in an aboriginal Australian people he was studying. They at first denied it existed among them, but said they were aware of it since it was widely practiced among a neighboring people. As Roheim got to know these people, he found the practice of masturbation to be common. He learned that men often masturbated together, both ritually and recreationally, and that children would masturbate openly in the presence of adults without negative comment.

It takes little imagination to translate this situation into our culture. What therapist with a teenage male patient has not inquired about masturbation, only to be informed that he never does and never would do this, although he is aware of many acquaintances who indulge in the practice. When interviewing male victims from any culture, we need to be acutely aware that the first account we are likely to get is how things are supposed to be and not how they actually are.

Erotic Traditions

Frederick Whitam, a sociologist with great interest in matters sexual, writes of erotic traditions in his book *Male Homosexuality in Four Societies.* Although he does not delineate all of the world's erotic traditions, he does outline a Mediterranean erotic tradition and a Southeast Asian erotic tradition. By "erotic tradition" he seems to mean a series of rules regulating the kind of acceptable sexual activity and expression within these cultures. Cultures vary a great deal in terms of what they permit and do not permit the individuals to do with social sanction. For example, the Rwala Beduoins historically killed anyone caught engaging in "homosexuality" (Ford and Beach 1951). Other cultures offer a clearly-defined and socially acceptable role for the male homosexual. Such societies would include those of the Sioux Indians and Yokut of Central California. Among the Sioux, individuals who experienced certain dreams either committed suicide or adopted a female role. They were allowed to engage in sexual relationships with otherwise heterosexual men without social stigma on either participant (Erikson 1950). In the Yokut tradition, homosexuals were given the specific vocation of mortician (Wallace 1978).

Whitam talks of a Mediterranean erotic tradition in which he seems to include Spain, Italy, all of Latin America, and possibly the Arab world. All of his specific data on this tradition is drawn from Latin America. Although he cites a Portuguese government study which found that eighty percent of males classified as heterosexuals regularly have secondary homosexual contact. No statistical data for other Latin societies is presented.

Whitam notes variation within Latin countries in regard to their tolerance for homosexual behavior, with Cuba and Argentina being the most homophobic. He provides the richest data on Guatemala, which he describes as relatively permissive of sexual relationships between young males and older males, and sexual relationships between men in general.

Whitam talks about two types of males who participate in this Guatemalan pattern. One is of ostensibly heterosexual adult males who use homosexual males, often adolescent in age, for a sexual outlet. Their motivation seems to be either unavailability of female partners or a quest for variety. The second group are younger males with strong homosexual inclinations who are willing to participate in this system.

Whitam links these sexual patterns to the strong patriarchal structure of Latin societies, suggesting that male dominance not only includes authority over females in sexual and other areas, it extends to the domination of stronger males over the weaker males. If it is an assertion of power to conquer a female sexually, it is an even greater triumph to conquer a man sexually because of the man's greater ascribed status and power in this cultural system.

The Latin *macho* who occasionally or frequently turns to sex with a younger or homosexual male must follow certain rules to remain within his society's parameters. If the intercourse is anal, he must be the active partner. He is the recipient, rather than the giver, of fellatio. There is also often a payment demanded for the service. Whitam feels that the Latin question is not who is gay and who is not, but who penetrated whom.

Similar data comes from a less scientific source. The distinguished Mexican poet Octavio Paz. Paz is a perceptive observer of his own society. In his classic work, *The Labyrinth of Solitude,* a study of the development and nature of the Mexican personality, he turns his attention to sexual relationships between males (1961). This perceptive and respected participant in Mexican culture comes by other means to conclusions similar to Whitam's:

> It is likewise significant that masculine homosexuality is regarded with a certain indulgence, as far as the active agent is concerned. The passive agent is an abject, degraded being. Masculine homosexuality is tolerated, then, on condition that it consists in violating a passive agent. As with heterosexual relationships, the important thing is not to open oneself up and, at the same time, to break open one's opponent.

In addition to his discussion of the Latin world, Whitam turns his attention to the Philippines. He classifies society there as belonging to a Southeast Asian erotic tradition which is tolerant of all forms of consenting sexuality, including homosexuality and prostitution. He describes an institutionalized sexual activity between what he calls "call boys" and older men. The call boys typically range from fifteen to twenty-five in age and are not despised for their sexual activities. There is another identifiable group in Philippine society called the *Bayot* who enjoy sexual contact with the call boys. Either the young males or the Bayot may initiate the relationship. The *Bayot* apparently continue this kind of relationship throughout their sexually active life. The call boy gives up this behavior sometimes in his twenties. He is viewed by Whitam as predominantly heterosexual, and will eventually marry and have a family. Structurally, Whitam interprets this institution as intended to preserve the required virginity of Philippine females. As the male adolescent's sex drive develops, he finds himself in a society which demands female virginity as a condition of successful marriage arrangements.

The Philippine system allows considerable sexual activity without damaging the traditional arrangements for marriage between males and females. The ability of males in this age range to engage in sexual activity with other males and then shift to heterosexuality in their twenties is a pattern found over and over in the literature. It seems to fly in the face of both social learning theory and psychoanalytic theory. I suspect that the ability to make such shifts is dependent on the events occurring in neurally critically developmental periods prior to age five. This was discussed in more detail in the chapter on theory.

MELANESIA

It is in Melanesia that the pattern of males shifting from early homosexual object choice to later heterosexual preference is most dramatic and best documented. It is also here that institutionalized sexual use of young males by older males reaches its apogee. The term Melanesia refers to a cultural area including New Guinea and numerous smaller islands in its vicinity. In this area, many but not all, societies institutionalize homosexual contact between older and younger males.

New Guinea is probably the world's most valuable anthropological data bank. Because of its isolation, the rugged topography of its highlands, and the malignant nature of the lowland climate, it remained the least disturbed area occupied by primitive people anywhere in the world. Some of its highland peoples were totally unknown until after World War II. Traditional cultures remained largely undisturbed in some cases until the nineteen sixties or seventies. Unlike most ethnographic cases, anthropologists have been able to study largely undisturbed cultures in the New Guinea highlands in an age (1950–1980) when anthropology was sophisticated enough to collect extensive, high quality data without the same ethnocentric biases and faulty techniques that contaminate earlier studies.

These are fierce warrior cultures practicing head-hunting and cannibalism. Warfare was chronic and endemic. Certain generalizations can be made about all of the societies who ritualized homosexual practices between older and younger males (Lidz and Lidz, 1989). Relationships between the sexes are characterized by hostility and suspicion. Woman have low status. Men fear woman and often live separately in communal men's huts. Boys are allowed great intimacy and closeness with their mother's until the age of initiation—usually seven to ten years. Then they are traumatically separated and go through a prolonged initiation that would be called physically and sexually abusive in our culture. The best studied of these peoples are the Sambia—studied in great depth by

Gerald Herdt (1981) and visited by the analyst and sexologist Robert Stoller (1985). Lidz and Lidz make extensive use of Herdt's Sambia material in their psychoanalytic interpretation of masculinization in New Guinea (1989).

Like most of their neighbors, Sambia boys enjoy an early intimacy with their mother characterized by protectiveness and even indulgence. The Sambia father sleeps in the family hut, but in a separate area which his wife may not enter. In his own initiation, the father has been taught to be hostile to his wife. Sambia men fear contamination by menstrual blood and vaginal fluids to the degree that men and women walk on segregated paths to avoid a man accidentally touching a bush that has come in contact with these fluids. The men believe their vitality sapped by all orgasm, but particularly by orgasm resulting from heterosexual relationships. Such intercourse leads eventually to premature death via semen depletion. They believe that it is semen that turns boys into men and that a lifetime supply must be obtained by fellating older males during youth.

The initiation process begins between ages six and ten. The boys are abruptly taken in groups from their mother amidst howls of grief. Some attempt to flee but are dragged back. The initiation rites are long and complex and will be only summarized here. The boys are first carried to the forest where they are severely beaten by the men. Throughout the process they are deprived of sleep and given minimal food and water. Sharp canes are thrust down their nostrils with comments that this is because the mothers' bad influence entered their body through the nose. This continues until blood is drawn. This is believed to be the mother's womb blood, a source of feminizing influence on the boy. The blood is collected on leaves. Later the men select a mother and in a public rite force the bloody leaves down her throat while verbally berating tribal women for being bad mothers and inhibiting their sons' development.

The boys are also taken to a forest glade via a path that Herdt compares to a birth canal opening into a womb. Here their entire body, including their genitals, is scrubbed with nettles. This is to remove their childhood skin so it can be replaced by a new masculine skin. Herdt was so appalled by the brutality of these scenes he could barely watch. In another public ceremony, the mother's attack the boys with sticks and assault them verbally as if to further emphasize that they can count on nothing from their former protectors.

Mixed in with these ordeals, the boys are introduced to the idea that they cannot become men unless they drink semen. They are introduced to bachelors and older initiates whom they must orally copulate. From this day forth the boys live in the men's hut. They regularly orally copulate older males in order to masculinize themselves. Initially many boys are shocked by the demand but most accommodate and the practice becomes erotized for both participants (Lidz and Lidz 1989). As they grow older, they reverse roles and allow themselves to be orally copulated by subsequent groups of initiates. They will not see their mothers or sisters for ten to twenty years when they will marry. From the time they enter the men's hut until they marry the boys must avoid all contact with women. When contact is unavoidable, they must look away or wear a mask.

When the time for marriage arrives, it is expected and, according to Herdt, actually happens, that these males abandon same sex relationships, take up relationships with female peers, marry, become fathers and warriors, and rarely return to any kind of same sex activity. Herdt observed only one deviant in this culture who seemed to retain a preference for sex with younger males throughout his life.

Sambia men in general seem to make the shift from an early heterosexual attachment to their mother to an intense sexual involvement with other males and then back to an enduring heterosexuality. Herdt found no evidence of the kind of angst about sexual identity that plagues male victims in this culture. It does, however, seem that this brutal process of masculinization may forever poison the ability of men to relate lovingly to women. Love and intimacy with women must be given up to prevent regression back to the symbiotic attachment to the mother that preceeded initiation. Hostility, fear, and devaluation of women are techniques to assure that no such regression takes place. American culture produces men like this. Jim, whose case is discussed and illustrated in Figure 4 in Chapter 5, has a Sambia type personality structure. Jim's personality was, however, created as an accident of personal history rather than as a part of a cultural design. He will not fare as well in American culture as he would among the Sambia.

For most primitive and ancient societies we have only anecdotal evidence about their sexual attitudes and institutions. For the Sambia, we are replete with data. Perhaps enough to help us understand why Sambia society would design such cruel institutions. Erik Erikson long ago (1950) developed the concept that difference cultures zero in on crucial aspects of child development to accentuate the personality traits they need in their members if the society is to accomplish its vital tasks. In the Sambia case it would seem that their goal is to produce not balanced human beings who can love and work, but fierce warriors who can survive in a world of warring cannibals and headhunters. To do this, they must wrench the boy from his mother's breast and transform him into an emotionally hardened warrior. This cannot be done without both the period of loving dependency on the mother and the subsequent harsh masculinization. Only by violently removing the boy from the maternal paradise and forcing him into the brutal world of the men can they tap the rage generated by forced separation from the mother and channel it by cultural means into a generalized rage that is useful against this society's many external enemies (Lidz and Lidz 1989).

Siwa

Leaving Melanesia, the literature becomes far less rich. The closest thing to what the West might define as pedophilia comes from the oasis of Siwa. This is in the North African desert near the border between Egypt and Libya. According to Ford and Beach (1951), all men in this culture, and all boys, engage in anal intercourse with each other. Prominent men in these cultures lend their sons to each other. There is no social sanction upon this. The fact that fathers are exchanging sons with each other for sexual purposes suggests that this practice does not so inhibit heterosexuality that men are unable to function as husbands and fathers.

Australia

There is also relevant data from this island continent. Australian native populations have sexual practices which are extremely unusual from the Western perspective. Perhaps the most shocking is the custom of subincision. At the time of puberty, the boy's penis is literally slit open to create what this culture regards as a vagina-like structure. This is at least suggestive of a deeply rooted envy of females and a desire to possess their genitals in a sort of aboriginal reversal of penis envy.

Ford and Beach also describe sex as common between unmarried men and uninitiated boys. Since boys are generally initiated at puberty, this is an institution which may somewhat parallel pedophilia in our society. According to the authors, it is not uncommon for a fully initiated man who has not married to take a boy of 10 to 12 years of age and to live with him as he would with a wife until the older man marries. Roheim (1974) describes an Australian group in which a young man must become the "boy-wife" to his future father-in-law. The implication is that here, as in Melanesia, a period of homosexual activity precedes and then is super-seded by heterosexuality.

SECONDARY OUTLET

This concept is developed by Whitam (1986) as a partial explanation for the homosexual behaviors he explores. The idea is that males, when their sexual contact with females is culturally or otherwise limited, will turn readily to other males for sexual gratification. Frequently, the pattern seems to be one occurring between older and younger males. The literature from Melanesia suggests that the lower threshold for involvement in these kinds of practices can be as young as six years of age. Elsewhere pubescent boys seem to be the youngest group involved in the practices.

The concept of secondary outlet may apply clearly in American prisons and in all-male military institutions. It may also be similar to the concept of situational molester developed by Howells (1981). Situational molesters may be men deprived of their regular or preferred outlet who will take advantage of a sexual opportunity with another, often younger, male as a secondary source of gratification.

Implications of the Literature

The anthropological literature reviewed here allows some important inferences about the nature of male sexuality. If this data is accurate, basic sexual orientation does not follow the patterns that would be predicted by a social learning or addiction model. The anthropological testimony is that in spite of intense homosexual stimulation in latency and puberty years males emerge from this process as functioning heterosexuals. This phenomenon seems best explained by a theory that sexual orientation/ preference is laid down in the first six years of life and is virtually impossible to change after that. This kind of theory has been developed by Jonathan Winson (1985) using data from neurobiology and John Money (1965) using data from the treatment of hermorphroditic chil-dren (see chapter on theory for elaboration).

Societies can devise institutions which force males into homosexual contact in latency and adolescent years, but the behavior does not become permanent. The Sambia case suggests that affective relationships with women are damaged, but this is more likely caused by the brutality of the initiation process rather than its sexual aspects. The available data would suggest that cultural attitudes have a tremendous impact on how males handle homosexual contact in childhood and adolescence, but that changes of sexual object culturally dictated during these periods do not become permanent. It is possible that the sexual components of the male psyche are always plastic or bisexual. If a hypothetical culture required permanent homosexual activity, it is likely most of its males would comply. There are no anthropological case studies of this. A society which engineered permanent, exclusive homosexuality in its males would be at great reproductive disadvantage in the struggle for survival against other societies, so such "field experiments" are unlikely.

These data also imply that basic heterosexuality (and probably homosexuality where it is the preference) arise early in human development. In no case does the anthropological literature deal with boys sexualized to other males prior to age six. It would seem that if the male has become heterosexual in preference prior to that time no amount of cultural pressure can change the male's ability to respond sexually to females when it is again permitted by the culture.

It is also clear that in many parts of the world young males are readily channeled by culture into socially sanctioned homosexuality. In the more benign cases such as the Philippines and Guatemala, this process seems psychologically harmless generating none of the problems arising out of the molestation of males in more homophobic cultures. Presumably those boys with a pre-existing homosexuality can continue this with less social opprobrium that they would encounter in the United States. Those with a strong pre-existing heterosexuality would most likely return to that when culturally approved options become available. In the meantime, key figures in the life of young males are not reacting hysterically and homophobically to a course of events which is culturally approved and culturally regulated by institutions facilitating sex between males.

The same kind of reasoning may explain why researchers in the Netherlands have found that sexual contact between adults and children are non-traumatic if they are consensual (Bruinsma. Personal Communication, 1992). The Dutch and probably several other North European cultures seem to be far less homophobic than American culture. Out-comes in the Netherlands may parallel those in Guatemala without the angst and turmoil that characterize male victims in America.

Stated differently, this information suggests that the male *homo sapiens* can adapt his sexual behaviors to meet the demands of culture and reality and that this adaptiveness includes a much wider range of behaviors and more dramatic shifts in sexual behavior than would be predicted by data drawn solely from North American sources. Males seem to return to their original object choice when cultural conditions permit. In all the cultures examined here, men shift from homosexual objects in latency and adolescence to heterosexual objects in adult life. In the Sambia case, an early and intense attachment to the mother is documented. Lidz and Lidz (1989) describe this as a pan-Melanesian fact of life. I suspect it is also true in other societies where data from the earliest part of life is lacking. Indeed, it is almost inherent in the human condition that our earliest intimacy is with the mother. Cultural conditions facilitating intense, and eventually sexualized symbiosis between males and their mothers in early life are probably common world wide. This kind of relationship with the mother, in my judgment, predisposes men toward female object choice.

One alternative interpretive hypothesis is that sexual orientation is inherited. This is discussed in the chapter on theory and will not be reviewed here. Other hypotheses are that male sexual preference is completely plastic and subject to cultural manipulation or that all men are bisexual and simply choose the object dictated by culture. Bisexuality may be common world wide, but is so poorly studied it is difficult to evaluate its role. In cultures which permit adult men to choose either male or female objects for sexual love, some seem to choose almost exclusively males, others almost exclusively females and some both. This suggests the truism that individual men do have sexual preferences and will turn down opportunities to have sex with a partner of a sex that does not appeal to them.

Sexual object choice is culturally prescribed in small face-to-face societies. But in such places as Guatemala, the Phillipines, and Portugal men are culturally free to choose male or female partners. In these cultures some men choose women and others men as sex partners. The underlying model of male sexuality seems to be one in which males develop a preference in early life. This preference always remains a potential that at times dominates sexual expression. At other times preference is buried by cultural demands. But there is also a potential in most males to enjoy sexual relations even if they are not with the sex of preference. It is here that culture enters. In some cultures such as American, only heterosexuality is approved. Homosexuality is actively devalued in most segments of American society. Several primitive societies require shifts of sexual objects as a part of normal growing up. Another group of societies are relatively neutral about mens' sexual preference. These societies usually have institutional arrangements for both heterosexual and homosexual preference. Males seem to adapt easily to the latter two kinds of societies. They are able to experience sex with males and females as well as sex between older and younger males without the kind of trauma that is well documented for the male victim in the United States. I would hypothesize that the male sexual psyche is two tiered. There is a deep level that contains a fixed object preference for male or female. A group of males of unspecified size probably is truly bisexual even in this deepest core of the sexual psyche. Above this nuclear level there is a less basic sphere where plasticity in sexual object choice is the norm. This allows the male to adapt to whatever cultural conditions require.

It would seem to me that biology would require this kind of arrangement. If Sambia men could not return to female objects there would be no Sambia. There must have always been natural selection operating against human populations that turned out a high percentage of homosexuals. Yet in the Sambia case it is clear that the plasticity of the male sexual psyche also serves an adaptive function. These people need male bonding to create fighting groups that give them a survival advantage in a militarily competitive world that has existed for millennia. This culture also needs the rage that is generated when young males are traumatically separated from an intimate relationship with the mother and forced into a harsh masculine world. Erik Erikson (1950) has demonstrated in several other cases how societies manipulate early childhood to produce personality types that are adaptive to their society's survival needs. I suspect this two tiered sexual psyche in males is a structure that has developed evolutionarily to give societies flexibility in the production of personality type while assuring a heterosexual outcome for most of its males.

The fact that there are many societies in the world which allow males to shift their sexual object choice and which permit or require sexual contact between older and younger males, is consistent with recent research on the males who survive molestation with minimal problems in American society. I would suggest that these are victims who find themselves in families and/or social systems which give them support to get through their victimization. I would suggest that some parents or other key figures in a victim's life have an intuitive awareness that if the cultural system is supportive the damage can be contained. I would add that the damage can be contained because once basic or core sexual identity is established, it cannot be altered by molestations occurring outside of critical developmental periods. What can happen though is much *Sturm und Drang* in the upper levels of the sexual psyche, *Sturm und Drang* that can indeed lead to severe damage if not well managed. More will be said of this in another chapter.

In no way should this information be interpreted to mean that we should adopt a laid back, casual attitude toward sexual contact between adults and children in American culture. Like the Sambians, we must adapt to the cultural reality we are given. American cultural reality is that many of our males are severely harmed by molestation. As therapists we can, however, use insights from other cultures to better understand the adaptability of the male psyche and to give us clues as to how to minimize sexual trauma once it has occurred.

We can help develop supportive families. We can make victims aware that their life need not be destroyed because they have had sexual contact with another male. We can be encouraging to parents that the damage can be repaired. We can point to examples of individuals in this culture, as well as others, of men who have survived victimization with an intact sense of masculinity and an ability to function sexually.

CONCLUSIONS

This chapter has ranged over a wide variety of cultural data about male sexual orientation. The anthropological data varies widely in quality. Usually it lumps homosexuality and sex between adult males and adolescent and pre-adolescent boys into one category. For this reason, the focus has been on erotized relationships between males rather than a specific focus on molestation and pedophilia. Still the reader must keep in mind that most of what is being discussed is sexual contact between younger and older males. Most of this would be called sexual assault or molestation in the United States. Nothing in this literature describes consensual relationships between same age male peers.

In spite of the often thin data, it does allow some fascinating speculations some of which seem to be confirmed by data from other sources presented elsewhere in this book. Several facts seem to stand out: Many societies permit far more young male-older male sex than does American society. In many societies such contact is not only permitted, but institutionally required. Whereever there is data, it suggests that men can shift from homosexual to a heterosexual object choice with little difficulty where the culture requires it. In no society examined does this shift cause a permanent change in male's basic sexual orientation. It is never accompanied by the traumatic sequelae amply documented by research on male victims in the United States. In the anthropological record, the thinnest, but most interesting data suggests that males have an innermost psychic core in which a very early object choice is made and there is an outer sphere of sexual functioning in which they may shift back and forth in object choice, depending upon cultural pressures and realities. All of this has implications for the understanding and treatment of male victims of sexual assault in the United States.

Chapter 7

AMERICAN SUBCULTURES

It is now time to bring the issue of culture closer to our own shores, and to deal with American subcultures. The term subculture has been selected after careful consideration. It may be controversial. What is meant by subculture is a group contained geographically within a larger culture and connected to the larger culture by economic and political bonds. Subcultures also may share many values and institutions with the broader culture that surrounds them. The major American subcultures— African-American and Mexican American—share many traits with the dominant Anglo culture. All three are historically Christian and have been deeply influenced by this religion. These three cultures have interacted on the North American continent for four hundred years. Most participants in all three cultures speak English although sometimes in dialectic form or as a second language. Complex subcultures such as the African-American, or the Mexican-American, contain smaller, more homogeneous groups that do not share all elements of the subculture. For example, immigrants from the Caribbean may be called African-American, but have cultural differences from African-Americans descended from slaves brought directly to what is now the United States. In diagnosis and treatment even the nature of these subcultures within subcultures need to be taken into account.

Although the majority of my clients have always been white, I have worked with enough African-American and Mexican-American victims of sexual abuse to make some remarks about how the values and usages of these subcultures impact the way abuse is experienced by these young males. It is essential to remember that cultures are composed of individuals. Complex cultures such as European-American, African-American, and Mexican-American allow a much wider range of personality expression than primitive cultures such as the Sambia. It is probably accurate, however, to say that there are certain personality configurations that occur more commonly in each subcultures than in the dominant Anglo culture. The focus of this chapter will be on the content of African-

American and Mexican-American that is relevant to understanding and treating male victims from these cultures. It should be kept in mind that only the most common personality patterns and cultural practices in these cultures will be discussed. It must be kept in mind that there will be many individuals and families within these subcultures to whom these generalizations do not apply.

Differential Incidence of Sexual Abuse?

One of the first questions to arise from the issue of subcultures in America is: Do these groups experience sexual abuse of young males at differential rates? The literature does not seem to answer this definitively. Showers, et al. (1983), find in a hospital emergency room population that boys referred for suspected sexual abuse are referred in approximately the same percentages as boys of these subcultures are found in the general population. Cupoll and Sewell (1988) obtained different results. They found African-Americans over represented in the referred male victim population. Hispanics were underrepresented, and whites appeared in the same numbers as would be expected in terms of their representation in the general population.

My own sample offers yet different data. It should be kept in mind that I am sampling those not referred for evaluation, but those actually involved willingly in a treatment process. My sample is seventeen percent Hispanic, whereas the community is twenty-eight percent Hispanic. African-Americans represent seven percent of my sample, as compared to seven and seven-tenths percent for the community. Whites are overrepresented, constituting seventy-six percent of my sample, as opposed to sixty percent of the general population.

It is difficult to make any sense of these figures. The available data is inconclusive. My working hypothesis is that probably the three major North American subcultures have roughly equal rates of sexual abuse of young males. Differences in the samples may reflect differences in community agencies where these samples are drawn. It is likely that different cultural groups respond differently to societal institutions dealing with sexual abuse. It is also likely that the sophistication and sensitivity of these agencies in dealing with other cultures vary from community to community. Police departments, hospitals, and social service agencies presumably vary in their response to minority concerns from community to community. In some communities members of minority groups may be more willing to work with these agencies than in other communities. In racist communities, these agencies may prefer to ignore sexual abuse problems for a variety of reasons. Whites are likely to be over-represented in treatment samples because of greater affluence, greater trust of authorities, and a culturally determined orientation to seek therapy at least among middle class whites. Hispanics do seem to be under represented in all samples. This may be due to first generation distrust of government agencies and fear of deportation in the case of the undocumented.

HISPANICS

The first thing that needs to be said about "Hispanics" is that this is an extremely variable group. All U.S. statistics seem to be collected with this label. Under this term, an aristocrat from Madrid, a businessman from Veracruz, Mexico, an adolescent from a Los Angeles barrio, and a Maya Indian from Guatemala City would all be labeled as participants in the same culture. The absurdity of generalization across such boundaries is obvious. Differences due to social class and a rural/urban dichotomy are much greater in Hispanic populations than either Anglo-American or African-American populations.

My referrals have included Mexican-Americans who are either recent immigrants or whose families have long-term, sometimes generational, residence within the United States. There are appreciable differences between the new arrivals and the long-term residents, even though both are ultimately of Mexican heritage. Some generalizations, however, can be made, with the cautions stressed earlier in this section.

Any discussion of masculinity in Mexican males needs to begin with the concept of *machismo*. This is not because the *macho*, is the most common type of male seen in the treatment of Mexican male victims, but because of the centrality of the concept of *machismo* in Mexican thinking about maleness. To Anglos, this is usually a negative word connotating a strutting patriarch who dominates and/or abuses women. It carries no negative connotation in Mexico. In all but the most sophisti-cated circles, it is the ideal of what a man should be. Strong, fearless, ready to fight at the merest aspersion upon his honor. A sexual object irresistible to women. Passionate when his relations with women are good. Vengeful and even violent when he feels betrayed by a woman. Usually hard drinking. Proud. A man who never cries or shows his softer side. This is a flamboyant male who prides himself in an exaggerated sense of masculinity. He is a classic, if often benign, patriarch. He is the head of his family and makes all major decisions about family business. His relationships with other men can be stormy whenever issues of dominance emerge. He expects women and children to be submissive. This is the yardstick by which most Mexican boys will measure themselves.

It is very difficult to live and feel the macho role when one has been molested by another man. That means to these boys that they have been debased in terms of their cultural understanding to the status of a woman, used by a *macho* for his pleasure. Or as Octavio Paz has said, "violated as a passive agent" and "broken open by his opponent" (1961). Boys who try to adhere to the *macho* ideal do come into treatment for victimization, but less often than some other types. When they do come into treatment, they are difficult cases. They must deny at least in emotional terms how they feel about what has happened to them. Otherwise their *machismo* would be deeply compromised.

The most common type of Mexican American boy coming into treatment for sexual victimization by men presents with varying digress of what I would call broken maleness. They seem to quietly or with great anguish acknowledge that something has happened that has compromised their ability to live up to the *macho* ideal. In some cases this has lead into an open hatred of homosexuals, often explicitly because they characterize their victimization as a homosexual act on their part as well as on the part of the perpetrator. In other boys their sense of maleness is so shattered they have surrendered. They either see their masculinity as hopelessly damaged, or they have reluctantly accepted that they are bisexual or gay with all the negative ramifications this has in their cultural setting.

Another kind of Mexican male I see in practice is the fragile, somewhat feminine, overprotected male child. These boys are intensely involved with their mother. Often both mother and child are heavily involved in the Roman Catholic Church. Their parents are fearful that they will become involved in the American gang and drug culture, and tend to separate them from other children to avoid temptations. These boys are often fearful of peers and have poor peer relationships. They are relatively easy prey for child molesters and hence show up frequently in victim caseloads.

Mexican and Latin American cultures, like most others have a deep split between how things are supposed to be and how they really are in the sexual area. One senses much conflict beneath the surface about homoeroticism in general which would certainly spill over into the area of the molestation of boys. Such things are seen as full of shame and not to be discussed with outsiders. To get into these areas with Mexican males in general and with Mexican victims of sexual abuse in particular often takes a long period of relationship building and demonstration of empathy on the part of the therapist.

The reader may note an absence of any reference to molestation of Mexican boys by women. In general boys of all cultures seem to be brought to treatment most often as a result of molestation by males because this is almost universally perceived as more damaging. The *machismo* complex in Mexican culture aggravates this tendency. The *macho* would regard molestation of boys by older women as a male triumph, not something about which one seeks help. The reality may be different particularly where very young boys are involved, but I have never had a Mexican-American boy brought to me for treatment of victimization by a woman. I have, however, treated perpetrators from this culture and discovered in the course of treatment that the boy has been molested by a woman.

No discussion of Mexican culture, as it relates to sexuality, is complete without stressing the role of the extended family. High cultural value is placed on the maintenance of the extended family and upon maintaining connections between members of this extended family. This is a much tighter system than the dominant Anglo-American nuclear family. It is expected that family problems be maintained and managed within the family. Anything that will divide and destroy the family unity is to be avoided. This may be why Mexican-American victims are underrepresented in statistical studies.

The greatest relevance of this to our discussion is that, when molestation occurs within the extended family, the family unit is subject to severe stresses pulling in opposite directions. On the one hand, the child's parent is most likely to feel that the child has been wronged and damaged. On the other hand, they are aware that an open accusation or, particularly, reports to authorities, may create a deep and irreversible division within the family. This makes working with victims of extended family members particularly difficult in the context of North American reporting laws.

Culture and Treatment

The discussion of Mexican and Mexican-American cultural attitudes to this point raises issues relevant to the treatment of the Mexican-American male victim of molestation. There are cultural reasons that would make this population less likely to seek treatment and to disclose the extent of what has actually happened. Already noted are shame about damaged *machismo* and protecting perpetrators in the extended family.

In working with immigrants, the clinician needs to be aware that they are off-balance and disoriented in a new culture. Their attitudes toward officialdom will be drawn from their experience in Mexico and with American immigration authorities. In both cases the lessons learned are likely to be that authority is to be feared and avoided when possible. This would extend to police, child protection agencies, and even agencies providing treatment. It is up to the clinician to demonstrate that, even though they have been referred by a government agency, they can trust and invest in the treatment. They are unlikely to do so without considerable testing. In spite of the baggage they bring with them from Mexico, immigrants are probably easier to reach out to and form a treatment alliance with than are many long term Mexican-American residents of the United States. This is particularly true if the therapist is Hispanic or bilingual. If such an alliance is to be established, the therapist must be aware of the basic values and traditions of Mexican culture, as well as some of the facts about its subdivisions along class and ethnic lines.

Mexican-Americans who have been in the U.S. for a long time are in many ways more difficult for the non-Hispanic therapist to reach. Long-term residents may have had more negative experiences with racism in the United States, and may have had more and worse experience with our societal institutions. I believe they can be engaged by the non-Hispanic therapist, but the period of testing may be even longer than with the immigrant.

AFRICAN-AMERICANS

This culture seems to be somewhat more homogeneous than the Hispanic. The same cautions, however, are necessary regarding subdivisions. There are important divisions within African-American culture following lines of social class. There is a value on cultural solidarity which does seem to be holding the majority of African-Americans together around a number of shared values and institutions. African-Americans do not have the wide diversity of national background that is found among Hispanics. Most are long term residents of the United States. The clinician, however, needs to be careful to identify cultural differences between this population and more recent immigrants from the Caribbean, Central America, and Africa.

Most of us are aware of the long, destructive experience of Africans in America. It is no surprise that most participants in this culture have a deep distrust of the white-dominated institutions of American society. This distrust spills readily over to white therapists, and even to theories and treatment approaches derived by whites. Closely related is an extreme sensitivity on issues involving racial self esteem. This is predictable in view of the degradation to which African-Americans have historically been subjected in this country. Much of this degradation was aimed directly at their sense of self-esteem. One of the results has been that African-American culture has turned inward and works very hard at keeping outsiders unaware of anything that might bring shame on the group as a group.

In discussing the confirmation hearings for an African-American, Justice to the United States Supreme Court, Kim Crenshaw, an African-American professor at the U.C.L.A. Law School made the following comments about degrading allegations being exchanged between the candidate and an African-American woman.

> For us African-American people, anything that occurs within the race, whether in the workplace, within our families or private lives, is a deeply personal affair. For that to be made so public is in a sense a violation of our collective privacy (*Los Angeles Times* (Oct. 12, 1991).

Obviously, even writing these words about the treatment of African-American victims of sexual abuse raises some of the same pitfalls of invasion of racial privacy. I indeed considered not including this section in the book because of the delicacy of this matter. This section was reviewed by an African-American therapist with extensive experience. Some of the content was altered at her suggestion. In spite of the sensitivity of the topic, I decided to include this section because clinicians need to be aware that there are many African-American male victims who need treatment. There are relatively few specialists in this field and all African-American victims cannot be treated by African-American therapists. Those of us who are not African-American who must work with this population need some understanding of the issues involved. It is in this spirit that these remarks are offered.

The first cultural value to be encountered is homophobia. This is no surprise, since it is shared with both Anglo and Hispanic culture. If anything, homophobia is more intense and rigid in African-American culture than in either Anglo or Mexican cultures. Unlike Mexican culture, there seems to be no major distinction between passivity and activity. Sex between two males is considered homosexual, regardless of who does what to whom, and, I suspect, regardless of the ages of the participants. These attitudes, again, are not unique to African-American culture, but seem more intense within that context.

There is, indeed, homosexuality and molesting of boys among African-Americans. Any candid African-American professional will tell you that, and there are statistics to back it up. In working with African-Americans on this issue, a high level of denial is likely to be encountered. The rhetoric versus reality dichotomy here seems to be the sharpest of the three cultures under discussion.

As with the Mexican and Mexican-American cultures, some comments on family structure are relevant here. African-American culture does not share the pattern of a homogeneous patriarchal family found among Hispanics. Women are far more influential in contemporary African-American families. Indeed, in a high percentage of African-American families, no father figure is present. A significant segment of the African-American population is increasingly regarding this as a problem and trying to reinvolve men in family life and particularly with young African-American males.

The historic degradation and destruction of the African-American male have led, in many cases, to the emergence of a strong female in the African-American family who has to take the role of both mother and father to the male child. Cobb and Greer in their book, *Black Rage* (1968), suggest that this matriarchal mother had to produce a passive, non-assertive male in order to protect him from physical extermination by the whites. These authors describe a "paradigmatic" African-American male who was culturally esteemed for centuries. This type of male suppressed his assertiveness and anger in order to conform to the demands of white society. He gave up key elements of his maleness in order to succeed in his time and place. Grier and Cobb describe him as often despised for this lack of assertiveness and masculine power by both his wife and sons.

This kind of historical background can be expected to make issues of maleness of intense concern in this cultural context. Obviously many African-American males have now escaped this devalued role, but it is part of the heritage of the culture, of the life of the fathers and grand-fathers of contemporary African-American men. As such it makes issues surrounding the expression of male identity an especially sensitive topic. Anything that demeans masculinity is frought with anxiety. I suspect that talking about molestation of boys by older males is one such issue. On this basis, the clinician can expect greater shame and reluc-tance to discuss victimization among African-American boys than among Anglos or Mexican-Americans. This will also make it difficult to discuss homosexual feelings and conflicts mobilized by sexual assault by other males.

African-Americans seem to me to have very complex attitudes about homosexuality. The boys I have treated have been homophobic as have their parents. This may be related to the culture's sensitivity about male identity. Homosexuality does not seem to be on this culture's list of approved forms of male sexual expression. It may be connected with the historical figure of the passive, devalued man. I believe it will be very difficult for any therapist involved with this population to convince most African-American boys or their parents that a gay life style is acceptable. This is particularly true for the less educated members of the population.

It is a truism that African-Americans have lived at the bottom of American society for centuries. As a result of this, in a situation where their needs for basic survival depend upon careful observation of their social environment, and particularly the feelings and reactions of other human beings, African-American culture has developed this into one of its strengths. Many of the participants in this culture have a shrewd common sense about other people and their motivations. They have often developed an ability to look at the concrete and practical meanings of complex human interactions. The flip side of this same coin is that, at times, African-Americans can be highly suspicious about the motives and self-interests of others. Additionally, survival issues have so over-whelmed the culture for so long that, as a generalization (with many exceptions), there is little interest in the kind of metapsychological interpretations and speculations characteristic of the psychodynamic approach. This has obvious treatment implications.

Related to the authoritarian African-American family, which is typically headed by a patriarchal male or a matriarchal female, are authoritarian child-rearing practices. As a generalization, the opinions, feelings, and wishes of children probably are taken less into account in African-American culture than they are with the other two major cultures. Traditional standards seem to be that children are to be quiet and respectful of their parents and that parents take a forceful, directive role in the child's life.

Treatment Implications

The material we are discussing here has treatment implications. Forming a treatment alliance with African-Americans is probably more difficult for the therapist from a different cultural background than it is with either whites or Hispanics. The early part of the treatment process needs to be handled with extreme caution. The therapist needs to proceed more slowly in the initial stages than he/she would proceed with members of the other two cultures. As with the Mexican-American culture, it is essential that the non-African-American therapist respect the cultural institutions and values of African-American culture. Lectures on patriarchy, matriarchy, and the evils of homophobia are unlikely to be appreciated or effective.

This case vignette illustrates many of the principles under discussion here:

For some time I treated a young African-American boy whose treatment I came to share with another therapist. The boy had been repeatedly sodomized and orally copulated by an older boy. I had treated the boy for roughly a year prior to referring him to another therapist for a group therapy experience. I continued to provide individual therapy. This boy seemed to me to be prehomosexual. I had previously tried him in one of my own groups which consisted of older boys. He made a sexual advance on one of the boys which alienated the group and made further participation impossible. The other therapist had a group for younger boys but few African-American clients. Things did not go well at first. After roughly one month, the father was anxious to pull the boy out of his group. I felt that the group experience was essential to his treatment, and could not offer a suitable group in my practice.

The other therapist was deeply troubled by the patriarchal structure of this family and by the homophobia of both parents. I found this couple admirable in terms of their long, carefully worked-out marriage, which had survived in a social environment which destroys all too many African-American families. Probably, in order to keep her husband, the mother deferred to him and allowed him to set the terms for their relationship and for their child-rearing.

At the onset of treatment with me, both parents made it plain that they would regard their son's developing into overt homosexuality as an unmitigated catastrophe and a failure on their part as parents. I had a strong feeling that the child was likely to be homosexual and that, eventually, the parents would have to accept this. I had been slowly working in this direction.

After two or three sessions, this patriarchal father had been told by a white therapist to change his authoritarian attitudes toward his children, to be more permissive, and to encourage his son's developing homosexuality as an alternate and acceptable means of sexual expression. I cannot quarrel with these long-term goals, but to insist on them at this stage in treatment would mean the loss of the case. I urged my colleague to slow down the pace of confrontation. I also felt he needed to understand the numerous, specifically cultural problems that this couple were addressing in what seemed to the other therapist like purely dysfunctional attitudes.

The couple's priorities appeared to be to keep their marriage together, to provide a two parent home, and to help their son grow into a male who would be respected within the context of African-American culture. I cannot fault these goals. They, of course, involve value judgments, but so does the other therapist's position. Unfortunately, in this case I believe that the family's goal cannot be reached. This child is unlikely to be heterosexual.

This case stresses many basic principles in working with African-Americans as a therapist with roots in another culture. It is essential to understand and empathize with the values of the culture with which you are working. In the case of African-American culture, it is often necessary to slow the pace of treatment considerably, at least until rapport is established.

Once some rapport is established and treatment fully engaged, patient and therapist are likely to come up against differences in cultural attitudes. Usually, this can and should be discussed. It needs to be handled sensitively. It is an issue for the middle of treatment not its beginning. It is best that the patient bring the issues up. If not, the therapist should bring up these issues only when they are implicit in current treatment issues.

With the family just discussed, I eventually spoke about the different attitudes that Anglos and African-Americans typically have toward homosexuality. I indicated my understanding of this without making the judgment as to which attitude was "correct." This gives the family permission to assess their own attitudes as part of a culturally determined value system. Once identified in this way the family has greater freedom to change a dysfunctional attitude because now it has been identified as something culturally determined rather than some kind of moral absolute.

If a non-African-American therapist wishes to work with this population, they should get all the help they can from African-American peers and community members. Case consultations with African-American therapists are highly desirable. In group therapy, African-American guests in the therapy sessions are desirable. In a perpetrator group I once found it necessary to do this after being confronted with repeated denials that there was any homosexuality at all in African-American culture. I knew that the African-American adolescents in the group were not leveling with me, but there was no way, as a white therapist, I could convince them of that. For that reason, I invited a young, street wise African-American counselor from a residential program to join us for some group sessions. He was able to cut through their evasion and get them to deal with the reality of their own culture.

African-American attitudes about child-rearing and the role of children demand a different treatment approach than the standard child guidance clinic usually offers. The traditional therapeutic approach, which permits nothing to be said to the parent about the child's treatment, runs against the grain of African-American culture. It is in conflict with this culture's attitudes about parental authority, and runs afoul of African-American suspiciousness about the motives of outsiders. Whatever you are doing, you need to do it openly and candidly in front of the parents of African-American children. They need to know what is going on and why you are doing it, and what you hope to accomplish. The child guidance approach of the secret interview with the child will probably result in early termination of treatment. A parent can be an ally in this kind of case if properly informed and motivated. The toxic, intrusive parent probably is going to destroy treatment no matter what is done.

CULTURAL OVERLAPS

In this part of this chapter we have stressed the differences between the three main subcultures coexisting within the United States: the Anglo, the Mexican-American, and the African-American. None of this material should imply that we do not share a basic core humanity with themes which need to be addressed in any treatment program. I believe that mankind basically has one psyche which is complex and rich enough to allow for different manifestations of the same themes in different cultures.

All human beings have a need for love, both to give it and to receive it. We also need connections to others and the affirmation of others to assure us that we are okay. In my judgment, all human beings share a series of conflicts centering around dependency versus independence. We also have similar conflicts about aggression and passivity and about a sense of identity and autonomy. All of these themes become interwoven in all cultures with themes of gender identity and cultural identity. Beneath all of this, however, I believe we all must wrestle, as Kohut suggests, with issues of nuclear identity and the cohesiveness of the self. Nuclear identity and the cohesive self involve a striving to reach our full human potential, to achieve certain nuclear goals for our lives that are defined by our earliest experience, and to achieve a sense of full identity and autonomy within our culture and gender.

Although cultures have much in common, they also vary in what they accentuate. Some cultures will accentuate aggressiveness. Others will emphasize cooperation, or acquisitiveness, or homophobia. All three North American cultures share certain traits which are also relevant to the treatment of male victims. All have their own stereotypes of male roles. The available stereotypes may vary in number and nature between the three cultures, but none permit a wide latitude of freedom in male personality. All three cultures are, to some degree, homophobic. All tend toward the creation of patriarchal or authoritarian relationships between the sexes.

All three cultures appear, to me, to equate sexual expression with either domination of others or submission to others. We do not seem to have a playful, erotic subcultures like those of Southeast Asia. Returning to the opening sections of this chapter, it is obvious that the nature of American subcultures creates a situation in which victimization is highly traumatizing to its participants. As noted earlier, culture is a given. Therapists must make do with what we are given in this area. Although human beings have much in common, the therapist needs to keep in mind the unique culture of each patient and to tailor treatment efforts to the specific contents of these cultures.

Chapter 8

ASSESSMENT

In this chapter begins the transition from material that is largely theoretical to a practical application of that material in the treatment of young male victims of molestation. Throughout the rest of the work, data from the literature as well as the theoretical matrices developed earlier will be integrated into a program for treatment. Before treatment begins, an assessment of the young male victim is essential. In this chapter, methods of making that assessment will be presented. Once a boy is known as an individual, a treatment plan can be devised to achieve basic goals of treatment derived from the literature, theory, and clinical experience.

It needs to be stressed that the kind of assessment suggested here is one intended to begin treatment. This is not a model for forensic assessment. Procedures necessary to gather information quickly for a court report are often intrusive and make follow-up treatment difficult. In a treatment situation it is essential to gather diagnostic information simultaneously with procedures designed to begin the therapeutic alliance. Where the clinician is assessing as the beginning of treatment, there need be no haste that damages the relationship with the patient. The reality is that assessment is always part of the ongoing treatment process. As new information emerges from the treatment process, the clinician is constantly modifying his understanding of the patient and his treatment needs.

Methods of assessment must be tailored to the age of the victim. This population must be broken down into smaller age groupings, and appropriate procedures selected according to developmental age. It is obvious that the techniques used to gather information about a two-year old are going to be very different from those used to gather information about and from a seventeen year old. The matter is further complicated by the fact that it is well known that some children have not reached a level of emotional development corresponding to their chronological age.

There is a certain amount of trial and error necessary in the assessment process with the young male victim. Evaluations involving play may be suitable for some boys at twelve, whereas others might reject such an approach at age ten. A predominantly verbal interview might work with some eight-year olds, whereas it might be totally unsuccessful with a developmentally retarded fifteen-year old. The assessment process needs to be a flexible one in which whatever works to gather the necessary information is used. A variety of tactics and infinite patience are often required.

An immediate question might be raised about the gender of the interviewer. Being male, I can only offer part of that data. In general, I have little or no trouble gathering information of a frank sexual sort from victimized boys younger than about twelve. The overwhelming majority of adolescent males will eventually discuss their victimization with me candidly. However, many of them are guarded. Occasionally, I encounter an adolescent male who simply will not talk to a male interviewer because of his rage, fear, and homophobia resulting from their molestation. Such an adolescent would obviously be better served by being interviewed by a female.

I would not, however, discourage male clinicians in this area, since I would "guesstimate" that this is an issue with perhaps one percent of the boys who are referred to me. Indeed, some boys are more comfortable, sharing information with a male clinician. There may be a difference in the kind, quality, and speed with which the information is gathered, but eventually a male clinician will usually be able to bring together as much information as a female clinician.

The boys who are more comfortable with a male interviewer are most often those with a precarious sense of masculinity. It is important for them to be viewed positively as undamaged males in the eyes of women. They feel that molestation is a profound disgrace. To reveal this damaged masculinity to a woman is more difficult than sharing it with other males. It needs to be stressed that these issues are individual. The sensitive clinician needs to constantly be listening for clues about the patient's comfort in the interview process.

AGE DIFFERENCES

The age at which the young male client is brought for treatment is critical to the determination of the mode of assessment. The birth to eighteen year old population breaks down into a number of subcategories, with often fuzzy boundaries between them. These basic groups would be infants up to roughly one and one half years of age, toddlers one and one half to three or four, the early school-age child from roughly five to seven or eight, the latency-age child from perhaps eight to twelve, and the adolescent. Boundaries are fuzzy because of individual differences, and because of the developmental level which each child might have attained, in spite of chronological age.

In my practice, assessment of infants and toddlers has generally been for forensic purposes. Such children are relatively infrequently identified by parenting figures as needing specialized treatment for sexual problems, and are not often referred for treatment *per se*. The task here is usually initially to prepare a report for a court or agency to lay a foundation for further protective action. The parents will usually need to be convinced that at least brief parent guidance may be necessary to help them cope with the results of sexual abuse when it has occurred. With the very young infant, most information obviously must be obtained from the parenting figures and others who have observed the child. The clinician can also get some clues from direct observation of the child and its interaction with key figures in its environment.

With toddlers, some observation of play can be productive. Some verbal information can be gathered from the child, but needs to be processed in terms of the cognitive distortions characteristic of children this age. Much of what they say cannot be taken literally, but must be analyzed symbolically. Once language is acquired, children can communicate something about their victimization, often with the assistance of anatomically correct dolls. A play session in which the child's spontaneous play behavior is observed is also valuable.

With latency-age children, parents and key figures in their life also need to be interviewed. These children are, however, more able to communicate directly verbally, as well as symbolically, through play. Assessment in this age range becomes an easier task. The number of referrals increases dramatically in this age group. This is partly because many children are first molested in this age range. Children at this age are also often able to communicate clearly to parent figures that they have been molested. Behavioral symptoms especially sexualization may have progressed to the point where even parents who need to deny can no longer do so. With the adolescent, the focus moves more in the direction of interview and increasingly away from play and symbolic discussions. With the proper techniques, a great deal of information can be gathered quickly from most adolescent male victims by direct interview.

All victims are prone to distort their experience, either to protect their self-esteem or to reduce guilt and shame they may feel about what has happened to them. As a result, it is wise at all levels of development to rely on any existing documentation, such as police reports, probation reports, reports from child protection agencies, and any other professionals who have observed these children. Reports from the key figures in the child's environment are important at all stages of assessment.

Assessment should be regarded as an ongoing process. Some young males will give a lot of information in the initial interview. With others, it is necessary to tell them that you are not even going to discuss the incident at this time, and that you simply wish to get to know them. Getting the frightened and ashamed victim to talk freely should be regarded as an ongoing process. It is not unusual for young male victims in treatment, particularly adolescents, to disguise their victimization for months, until they are ready to disclose. In non-forensic situations, it is desirable to take the assessment at the pace at which the child is willing and able to go, and not to rush the gathering of data to the detriment of the treatment relationship.

The proper course of action in the assessment process is to give a great deal of control to the young male victim throughout the process. The sexual assault on the young male has already damaged his sense of self-esteem, his sense of control of his environment, and his sense of mastery. It is inappropriate for a clinician to impose further insults upon the child's identity, autonomy, and mastery in the treatment process. Unless there are urgent judicial needs, the intake process should proceed at a slow pace, according to the cues offered by the child. In spite of this caution, it is often possible to get an extensive amount of information even in the initial interview. A sensitive clinician can pick up when the child is beginning to become wary of further disclosure and back off.

Family Assessment

It is also essential to gather information about the family system in which the child lives. Parents are often involved to some degree in ignoring or even setting up the process which results in victimization. Their involvement is usually essential to successful treatment. Supportive families can be highly restorative. Those who do not handle the victimization well can be destructive. It is important that the entire family be interviewed, and the nature of the family system ascertained as part of a complete assessment. This is best done with a complete family interview and, if possible, in ongoing family therapy as part of the treatment plan.

TESTS AND RATING SCALES

Valuable information can be gathered from parenting figures and sometimes from the children themselves by the use of pre-existing rating scales, such as Friedrich's "Child Behavior Checklist" and "Child Sexual Behavior Inventory." In a thorough assessment, a battery of psychological tests is valuable. These should include such standard instruments as the Rorschach, and the Children's Apperception Test. Various projective drawings also yield valuable insights. These include but are not limited to draw-a-person, house-tree-person, and kinetic family drawings. What the child draws when encouraged to draw something of their choice is also significant. For older victims the MMPI often yields valuable data. It is of particular value with adolescent boys who have also perpetrated. A great deal of research has been done on the MMPI with sex offender populations and more recently with victim populations (Olsen 1990). A measure of I.Q. is also valuable in all cases.

With adolescents who are also perpetrators or at risk of perpetration, there are a number of instruments that may be suitable. These would include the several self report check lists that explore sexual arousal patterns and thinking patterns that are correlated with sex offending. Examples are Farrenkopf's "Adolescent Sexual Interest Cardsort," and "Adolescent Cognition Scale." Caution is warranted in using this kind of instrument. They should be used with the permission and understanding of any adolescent who is not an admitted sex offender. They are intrusive, and can be damaging to the treatment relationship if their use is not carefully managed. In a sense, this same caveat applies to all testings except behavior rating scales done by parents or done conjointly by the clinician and the patient.

Adolescents in particular seem to resent psychological testing and cardsorts. The dynamics seem to be in part a control issue. The patient believes that he has entered into a one-to-one treatment relationship with the therapist, and that the therapist will have the information that he, the patient, provides with perhaps a little bit of additional information from the family. Testing can be seen as by passing of his own ego barriers and a sort of voyeuristic peeking into his interior. To avoid damaging the treatment relationship it is better to refer this part of the assessment when possible if you will also provide treatment.

One of the particular values of psychological testing is that it assesses a much wider range of issues than just the child as victim. Male victims have many problems which pre-existed or coexist with their issues about victimization. It is relevant, for example, to know if a victim has a thought disorder or is mentally retarded. Any number of more subtle questions could also be posed through the medium of psychological testing.

WHAT IS ABUSE?

The above remarks beg a basic question: What is it that we are assessing? What is abuse and, what is not abuse in the area of sexuality? This question is the object of some controversy within the community that treats sexual abuse. It is an object of even greater controversy between that community and the broader society in which it is immersed. Some writers use a very broad definition of sexual abuse. For example, Bolton, Morris, and MacEachron (1989) develop a model called "The Abuse of Sexuality." This perspective places "sexual abuse" along a spectrum. At one end are hands-on felonious offenses. At the other end are sexually repressive family environments seen in this model as a form of sexual abuse of the child. All points on the spectrum are considered abusive because they result in distortions of the child's sexuality.

Few clinicians would argue that there is not a hierarchy of offenses in which some are more toxic to the victim than others. Disagreement arises in where the lines are drawn. I believe a useful metaphor would be the concentric circles that radiate from a pebble tossed into a pond. At the center there are clear-cut happenings which almost everyone in American culture would regard as abusive. These are the hands-on offenses which are also criminal acts when committed against children. Rape, would be a clear cut case. So would sodomy, oral copulation, fondling, and frottage where force is involved. Some researchers feel these acts are not damaging if done with consenting children. This position would find little support among clinicians in the United States.

It might have more support in American sexological circles. Most American therapists would consider sodomy, oral copulation, fondling, and frottage abusive with or without the child's consent.

As the outer circles of problematic behaviors are approached there is less and less consensus. Most U.S. therapists would probably rate a series of hands-off but intrusive sexual acts as abusive to children. These would include such things as exhibitionism, voyeurism, sexual harassment, deliberate exposure to pornography. Less agreement can be expected when we move into the area of children who are raised in highly sexualized environments or, at the other pole, sexually repressive environments. American consensus would clearly break down in this peripheral area. My guess is that most clinicians practicing in the area of sexual abuse in the United States would call this abusive. Sexologists and other academics and intellectuals would be more divided.

Particularly difficult for Americans are families who rear their children in highly sexualized environments. This would include exhibitionistic parents who wander about the home naked, bathe with their children and who engage in sexual activity in front of them. Here also are families who allow young children to view pornographic films. These behaviors seem to sexualize children in a way similar to the sexualization resulting from molest. I doubt that the other unfortunate sequelae of sexual abuse described in the research literature is generated by this kind of sexualization.

A more clear cut manifestation of a sexually abusive situation is where there is a pronounced sadomasochistic quality to the family environment. Here, the child is intruded upon sexually for purposes disguised as punishment. In structure, the relationship between parent and child is sadomasochistic. This would include spankings in which the child is required to be naked. Often, such spankings are conducted in public or semi-public locations to further humiliate the child. Unnecessary enemas are often another version of the sadistic, erotized assault upon the child. This form of sexual abuse is usually concealed within the boundaries of "parenting," and is not often identified as sex abuse outside of professional circles.

In all probability, most participants in American culture would only identify the hands-on offenses, plus exhibitionism, and voyeurism by outsiders as sexual assaults. Because of the nature of my practice, and probably because this society perceives the problem, my treatment efforts are largely limited to victims of the hands-on offenses. When I encounter young men victimized in the hands-off manner or by parental sadism disguised as punishment, it is usually in the course of treating perpetrators who never acknowledge any formal victimization, or adults who enter treatment for a nonsexually related issue, and discover this form of abuse in the course of treatment. My working definition of abuse would have to be limited to the hands-on offenses committed by a person significantly older than the victim. I believe there are other phenomena that are sexually abusive, but they do not occur in my practice with victims and are not a focus of attention here.

Essential also to a definition of abuse is the issue of the age difference between participants in a sexual act. The research literature is moving toward a consensus that there needs to be a five year separation in age to create a victim-perpetrator type situation. This may be necessary for research purposes, but it is not suitable for clinical purposes. Boys can experience the typical traumata of molestation across a much smaller age gap, particularly when the younger children are involved. For example, if an immature four-year old is forced into sexual acts by a precocious and sexually sophisticated six-year old, the typical sequelae of victimization can be expected.

The clinical situation seems to be that we must use a fluid definition, depending upon the age and developmental levels of the participants. I usually use a working definition of two to three years of age difference with many allowances for exceptions. I have actually encountered situations where I felt the younger of two children was the "molester"—An example would be a bright, streetwise ten-year old, forcing himself sexually on a sheltered, retarded thirteen-year old. The thirteen-year old may well need to be considered a victim for treatment purposes.

The victim's perceptions and reactions are highly important. If the younger child feels victimized, and/or shows behavioral and other subjective indicators of damage and distress as a result of the molestation, then that would suggest that a molestation has taken place. On the other hand if we are dealing with consenting sex between two adolescents, one seventeen and the other a pubescent thirteen-year old and no trauma is evident upon careful examination of the younger child, I would be reluctant to treat the younger individual as a molest victim.

Cultural Definitions of Abuse

As American society becomes increasingly multicultural, it is important that clinicians working in the field of sex abuse become aware that abuse is defined differently in different cultures. As is illustrated in another chapter, there are cultures which make normative behavior which would be criminal sexual abuse in this society. There are numerous examples of cultures which use physical discipline techniques which would cause criminal charges to be filed in this culture. There are also subtle differences among American subcultures which need to be taken into account in working with clients from those populations.

The main implication of cultural differences for assessment is that they will affect how incidents of sexual activity are defined by both the clinician and the client and his family. When treatment is court-ordered, this becomes particularly sensitive because the participants must be involved. If the assessment is to be successful, the clinician needs to be aware of the cultural attitudes toward sexuality characteristic of all of the clientele with whom they are working.

Forensic Cautions

As a general rule, my interviews are for clinical diagnosis and treatment, and not intended as forensic data-gathering. Most of the cases referred to me have already been settled by the court. For that reason, I have more freedom in collecting information than I would in a forensic setting. If a therapist is the first person to collect data about a victimization, some of these techniques should not be used. Legally, it is better that the first interviews be conducted in a forensic setting. Such interviews should be videotaped and carefully constructed to avoid leading questions. The infamous McMartin case has laid a foundation for blaming therapists for planting ideas in children's heads. Using treatment techniques to get information for use in court can contaminate evidence needed for legal proceedings. At least in California, it is best for a therapist confronting a previously unidentified victim to ask a few non-directive questions and report to law enforcement.

Molest allegations in divorce custody cases require the same kind of caution as those involving possible criminal charges. There does seem to be a small group of toxic parents who coach small children to make false allegations against the other parent in order to secure custody of the child. These situations are usually easy to detect. Evaluating, mediating, and reporting to family courts in these situations is another specialized form of work. Kaser-Boyd (1988) has offered guidelines for determining the truth of sex abuse allegations in marital dissolutions. It is beyond the scope of this book to elaborate on this. I would simply urge extreme caution in such cases.

The Interview

Interview techniques obviously need to be adjusted to the age of the child. In these paragraphs I am talking most specifically about interviews with verbal adolescent and preadolescent boys where most of the information is obtained by verbal interaction. A successful interview with a young male who has been sexually abused has one really essential element: rapport. If a trusting, communicating relationship can be established, the therapist will get pretty much whatever information is needed. Without rapport, you will be misled, shut out, conned, or manipulated.

Perhaps the most important factor in conducting an interview is that the clinician be comfortable with basic issues of sexuality. This needs to be communicated through a calm, relaxed, matter-of-fact attitude in such discussions. Such an interview should not begin with immediate questioning about victimization or sexuality. The clinician will usually need to deal immediately with the patient's anxiety or even anger about being in the interview situation. It is often useful to tell the patient that they can wait to talk about their victimization, and that it does not necessarily need to be discussed in this initial interview. Often, this kind of statement leads to a candid discussion of victimization later on in the same interview. Sometimes it does not. Patience is an essential characteristic for those wishing to work with young sexually abused males.

Some routine question about areas in which the child is successful are a good place to begin. I usually know where the child is successful by interviewing one or both of the child's parents before seeing the child. Early in an interview of this nature, I describe myself as a specialist in this area. I identify the child's probable anxiety about discussing such intimate matters, and indicate my awareness of how difficult it is for them to talk in this area. Frequently, I will address the need to know what happened in order to be of help, and that I will not be shocked by anything I hear. Nor will I blame them.

This reassurance is necessary in view of the shame and homophobia which are characteristic of male victims before they begin treatment. Talking about abuse is generally easier for males who have been sexually victimized by women. The major exception is the boy molested by his mother. Shame and denial are very high here as is the level of psychiatric disturbance.

My goal in initial verbal interviews is not a step-by-step detailing of the victimization process, nor an extensive, catalogue-type inventory of what kind of sexual practices in which the child has been involved. This material will come up more easily if allowed to emerge in the course of treatment when the patient is ready to discuss it. In a nonforensic interview there should be no hurry to get this kind of data. Haste can seriously damage the therapeutic alliance.

Resistance

Resistance has already been alluded to. The sources of resistance in the young male victim are multiple and generally well-known to therapists. Males in American culture and the major subcultures are not supposed to have sex with other males. Since most victims in my practice have been assaulted by other males, they are aware that even though they are a victim, they have violated a societal taboo. This is particularly strong if there was a pleasure component in their victimization, or if they returned to the perpetrator of their own free will. These are issues best avoided in the initial session with the patient.

Being victimized also violates our society's basic rules for male behavior. Males are never supposed to be victims. They are supposed to be adequate, to handle anything. They are not supposed to turn to others for help when they are overwhelmed by problems. Any young male talking to you about his victimization and seeking treatment for it is violating these multiple cultural taboos. Additionally, he is violating taboos against discussion of sexual matters with strangers (the therapist). As a child or adolescent, he is violating the taboo on having such candid discussions with adults. If the perpetrator was a male, the young victim may be extremely anxious about a one-to-one interview with an older male. I do not usually discuss this particular anxiety during a first interview. It introduces a very threatening idea before enough rapport is established to allow the patient enough security and comfort with the therapist to deal with this issue. With some very anxious victims, it may however, be necessary to deal with fear of the therapist in the initial session to avoid losing the patient. There are also measures that can be taken to reassure the suspicious and anxious victim. I usually start all interviews across a broad desk or with myself and the child seated at a table in the kitchen. Either procedure creates a symbolic barrier between me and the victim. If possible the initial interview should be conducted in a room with windows providing a view of the exterior so the victim does not feel locked up in a secret place with an unknown male.

There are also family issues that lead to resistance. If the victimization has been at the hands of another member of the immediate or extended family, there may already be a serious breach within the family. The family may be trying desperately to cover this up by coercing the participants into denial. If they have been referred by legal sources, they may have to deal with something that they do not want to deal with. If the molestation has not already been brought to the attention of law enforcement, the family may fear that there will be a deep division created in the family by reporting. Resident relatives may be forced to move out and/or be prosecuted. If this has already happened, there may be hard feelings within the extended family that family members want to repair at the cost of having the victim recant. Key family members may chose to deal with this kind of conflict by denying that anything has happened.

Other family factors involve shame, familial values that family business is private and not to be discussed with outsiders. If the perpetrator is within the immediate family, the situation can be explosive. A parent may be confronted with having to choose between a child and a spouse. In addition to an emotional choice, this may also bring financial hardship upon the entire family if an employed parent is incarcerated. Often, these issues have been addressed, at least mentally, by the victim's parents prior to the initial interview. Even if the perpetrating parent is incarcerated, the spouse may be looking forward to reconciliation and may want the child to minimize or deny the offense.

The Absent Teenager

The major part of the clinical material presented in this book has been drawn from, latency, preadolescent, and early adolescent boys. Most of the male victims I have treated as middle and late adolescents have come as perpetrators who are also victims. Over the years, I have received only a handful of referrals of boys fifteen to seventeen who were willing to undertake treatment on a voluntary basis. A somewhat larger number have been brought by parents, insisting that the boy be treated. Such boys are often unwilling to be involved in any discussion of their sexual abuse. Other therapists report similar experiences.

In middle to late adolescence males seem obsessed with how they appear in the eyes of their peers. It is a time when boys want to fit in and be like other teenagers. Discussing deviant sexual experience is particularly hard for this age group. Attempting to conform to the sexual stereotypes of adolescent sub-culture seems to motivate much concealing or denial of their own internal reality. In an age-appropriate way, their bonding to adults has been weakened, while their bonding to peers has strengthened. This makes it especially difficult for them to work individually with an adult therapist in this period. In this age range, boys tell each other things about their sexuality in my waiting room that they would never share with me directly.

Interviewing the Youngest Male Victims

For the younger victims evaluation of play becomes an increasingly important part of diagnosis. Middle and late adolescents will almost always be evaluated without observation of play. The younger the child, the more emphasis needs to be placed on play techniques. They will be useful with the more immature children between ten and twelve, and most children ten and younger.

I find the most useful toys for play interview of male victims to be stuffed human and animal figures. I maintain an assemblage of these for use with the young victims. They include a large, benign looking gorilla, about three feet tall, which seems to evoke father associations in most boys. There is also a benign-looking mother figure. The gorilla has a young son, a smaller gorilla. There are also several young female and young male figures. There is a perpetrator figure with a prominent penis, and a somewhat adolescent-looking monkey who also has a prominent penis. Some of the female dolls are also anatomically correct. The collection also includes a foam bat, with which the patient can harmlessly strike the figures.

The office is arranged in such a way that a large sofa can be used as a kind of stage. Usually I will pile the figures in a heap on the sofa before I bring the child into the room. I then allow the child to seek out the figures as he sees fit.

I have another cabinet which includes more standard play instruments, such as building blocks, small cars, smaller human figures without genital features, and a variety of animal figures. In general, these toys do not evoke nearly as productive and revealing play. I discourage their use, except with the more resistant child who will not work spontaneously with the stuffed animals. I do not conduct highly structural interviews with the anatomically correct figures to ascertain details of their victimization. If most children just play spontaneously, they will produce this material in due time. This technique can often be used with children as young as three years of age. For children less than three, for younger children, most information will have to come from parents, behavior inventory, and direct observation of play and behavior by the clinician.

Behavioral Clues

Sometimes clinics are brought patients who are not clearly identified as victims at the beginning of treatment. They are brought in for a variety of behavioral problems. Since victimization of young males is such a taboo topic in our culture, clinicians need to be sensitive to these behavioral clues to identify molestation, if it is a hidden problem.

My experience is that the cardinal indicator of molestation is sexualized behavior. Friedrich provides some research support for this hypothesis. In a 1988 study he compared thirty-three boys with conduct disorders with thirty-one boys who had been sexually assaulted. He found the main distinction to be that the sexually abused boys were less externalizing and more sexualized than the conduct disorder group. Children brought to treatment for sexual misconduct may be victims of molestation. Such children should be interviewed regarding molestation with the forensic cautions already described.

With adolescents, a history of molestation by males may be hidden behind an intense homophobia. I refer here to something above and beyond the normal homophobia of American adolescents. It is an obsessive hatred, often mixed with homicidal impulses toward gays. This can come from other sources, but previous victimization by males should be probed as a possible origin. At the other pole, the strutting, macho adolescent, who often brags of his heterosexual prowess, can be a victim in the process of overcompensating.

Differential Diagnosis

Practitioners treating the young male victim will encounter a wide spectrum of abuse survivors requiring considerable skill in differential diagnosis. These will include victims who have truly survived relatively unscathed, seriously damaged victims who are in denial about what has happened to them and do not wish treatment, non-victims who make false allegations, and victims who have been molested but recant to protect those to whom they wish to remain close. Distinguishing which of these issues or what combination of these issues involved is an important part of both diagnosis and treatment planning.

It has long been orthodoxy that sexual victimization of any kind is always damaging. This assumption has recently been challenged by research investigating what enables some victims to tolerate abuse better than others. Researchers are beginning to discover some victims who have not been devastated and who are coping well, and may have indeed spontaneously recovered. They are beginning to investigate the factors involved in this process (see Literature Review). These patients probably rarely seek psychotherapy, since they are not in distress. They are, therefore, very poorly known in clinical circles.

At the other end of a continuum, clinicians will find young males who have been so thoroughly sexualized and seduced that they are not consciously ambivalent about what has happened to them. The word "consciously" is used here because I suspect that there is tremendous unconscious turmoil in these situations, but not conflict that is accessible to therapeutic intervention. These boys are difficult to impossible to treat and at high risk of becoming perpetrators. I have seen this most often in boys molested by their fathers or other men to whom they were very close. (See the appendix on boys molested by parents for further exploration of this issue.)

ASSESSMENT AND TREATMENT

The purpose of assessment is to plan treatment or document fully that it is not necessary. Where boys have clearly been molested and damaged in the process, the kind of treatment outlined in other chapters is indicated. Those who have been molested, but recant due to family pressures or shame will need special handling before the basic lesions of molestation can be addressed. In cases of false allegations, focus needs to be placed upon repairing damaged relationships and the character distortion and corruption involved in such behavior. If a parent or other important figure in the child's life is responsible for the false allegations, this is in my judgment another form of child abuse.

If a boy seems to be functioning well in spite of molestation, brief exploratory treatment to confirm this hypothesis is the course of choice. In these situations the parents should be involved and alerted to danger signals. Parents also need to know that an apparently well functioning victim may develop problems at a later developmental stage, and that treatment may be indicated at that time.

SUMMARY

This chapter has focused on determining what has happened to the male victim and how it has impacted him. What is presented here is an ongoing assessment process that can be spread over weeks and months. It is designed to be as non-intrusive as possible. Priority should always be placed on developing the treatment alliance rather than gathering data. Too much haste will damage treatment. Treatment actually begins in the first interview and assessment continues until the last.

Chapter 9

BASIC GOALS AND
STRATEGIES FOR TREATMENT

This chapter focuses on goals and strategies of treatment with young male victims of molestation. There has been a recent surge in publication in this area. Porter (1986) published the first book-length work involving the treatment of this population. His treatment goals include a strong emphasis on combatting the denial. He also urges dealing with fears about homosexuality as well as guilt which arises out of the pleasurable aspects of being molested. He also urges that the therapist deal with issues of rage and grief. He describes a variety of unfortunate sexual outcomes of untreated sexual abuse in males including compulsive, self-destructive, and aggressive acting out. Presumably aggressive acting out includes perpetration against younger children. Porter emphasizes empowerment and treatment techniques necessary to help the victim develop a sense of power which has been robbed from him by molestation. Porter feels that the preferred and central method of treatment for the young male victim is group therapy conducted by a male and female therapist.

Hewitt (1990) concentrates on preschool age male victims of sexual assault. She subdivides this group into smaller age and developmental stage categories and stresses the necessity to include this child's developmental stage in treatment planning. She also stresses the need to work with caretakers to assure the child a safe and protective environment. Other key treatment goals are helping the child to develop control of sexualized behaviors. She also targets relief of the guilt and self-blaming. Like Porter, Hewitt talks about empowerment. To empower the child she advocates such techniques as teaching a child how to say no to sexual advances, and the use of play techniques to allow repetition of mastery concepts.

Hewitt is also concerned with the prevention of perpetration. She believes that the risk of perpetration is much reduced by restoring sense of power and control to the child. She stresses a need for sex education and to help the child separate erotic feelings from a need for affection. Finally, she notes that homosexuality may be an issue for the boys and their parents. Due to the young age group she discusses, she feels she cannot deal with this issue at this developmental stage.

Froning and Mayman (1990) pick up where Hewitt leaves off and deal with the older part of the young male spectrum through the end of adolescence. Their treatment goals are multiple. They stress the importance of dealing with homophobic concerns and possible homosexuality in later life. They advocate dealing with this in group and presenting homosexuality as an acceptable alternative life style. These authors share the concern of others with the potential of male victims to turn into perpetrators. They feel this outcome is best prevented by attacking denial and keeping the memory of the incidents and feelings surrounding their own victimization at a level of conscious awareness. This serves to prevent perpetration by creating a bond of identification and empathy with potential victims. In addition to potential perpetration, Froning and Mayman suggest targeting of compulsive masturbation and other addictive sexual behaviors. They suggest behavior modification techniques which may be useful here.

Froning and Mayman urge also the reduction of rage and anger and give some activity techniques for doing this. Empowerment is seen as an important curative factor with the young male victim. To empower the child they advocate giving him a great deal of control in the therapeutic situation. Shame and guilt are also a focus for therapeutic concern. They believe it is necessary to challenge frequently occurring cognitive distortions. These distortions include such beliefs as that the victim could have fought off the assailant, or that if there was not something wrong with the victim, his body would not have responded pleasurably. Other treatment goals include reduction of anxiety and fear and the addressing of the sadness and loss that is involved in victimization. These losses include loss of childhood, of innocence, and of control. Froning and Mayman stress the importance of group therapy, particularly to address issues of loneliness and isolation.

Finkelhor and Browne (1985) although not writing about treatment or just about male victims, share a list of sequelae of child sexual abuse which overlaps with those outlined by Porter, Hewitt, and Froening and Mayman. The first is traumatic sexualization. A second is stigmatization which includes issues of guilt, shame, and low self-esteem. Betrayal includes a range of reactions to the breech of trust by the perpetrator. These include distrust and disillusion, as well as anger and hostility. Grief and loss may be involved if the perpetrator was a trusted and important person in the victim's life. The powerlessness implicit in being a victim leads to a variety of related reactions which include anxiety, and a real impairment in the ability to function. Finkelhor and Browne see aggressive behaviors resulting from the underlying feeling of powerlessness as a kind of compensatory mechanism. This opens a route through which the victim may combine sexualization with compensatory aggression and to become, thereby, a perpetrator.

Common Ground

The traumatic sequelae of sexual abuse in males and the treatment goals for addressing them identified by these culled from the current literature can be grouped into seven clusters: (1.) First would be the sexualization cluster. This would include all of the compulsive and inappropriate sexual activity seen in victims. This begins in the youngest with excessive masturbation and sexual advances on other children. Later in life it may lead into to victimizing others, or the various sexual addictions and obsessions of adult life.

(2.) The second cluster could be called the self-esteem cluster. Central elements here are blaming oneself for the victimization and guilt about any pleasure involved or about violation of what the child perceives as rules about sexual behavior. This complex includes depression which has its roots in the self-blaming process. Possibly substance abuse in later life belongs here if it is regarded as a sort of self-medication for the anxiety and depression resulting from the blows to self-esteem arising out of victimization.

(3.) A third cluster relates to trust and betrayal. This is particularly salient where the perpetrator is a parent. The overwhelming majority of perpetrators are individuals with whom the child had some kind of trusting relationship so trust issues will almost always be important in the treatment of male victims. The ongoing issue for these boys is, "Whom can I trust, and under what circumstances?"

(4.) Another cluster relates to anger. This is provoked by many aspects of victimization including loss of control, a sense of being spoiled as a male, being derailed from basic developmental tasks, and being introduced to unwelcome homosexual feelings and conflicts. Often the anger only unfolds with time. It may be repressed or denied close to the time of the offense. As the child matures and becomes increasingly aware of the damage done by victimization, this anger typically escalates. Sometimes it reaches homicidal proportions and is directed toward the perpetrator, or perpetrator surrogates. Other times it is turned inward and fuels the development of depression as reaction to victimization.

(5.) A sexual identity cluster constitutes the next group. The most typical features here involve homosexual panic in victims who fear they have been made gay by what happened. The literature appears in consensus that being molested by a male forces most male victims to confront the questions, "Will I become gay as a result?" A less common variant is a homophobia where the victim is threatened and hostile about any expression of homosexual behavior in anyone. Bitterness and at least fantasies of violence characterize this group. Many "gay bashers" are probably drawn from victims whose reaction has taken this course.

(6.) Another cluster can be called the power cluster. This is where the issue of empowerment becomes important. A victim feels deprived of control. The trauma has left him with a sense of having little or no power as a resource of the self. Related are issues of self-control. The premature release in a child of powerful sexual feelings, confront him with strong impulses that his ego is not yet ready to manage. Impulsive acting out is often the result.

(7.) Finally, there is a loss cluster. This is most prominent where a victim has lost a parent as a result of molestation. Children are frequently removed from molesting parents. It is a rare case where the child does not have some kind of bond even to a molesting parent. Although clinically necessary, the child will experience varying degrees of loss depending upon the nature of the situation. Sometimes this loss is compounded by the loss of the other parent's psychological support due to their anger about the removal of the offending spouse. The distrust so common in victims causes further losses by impairing the ability to relate to others. This damages the child's ability to grow appropriately in the areas of interpersonal relationships. The sexualization caused by molestation often leads to another loss, the loss of impulse control.

These problem clusters drawn from the most recent literature on treatment seem to represent a consensus on what needs to be targeted in treatment planning. I doubt that any clinician, working from any theoretical framework from psychodynamic through behavioral-cognitive, would dispute this list. Throughout the rest of this work we will return to these clusters to explain the rationale for the various treatment procedures under discussion.

In this work, a specific perspective is taken on the kind of damage done by molestation of young males by males. The main damage is seen as a blow to the boy's developing sense of masculinity which "derails" him from the male developmental line reviewed in the last chapter. This perspective is easily adapted to focus upon the problem clusters just described. The major reason for spending so much time on the development of a psychodynamically based theory of how molestation impacts males has been to lay a foundation for a specialized treatment program aimed at repairing the specific damages. I believe that any clinician using an approach to the treatment of male victims which takes into account the need of the male to strive for male identity will see substantial improvement in the seven symptom clusters derived from other authors.

At the End of Treatment

The ideal end result of the process of treatment outlined here would be a male who had arrived at the optimal end of his developmental line of sexual identity. This would mean a relaxed and accepting position toward his sexual activity, fantasies, and feelings. He should feel free of significant components of fantasy involving hurting, humiliating, or dominating others. Needless to say, he should be free of actually carrying out such behaviors in reality, and should have either no interest in molesting children, or an abundant ability to control such impulses. In the area of ambitions, he should be able to realize ambitions in the sexual area, whatever these may be, ranging from marriage and family through to the maintenance of a long-term gay relationship. Feeling secure in his own masculinity, he is able to love women and to treat them with respect. He is also able to love other males, and to work with them. This does not mean, however, that he is afraid to or unable to compete with other males when and where appropriate.

These are ideal goals. Many patients will be too damaged in nuclear self to actually attain them. In these cases, the patient needs to be helped to develop compensatory structures or defenses to keep them out of the most catastrophic sequelae of victimization. These fall into two general areas: the prevention of pedophilia and/or sexual acting out toward younger children, and the prevention of inappropriate sexual or aggressive acting out toward any other human being. This second category would include violence directed at gays or women as a compensatory mechanism. Hopefully, even the most damaged patient will be willing to work toward such a goal.

For reasons to be discussed momentarily, the achievement of masculine identity and the ability to accomplish the nuclear goals of the self in regard to masculinity will be helpful in the repair of the damage done in all the cluster areas that have been examined. With a strengthened masculinity in a stronger nuclear self, there will be no need to erotize male/male relationships in an effort at self repair through fusion with a stronger male. There will be no need to compensate for feeling passive and unmasculine through defensively exaggerated pseudomasculinity and obsessive sexual conquests. Sexual needs can be met in an age appropriate way. The strengthened ego can censor inappropriate urges and gratify appropriate ones. Greater impulse control, somewhat reduced libido, and age appropriate sexual outlets will substantially reduce the risk of the victim becoming a perpetrator.

Several aspects of this kind of treatment program will address issues in the self esteem area such as guilt, shame, depression, and the "damaged goods" syndrome. The strengthened self will be able to discard the irrationality of assuming blame for being selected as a victim. A greatly enhanced competence will allow the recovering patient to boost his sense of self worth and well being by achieving long sought after nuclear goals. Reduction of compensatory deviant fantasies involving both sex and violence should also reduce shame and self-hatred.

With the male victim population, an inability to trust and to distinguish realistically who can and cannot be trusted is a sign of a self weakened by the trauma of molestation and/or by other trauma and developmental problems which preceded the molestation. In the course of strengthening and expanding the nuclear self and repairing the damage to the boys' masculinity, there should be an improvement in these critical ego skills. Much of this will be worked out in the selfobjects offered by the therapist and fellow members of treatment groups.

There are several elements of the self-psychology approach that should lead to reductions in the male victim's of rage and anger. One of Kohut's most important contributions to psychoanalytic theory is that rage is not a primary drive or a primary offshoot of the aggressive drive. He sees it as a response to a fragmented self, weakened, and inadequate nuclear self. Any strengthening of this self will reduce rage. To the extent that the patient's rage arose out of the victimization, it is compensatory for having been made to feel helpless and inadequate in the course of sexual abuse. As the nuclear self is strengthened, there is less and less need for the toxic compensatory mechanism of rage.

The sexual identity issues are probably the most difficult to deal with in treatment. Both the literature and clinical experience suggest that some boys are predisposed to become victims before they are molested. This suggests that in some cases the sexual identity issues and other sexual conflicts precede molestation. The problem of the "prehomosexual" boy looms large here and will be discussed shortly. The model proposed here is flexible enough to suggest that either an ego syntonic hetero-sexuality or an ego syntonic homosexuality is an acceptable goal. I believe the literature does not contradict (see especially Tyson 1986) the idea that a boy can be identified masculinely and still select a homosex-ual love object. In these cases his own nuclear goals seem to include a male love object with was selected very early, perhaps in a critical period. Where there is a deeply rooted homosexual object choice, the task is to get the boy to overcome powerful cultural stereotypes and to accept his nuclear goals as an acceptable choice.

The more heterosexual boys presumably were oriented toward female objects before their victimization. Without treatment they may drift into a temporary interest in homosexual objects. In such cases the boy needs to be guided back to his original object choice. This is based on the assumption that the original object choice is the most basic. Almost without exception boys in this situation wish help in strengthening their damaged heterosexuality. To help them do so aligns treatment goals with the nuclear goals of the patient.

Empowerment is implicit in a process which strengthens the nuclear self. As this self is strengthened, the patient will increasingly be able to accomplish his most cherished life goals, one of the headiest imagin-able forms of human empowerment. The importance of empowerment is stressed in virtually everyone treating victims at this time. In my judgment, most males connect power with masculinity and are pro-grammed during early stages of life to make this connection. Much of the reason for focusing on the development of healthy masculinity centers around this issue of empowerment. When males feel masculine, they feel powerful.

Some boys experience profound losses as a result of molestation. Perhaps the most extreme loss is loss of parents. Therapy cannot repair this loss. It can provide support and a place to do grief work. Skilled case management can sometimes find suitable relatives or foster parents to care for the child. Other losses are more subtle; premature sexualization involves loss of innocence and childhood. The young male victim is often propelled into precocious sexual activity that make him feel in some ways no longer a child. Peers and adults may also perceive the sexualized child as too precocious to be related to as a child. Predatory older people may further sexually exploit the boy, intensifying the loss of innocence and childhood. He may be related to as simply an object for pleasure to be discarded at the end of the sexual episode. The extreme development of this trend is male prostitution.

Some of these kinds of losses can be repaired when the nuclear self is strengthened. I believe that sexualization can to some degree be reversed by treatment. In any case a stronger self can better control and censor inappropriate sexual impulses. These processes help repair losses by restoring more normal relationships with adults and peers. The stronger self can also establish new relationships to partially replace those that have been lost. The loss inherent in derailment of normal male development can be repaired as therapy facilitates the resumption of growth toward mature male identity.

SELFOBJECT TRANSFERENCES AND THERAPIST GENDER

The approach suggested here places great emphasis on the curative value of selfobject relationships between the client and the therapist. This is the primary curative mechanism within self-psychology. The selfobject transference permits the reactivation of growth processes in the patient. It allows for those whose development has been arrested or has wandered into aberrant and dangerous byways to resume their growth by a normal human process of interacting with key supportive figures in their social environment. In the case of therapy, this figure is the therapist. I believe this approach practically requires a male therapist for at least a substantial part of the therapeutic process. Dimmock (1988) comes to similar conclusions:

> The problems described by this sample, as well as the information available in the literature, suggest a treatment approach focused on the clarification of sexual confusion, positive identification with the masculine gender, and the development of the ability to sustain intimate relationships.

Dimmock goes on to argue, later in the same work:

> The use of an exclusively male treatment approach is advocated as an effective means to accomplish the above goals. Through the development of relationships with other men to help affirm masculinity, respect vulnerability, and react with real emotions to the sexual abuse experience, the doubts male victims have about their adequacy as men, as well as the stereotypes they hold, can be altered.

Dimmock notes, as have I, that many males initially express more comfort with a female therapist. In spite of this, he believes that men must deal with molestation by men with "close, trusting relationships with other men." Dimmock is arguing here regarding the treatment of adult men, but I feel that his arguments can be extended down through adolescence to about age 7. I concur with Hewitt that preschoolers would be best served by individual treatment, and that the sex of the therapist is probably far less important in dealing with preschoolers, although I would still retain a bias in many cases for a male therapist.

The treatment of abused males has some things in common with initiation into manhood in primitive cultures. Boys who have been sexually victimized have been, in some sense, demasculinized. Either their masculinity has been severely damaged by what has happened, or, in panic, they have regressed back toward a symbiotic involvement with women. Participation in an all-male group headed by a strong male model has many parallels with male initiation rituals around the world. Because we are not attempting to produce fierce warriors and are not dealing, as a general rule, with the deep and profound symbiotic dependence upon women that characterizes Melanesian society, our techniques do not need to have the brutality connected with Melanesian practice. Unlike the Sambia, we have the luxury of producing softer men. Rather than fierce warriors, we seek to help men reach the end of the male developmental line, to become full human beings who can relate healthily to women as well as other men.

As noted elsewhere in this book, the needs described here are not limited to victims of molestation. The tremendous power of the men's movement in this country is a very good illustration of how "unmasculine" a component of the American male population feels, and how badly they seek masculinization through a ritual paralleling initiation in primitive societies. Robert Bly (1990) specifically develops the initiation model as a vehicle to strengthen masculinity in the modern world.

I doubt that there is serious dispute that older males have an important role to play in the lives of younger males. It is part of the folk wisdom of this and every other culture of which I have any awareness that men have an integral role in the development of boys, and that their absence in a boy's life cannot be replaced by a woman. Additionally, men bear an extra responsibility in the kind of situation described in this book. Most boys who come into treatment have been molested by older males. Often they are the very men who should have been guiding the boy toward male identity: fathers and step-fathers. To repair this lesion, these boys need to return to the kind of relationship in which it arose, an affective relationship with a father figure. Female victims of male perpetrators can shut men out of their life, usually at price, but they will not be ruined by such a course. A male who tries to exclude maleness from his psychic and social world is in deep trouble.

These remarks do not mean that women have no role to play in the treatment of boys who have been molested. Female therapists will be working with a major handicap when they attempt to address the core issues of damaged masculinity for reasons already spelled out in some detail. But boys who have been victimized have many problems not directly related to their maleness. A female therapist can do as much as a male therapist with these issues which are not gender specific. Boys who have been molested often have great hostility to women. Sometimes this is an effort to distance themselves from femininity to escape the regressive drawback toward symbiosis with the mother as a reaction to the damage of molestation. By hostility and devaluation of women, the male victim can defend against this regression which is both feared and desired. In other cases the hostility is rooted in preexisting conflicts with key women in their lives. A history of abuse and conflict with maternal figures may be one of the factors that make some boys predisposed to become victims. In the absence of adequate mothering, these boys may turn to males for affection they should be getting from mothers or mother figures. Some men will exploit this in order to victimize the boy. Mother and thereby women in general may be blamed, rightly or wrongly, for not being protective and preventing the assault in the first place. In all of these cases, eventual reconciliation with femaleness is an essential treatment need. It is my judgment that this will usually be best done toward the end of treatment when the boy's maleness has been strengthened and his general level of defensive rage reduced.

There are also specific developmental reasons that a female therapist needs to become involved at some point in the male victim's recovery. The mothering person always has a role in the development of a boy's masculinity. Young boys need female affirmation of their masculinity. They need a mother figure's permission and encouragement to be fully male. These issues can be best worked out in a period of individual therapy with a female therapist at a time in treatment carefully to best meet the boy's treatment needs.

Other Transferences

Much has been said here about the selfobject transference. There are other important transference phenomena that have been explored by self psychology. These transferences serve to support a fragile self and to promote the growth and extension of the self. They can be used in the treatment process to repair the psychic damage done by victimization. The most common of these transferences are the mirroring transference and the idealizing transference. The patient who need mirroring wishes the selfobject to reflect back on them as to what a wonderful, competent, lovable person they are. The analogy from early parent/child interaction is obvious. In the idealizing transference, the damaged self seeks an idealized, highly desirable object with whom it can identify, merge, and from whom it can acquire the traits that it idealizes. In the case of the victim population, this would most often be traits involving maleness, self-control, and power.

USE OF COMPENSATORY STRUCTURES

It was earlier noted that some victims, particularly those with borderline personality organization will be able to do little in the area of expanding the nuclear self. This is self psychology's way of describing the patient who will respond poorly to treatment. Other schools might call them "untreatable" or amenable only to supportive types of treatment. In all probability, these kinds of victims had serious problems before they were molested. Sexual victimization has made a bad situation worse. In treatment, the therapist, regardless of theoretical orientation, will be asked to address the borderline (or psychotic) issues as well as the impact of victimization. It is with this kind of patient that the therapist will need to rely on the development of compensatory structures to approach the kinds of goals described in this work. Compensatory structures can be defined as defenses, or tangible supports from the environment which are not part of the nuclear self, but nonetheless help

to assure long term, successful social functioning. Techniques for helping the patient develop compensatory structures include teaching of
ways for the simple suppression of the behavior or of fantasies which
underlie behavior. This is much done in behavioral-cognitive treatment. The knowledge of how to suppress a behavior or fantasy becomes
a compensatory structure when viewed from the perspective of self
psychology.

Sublimation and substitution can be useful, also, as compensatory
structures. If a patient's sexual and aggressive conflicts cannot be resolved,
sometimes they can be translated into achievement, career, and/or crea-
tivity in other areas. There are, of course problems with this kind of
approach. Helping develop compensatory structures is a form of supportive therapy. This process stresses bridging gaps in the core self
rather than repair of the core itself. Compensatory structures of any kind
are likely to break down under stress.

The development of compensatory structures to support an intrinsically
weak nuclear self implies a need for a lifelong system of supportive
selfobjects in order to maintain stability and to avoid fragmentation.
Practically, this may mean that the patient needs to be taught self-
monitoring. He needs to learn what kinds of things may trigger violent,
self-destructive, and/or inappropriate sexual behavior in them. Teaching "stress cycles" analogous to the abuse cycle well known in the treatment of sex offenders would be another useful supportive technique.

This kind of patient will need to be told that they will require periods
of supportive treatment, off and on at various intervals in their life, and
be encouraged to seek such treatment. This message needs to be incorpo-
rated in termination planning with any patient who cannot realize the
more comprehensive goals outlined earlier. The above remarks may be
familiar to those who also are familiar with the treatment of perpetrators.
I am describing under "compensatory structures" something very much
like standard practice in treating perpetrators of sexual abuse. I suspect
that it is the more disturbed victim who is at greater risk of becoming
a perpetrator. Hence the two populations, the more disturbed victims,
and perpetrators as a group may share in some of their treatment needs.
I would, however, stress the need for gentleness in implementing this
approach. I would not move heavily into formal behavioral-cognitive
techniques with young male victims. Some of these techniques such as
masturbatory satiation would be poorly received in outpatient practice
with children and adolescents.

The Pre-Homosexual Boy

Pre-homosexual boys are common in the victim population. They pose some significant treatment planning problems. In general, they are desirous of re-orienting heterosexually. In cases where homosexual behavior is reactive to victimization, this is relatively easy. The more difficult cases are the boys who were already oriented homosexually when they were victimized by someone much older. These boys were probably particularly vulnerable to sexual exploitation by older males because of their preexisting orientation. The problem posed by these boys is: Do we try to help them reorient themselves in terms of choosing a female sexual object or do we facilitate acceptance of a gay identity? More on that after some essential description.

Many writers are aware that the precursors of homosexuality appear very early in many males (Whitham 1986). Key manifestations of the pre-homosexual boy are cross-dressing, preference for toys and games culturally designated as female. In my practice, boys as young as six or seven, will acknowledge a sexual preference for males. Pre-homosexual boys who come into treatment may be different than those who do not. Most of the boys I see have a full awareness that they are male. They also wish to be and remain male. I recall none who presented with an enduring wish to be female. I would argue that, although these boys may indeed be pre-homosexual, the structure of the nuclear self in most of the young male victims seen in treatment is a structure that esteems masculine power and identity, while preferring a masculine sexual object. This may be dynamically tied to the seeking of a powerful male with whom to fuse in order to strengthen their own own masculine identity. This may be exactly the dynamic that made them vulnerable to victimization in the first place.

At least in the population of boys coming to treatment with me, very few show any desire to be female. Many show a strong sexual interest in other males. The majority of these boys are quite uncomfortable with their developing sexual orientation and usually explicitly state a desire to change it. Like the pre-heterosexual boy, the pre-homosexual boy generally usually expresses strongly and forcefully a wish to have his masculinity strengthened. Suggestions that a gay identity is okay usually fall on deaf ears.

Where does that leave us in terms of treatment goals? Our only hope is to individualize. Some boys make great progress in the kind of treatment

I am describing toward masculine identity and heterosexual orientation. Perhaps these are boys with a strong bisexuality which they tap in order to strengthen the preexisting erotic bond to females. Other victims seem intensely attached to male sexual objects and will need to make a synthesis of their masculine goals and ambitions with their intrinsic homosexuality. I would urge great caution here. It is only with time in treatment that the real underlying process can be uncovered. I have been very surprised when some boys I believed at intake to be intrinsically homosexual developed unmistakable interest in the opposite sex in the course of treatment.

It is my view that, as therapists, we have little choice but to accept the patient's, even the child patient's, basic goals for treatment. The pre-homosexual boy who comes to treatment requesting a re-orientation of his sexuality should be helped to the best of the therapist's ability toward these goals. With verbal patients and, particularly, older adolescents, I believe it is quite wise to explicitly discuss the formulation of goals in the area of sexual orientation. It is also appropriate to alert the pre-homosexual boy who is at a developmental stage capable of assimilating the information that changes in sexual orientation are quite difficult to accomplish.

CULTURE AND TREATMENT

I would like to conclude this presentation with some remarks about culture and the use of cultural factors in treatment planning and design. Much was made earlier in this work of the role of culture. It is my feeling that a drive for masculine identity is probably panhuman, occurring in all cultures with different manifestations. It seems to have either biological roots or roots in the earliest training and/or neural programming of the human brain. This, of course, does not mean that there is not a great deal of difference about how cultures conceptualize masculinity, and as to what kind of behaviors are worked out as to ways in which males can prefer sex with other males and still feel masculine. This resolution is poorly tolerated in mainstream America and its subcultures. In working with specific cultural populations, the way these cultures deal with male sexuality, relationships between the sexes, and the behavioral expression of sexuality needs to be taken into careful account. This was explored in more detail in the chapter on culture and will not be repeated here.

Chapter 10

GROUP THERAPY

This chapter explores methods of implementing the treatment goals and strategies discussed in the last chapter. Here they will be examined in the context of group psychotherapy. Emphasis will be placed on the eight clusters of problems which most researchers and clinicians agree are the focal treatment concerns for young male victims. Also of concern here will be operationalizing in the context of group therapy the second group of goals drawn selectively from self psychology and some other contemporary schools of psychoanalysis. This chapter rests upon the theoretical foundations laid in previous chapters.

Group therapy is a valuable modality for most victims of molestation. It helps to alleviate isolation and the sense that the victim has experienced something noone else has endured. The homogeneous victim group encourages sharing, disclosure, and mutual support. As will soon be explored, many things can be accomplished in group that cannot be done in individual or family therapy. Group seems to be a particularly critical experience for boys in the eight to fourteen year age range. Once they have experienced group, these boys usually prefer it to individual therapy.

Creating groups of boys from eight to fourteen may seem peculiar to the developmentally oriented since it spans the socalled latency period plus puberty plus young adolescence. I have arrived at this grouping pragmatically by experimenting with various possible combinations of ages in groups. The concept of a period of sexual latency from ages eight to puberty has not stood up well in clinical circles. I believe it is particularly invalid with molest victims who have been prematurely introduced to sexuality because of their victimization. Since the younger boys are already dealing with sexual issues, for better or worse, they have much in common with the younger adolescents and seem to work well with them in carefully composed groups. Another factor is that at least in American Cultures the age range from eight to fourteen is one in which factors relating to masculine identity are in an ideal configuration for the use of group at that time. Male victims in this age range seem very interested in maleness. They typically have a great hunger for father figures. They are very interested in sexual matters. This is an age in which peer groups are very important to boys in general in this culture. Even though I have designated this age range as eight to fourteen, this is somewhat arbitrary. I sometimes place twelve year olds in an adolescent group. Many eight year olds are too immature to work well with the older boys in these groups.

METHODS FOR EFFECTING INTERPSYCHIC
AND BEHAVIORAL CHANGE IN GROUP

The therapeutic group offers a number of opportunities to repair the damage done by molestation of young males. As was noted in an earlier chapter, human beings use a number of transference mechanisms for self-repair. These include the selfobject transference, as well as the mirroring, and idealizing transferences discussed in the last chapter. These transferences will be manifest in groups. They will involve both the therapist and group members. In groups for male victims transference issues involving maleness, power, and control of others as well as self-control are prominent and recurring. If they are identified they can be used in working through these vital issues.

A more widely known mechanism of change is identification. It is a truism that men whose masculinity is fragile need positive male role models in order to develop into competent male human beings. In group therapy, a powerful identification figure is offered by the male therapist. The group also offers a variety of other male models which can be used by the young victim. This is particularly true in an open-ended group where boys are coming and going. Those nearing the end of their treatment provide alternate examples of masculinity for younger boys just entering the group.

Group treatment also effects change by allowing boys to practice new patterns of behavior and to have them reinforced as they practice them. This is probably close to the secondary mechanisms of learning suggested by Winson. Certainly, the social learning theorists are both familiar and comfortable with this concept. In group, patients can practice social relationships with other males, both the therapist, who can be a father figure, and their male peers in the group. If the therapist is aware of the various kinds of transference mechanisms explored by self-psychology, he can make conscious use of them in this process.

The young male victim of sexual abuse has difficulty relating to male peers, as well as to older males. Male-to-male relationships in these cases often carry an excessive load of sexualization or fear and resentment. The peer group offers a chance to develop and practice non-erotized and non-hostile relationships with peers, as well as with the therapist. The group also offers an arena for males to work on issues of cooperation and competition with other males. Both have their place, and both need to be integrated into successful male/male relationships.

Power relationships can also be worked on and practiced in a group setting. Both Hewitt and Froning (1990) and Mayman (1990) recommend giving the male victim a great deal of power in the therapeutic relationship. In their victimizations, these young males have been severely deprived of a feeling of power. They need to experience a feeling of power and competence both in group and individual therapy over a prolonged period of time as a part of the restorative process.

In practicing self-assertion and the development of a healthy sense of power, the patient also needs to learn where the limits of that power are. We can help patients achieve realistic power in the world. We cannot make them omnipotent. The young male victim needs to learn where his realistic power ends and where the rights of others begin. He also needs to learn his responsibilities to others in social relationships. These are complex ideas which take a considerable amount of time and practice to develop and integrate the psychic and behavioral repertoire of the patient. The group is an arena in which they can be worked out through transference, practicing and reinforcement processes.

Cognitive Techniques

By this I do not mean the classical behavioral cognitive therapies, but something broader. There is a place in any psychotherapy for straight-out teaching by the therapist. In the case of child and adolescent patients, this often involves teaching what is acceptable and what is unacceptable in the context of reality and their own culture. Victims also need to know some of the things that most victims who come to treatment feel and believe, and what kinds of reactions to sexual assault can be expected. The fact that victims often experience some degree of physical pleasure while being victimized is a case in point. The increased tendency toward perpetration is another. These sources of anxiety and risk need to be explicitly discussed in group.

Also in the cognitive area is a frontal assault on denial. Denial is an ongoing process with this population. Details are forgotten or distorted. In some cases children who have been in treatment for more than a year will go through periods where they claim to have no memory of what happened to them. This can be a true denial in which the boy has truely repressed what occurred. It is often rooted in shame, particularly where sodomy was involved. It is in one way or another a defense to avoid painful feelings or memories.

The clinical literature seems to agree that these processes lumped under the name denial are toxic and need to be blocked in the course of treatment. Group can be helpful in preventing the development of denial, surpression, and distortion of reality. When new members arrive, each boy is asked to describe what happened to him. This serves as an ongoing reminder of the traumatic incidents. The therapist can remind boys of what happened if distortions and denial are creeping into his accounts. The group culture must be one which stresses that boys are not responsible for their victimization. In listening to the more mature boys discuss their victimization without shame, new boys are given permission to recall, discuss, and work through what has happened to them.

Cognitive techniques also include helping the patient make connections. They need to know what precipitates unwanted feelings or behavior. This would be particularly true of what precipitates sexually compulsive behavior or urges to commit sexual acts that are not acceptable to the patient, particularly perpetration upon younger children. Often unwanted homosexual impulses are also in this category.

Cognitive techniques can also include the classic Freudian making of the unconscious conscious. This can be done by analysis of dreams, analysis of fantasies, or analysis of verbal productions in group or individual therapy. This is tricky with children, but sometimes it works. One of the purposes of making previously unconscious material conscious is to make the patient aware of a potential problem. I encounter this most often with conflicts about homosexual impulses. Boys often either repress these or compartmentalize them in such a way that they have no meaning in a patient's psychic life much of the time. These feelings seem to emerge as impulses or fantasies that periodically trouble the patient, and sometimes lead to acting out. A similar pattern probably exists with urges to molest younger children. Few patients are willing to bring up this issue spontaneously. Sometimes the material is repressed. Other times it is concealed because of the burden of shame disclosure will bring. For these reasons it is often easier to get to this material through such methods as group analysis of dreams, fantasy, or drawings.

Where these feelings, fantasies, and behaviors are truly unacceptable to the patient, there is a place for behavioral-cognitive techniques such as covert sensitization. These need to be used with caution with younger children since most communities are not very tolerant of teaching young children such techniques as masturbatory satiation, or the showing of pornographic material to children in order to pair it with an adverse stimulus.

USING THE GROUP CULTURE

There are a number of "cultural" concepts that can be used in psychotherapy. In a non-anthropological sense, a psychotherapy group has a culture. Each group has its system of values, its practices, its social hierarchies. These things can be used by the therapist to effect change in the patients. To illustrate the use of group culture to effect change, I would point out that very few boys over eight years of age are tolerant of infantilism and immaturity in other boys. Such children will come under overt pressure, in a group setting, to grow up. At first the behavior is corrected by peer pressure. On a deeper level, the group offers the immature, dependent boy a chance for identification with and internalization of the value systems, or even elements of the psychic structures, of other boys in the group.

Peer groups will also develop value systems about masculinity. They will reinforce at least a verbal conformance to these value systems and allow an opportunity to practice verbalizing these value systems and receiving affirmation for doing so. This process can be used to strengthen the boys' sense of masculinity. Groups vary in their value systems regarding sexuality. One of my groups is very permissive regarding homosexuality. Another is extremely intolerant of it. Placement within a group that is permissive of homosexuality as opposed to a more homophobic group is an important element in treatment planning. Boys will seek out what they want and need. Those wanting to develop a strong heterosexual masculinity will be uncomfortable in a group that is easy going and tolerant of homosexuality. Needless to say, a boy whose sense of maleness includes sexual attraction to other males and who may be prehomosexual would be ill served in a group which devalues homosexuality.

I believe therapists will have little luck in changing the basic value systems of groups in regard to homosexuality. The treatment choice is to create separate groups with separate climates so the needs of all boys can be met. It is easier for the therapist to influence group values about perpetration against younger children. This is probably because American society is more uniformly condemning of child molesting than it is of homosexuality. It is also usually easy for the therapist to influence the group culture so that it condemns violence against females.

Where true selfobject relationships and other transferences exist between boys in the group and between the boys and the therapist, I believe that all of these changes can be internalized, and that boys do not simply conform to group norms until they are out of the group setting. In some cases change may be only a reaction to group pressure. I believe this is relatively rare. Most of the boys that I treat seem highly motivated to identify with the stronger and more responsible boys in group. Many of them have openly stated a desire to identify with me and my value system. This kind of process should according to the best theoretical and clinical data available, facilitate permanent change.

Use of Cultural Value Systems

Moving from the specific culture of the therapy group to the broader arena of cultural and subcultural value systems, a sensitive therapist can identify and clarify attitudes from the patient's own culture or ethnic group to help them integrate their sexual feelings into a stronger nuclear self. For example, with pre-homosexual boys, I will often discuss with them the permissiveness of some segments of American middle class culture toward homosexuality. With Hispanics, it can be useful to point out the permissiveness of Latin culture toward active homosexuality. If the Hispanic boy is pre-homosexual, it is probably culturally more advisable to guide them in the direction of the active manifestation of homosexual behavior.

THE RELUCTANT ADOLESCENT

Most therapists see very few middle and late adolescents (ages fifteen to eighteen) in treatment for sexual assaults perpetrated upon them.

Boys in this range rarely volunteer for treatment. Many of them are seen as perpetrators rather than victims. Sometimes parents insist on treatment because they have encountered media or professional opinion that sexually abused males need treatment. Others are brought by parents because of what they consider bizarre sexual behaviors and conflicts.

One of the difficulties in treating this population is that the individuation process itself seems, at this stage, to generate a withdrawal from adults. This is correlated with an increasing orientation toward peers and value systems embraced by peers. The hunger for father figures appears substantially reduced at this time. Many adolescent male victims are experiencing deviant sexual feelings as a result of being sexually assaulted when younger. They usually have profound feelings of shame and failure due to these feelings. There is tremendous pressure to be, to feel, and to behave in a narrow range prescribed by various adolescent cliques. In American culture these adolescent subcultures usually demand a strong display of sexual attraction to same-age females, backed up by considerable sexual activity. Most adolescents need to attempt to pour themselves into these predetermined subcultural molds. If they cannot, they risk anxiety, depression, and alienation.

At this stage, it seems to me that the ego is often strong enough to enforce massive denial about one's victimization, but not strong enough to support probing into the underlying problem. Yet, some boys do volunteer for treatment. Others are willing to accept it in a meaningful way after being referred for perpetration or other sexual problems. Sometimes the referral comes from substance abuse or behavioral problems which turn out to have their roots in victimization. If the boy can be convinced that there is a connection between the presenting problem or disturbing symptoms and his victimization, treatment can be effective in this age group. As a general rule, adolescent boys are much more willing to come into individual treatment than into group.

Group Therapy for Boys Eight to Fourteen

The lower age boundary on these groups is somewhat arbitrary. Many eight year olds are too immature for the kind of group described here. That can usually be ascertained in an assessment interview and/or a trial of two or three sessions in group. Important factors are attention span and social maturity. If the youngest boys are perceived by other boys as "babies" they will not be accepted in the group. Their presence can also cause regressive behavior in other boys and damage the group process for everyone. At the other end of the age and maturity spectrum some boys will outgrow these groups at twelve, and should be moved into an adolescent group at that time.

Male initiation rites whether in Melanesia, aboriginal California, or in Robert Bly's seminars have common foci. They teach the uninitiated or damaged male what it is to be a male in his culture and they help him form strong bonds with other males. This is an inherent part of what I feel is necessary to undo that damage done to boys who have been molested by men. It is no wonder that a therapy technique designed to achieve the same end would have structural parallels to male initiation around the world. In therapy, the all male peer group allows bonding with other males in a context that places strong value on masculinity. It also involves older men (and senior boys) in the group to teach and model what it means to be male. It also allows the male victim to experience working together, sharing, and mutual affection with other males. Group also relieves the sense of loneliness, isolation, and the sense of being different from other boys that comes from being sexually victimized. The techniques described here create a very intense kind of group experience which breaks down ego defenses and facilitates a great deal of disclosure. The disclosure usually comes much more rapidly than in individual treatment.

Some molested boys are so alienated from older males that they could never begin with individual treatment. For some boys at this age, the group dilutes the transference relationship to the therapist in a way to make treatment possible. Some of these boys have been so damaged by other males and are so angry with older males that they would be terrified or enraged to be in individual therapy. Group allows them to relate to and engage an adult male without the same degree of fear and rage that might arise in individual treatment.

Screening

All boys should be interviewed individually and with their parents prior to placement in a group. The nature of the group should be carefully explained to the child. In dealing with the eight to fourteen year old, I stress the fun aspects of group: the games, the refreshments, etc., but make it very plain that sexual issues will also be dealt with. Very rarely does a child who is suitable for group decline to participate after this kind of screening interview. The nature of the group also needs to be explained to the parents to elicit their support. If at all possible, the parents should be engaged in the treatment process themselves, through either family therapy, parent guidance interviews, or, in some cases, individual therapy for the parents.

The group techniques suggested here are ones I have devised, over the course of many years of experience with male victims in this age range. They will not be suitable for all therapists for a variety of reasons. To run this kind of group with boys in this age range requires a great deal of tolerance for disorder, and at least verbal chaos. These are, after all, boys in puberty who are probably considered by most adults to be in the most difficult age range with which to deal.

INTAKE CRITERIA

Not all boys are suitable for the kind of group described here. Obviously, they must be a victim of sexual abuse to participate. I do not have a problem with including boys who have been involved in minor acts of perpetration in this kind of group, as long as they are also victims. One of my reasons for this is that minor perpetration, mixed in with a lot of same-sex sexual acting out is common in male victims at this age. This mixture is so common that it would be very hard to draw guidelines that would allow only "pure victims" in the group. Another rationale for mixing "pure victims" and boys who have forayed into perpetration in the same group is that I believe that it is desirable to deal with the possibility of perpetration with all males who have been molested. The presence of some "light weight" perpetrators in the group allows this to be easily discussed and illustrated. The boys who have not perpetrated do not seem to have any difficulty accepting those who have, nor do they show any fear of them. I would, of course, screen out a sophisticated, aggressive, and predatory perpetrator from this kind of group. I work extensively with perpetrators as well as victims. Intuitively, it is easy to separate the victim who perpetrates reactively from the boy who has already developed into an entrenched perpetrator. It is the first group that I advocate including in the group for victims. The more sophisticated perpetrator needs specialized, offender specific treatment.

In assessing the appropriateness of a boy who has molested a younger child in addition to being a victim himself of the type advocated, several factors need to be weighted. Their perpetration should be part of a more pervasive pattern of sexualization. The boy is sexually active with peers as well as younger children. There is no pattern of seeking out only younger children. There is no force or sadism in the boy's pattern of sexual activity with others. There is no evidence of planning or entrapment in seeking victims. The boy shows ability to empathize and bond with others. Antisocial (delinquent) features are not prominent in any area of the boy's life.

Other basic intake criteria include a roughly normal IQ, with the lower limit being around 80, that the child be non-psychotic, and not have severe behavior problems. Some of the boys I see do have behavioral problems, but there are a few who are so angry and out of control that they cannot be handled in group. Occasionally, I encounter a boy who is so profoundly ashamed and frightened by his sexual feelings and victimization, he cannot or will not participate in group. This becomes particularly marked as the age of fourteen is approached. These boys need to start in individual treatment and move into group once they become more comfortable with the idea. Most boys initially reject the idea of being in a group. Unless the anxiety is intense, I urge them to try the group two or three times before they insist on individual treatment. Usually boys are comfortable in this kind of group after the first session.

Group Structure

For reasons that are obvious in the overall context of this book, I feel that most boys are best treated at least initially in groups that are led by a male and composed exclusively of males. The is in line with the group's focus on the development of male identity. As a practical matter, my experience has been that even where the group has another focus, boys in the eight to fourteen year age range do not work well with female peers in the same treatment group. (Remember I move the more mature boys out of these groups at twelve. These groups include only immature thirteen and fourteen year old boys.) I once inherited a general purpose therapy group of boys and girls in this age range. What happened was the group informally functioned as two groups with a boys' subgroup and a girls' subgroup. The two groups could never agree on what they wanted to do or what they wanted to discuss. Both boys and girls asked me to set up separate groups for each sex.

In addition to the above considerations, many young male victims have a great deal of hostility toward females. This is in part a reactive rejection of femininity in an effort to strengthen their sense of value as a male. In some cases boys have poor relationships with their mothers which sometimes include neglect and physical abuse. Anger and distrust of females may have been part of what made them vulnerable to the allure of male molesters in the first place. The presence of a females in the group on a regular basis would elevate the level of anger and shift the focus away from the strengthening of masculinity toward other issues.

Not all young male victims have anger issues with females. But even such boys would lose something if the group were led or co-led by a female or if the group had both male and female members. To deal with issues of damaged masculinity in the presence of females raises serious issues of shame and the compromising of their sense of masculinity in the presence of the opposite sex. For boys with a strong heterosexual orientation, the presence of female peers leads to concealing their sense of damaged maleness and a lot of flirting and posturing.

At some point in the treatment process, I believe it is desirable for the male victim to have a therapeutic experience with a female therapist. This can be done by referring for individual therapy. It could also be done by having a female therapist in group on an occasional basis to focus on specific issues. My sense is that the experience with the female therapist could usually be best integrated after the boy has had considerable treatment in an all male milieu. Obviously the male victim must at some time come to terms with his hostility to females. In most cases, this can best be done after his damaged masculinity has been strengthened and his general level of rage reduced. Some boys who are very damaged in their ability to relate to a man, may need to start with a female therapist and move at a later time into work with a male.

These groups, for both practical and theoretical reasons, are openended. The practical reasons involve a flow of referrals. The theoretical reason is to allow boys at different stages of development and repair of their masculinity to work together and share. The older, more mature boys in a group can provide role models, selfobjects, identification figures, etc., for the younger, newer boys in the group. These groups are intended to be of relatively long duration, with boys remaining in them from one to three years. Although the duration over time is long, the actual group session needs to be kept short. In general boys this age and in particular boys with these problems have short attention spans. A high level of anxiety and hyperactivity is stirred up by discussing sexual matters. One hour is about all these boys (and most therapists) can take. Once a week is my preferred interval.

The group must have basic rules. They are not listed, but are discussed at intake and enforced as necessary. These are just common sense: no hitting, no sexual behavior, no destruction of property, respect for peers and leaders, and no scapegoating. Obviously, any of these behaviors in group should initially be a target for discussion, but they must all be extinguished forcefully if discussion is not adequate.

Beyond these minimal rules, a high level of permissiveness in the group is desirable. There are no rules in these groups regarding the use of language. Profanity is acceptable and commonly used. This is for a variety of reasons, not the least of which is that many of the boys do not have the technical vocabulary to discuss sexuality without using street language. There are no concepts, feelings, or fantasies which cannot be discussed in group. Boys are, indeed, encouraged to share whatever is coming into their minds in the sexual area. As a result of this rule, much that comes up in group will involve primitive and/or hostile and aggressive feelings. In order to conduct this kind of group, the therapist must be comfortable with that material.

As part of the general framework of creating the most permissive possible group, consistent with survival of patients, therapist, and office, I let the boys make as many decisions as possible for themselves. There are a number of activities, both clinical and play, which can be engaged in by the group. I make it plain that I expect a certain amount of time to be spent on clinical issues, but within this basic ground rule, boys are often allowed to make decisions by majority vote about precise procedures. They have more or less complete control over the play activities at the first part of the group.

The purposes of these group rules and procedures are manifold. Clinically, I am anxious to stimulate as free a flow as possible of talk, feeling, and fantasy. When these groups get going, there is an intensity which breaks down defenses. Boys come out with all kinds of disclosures and feelings that would be harder to access in individual therapy. They pressure each other for disclosures, comments, and analyses that they would never put forth with similar pressures from a therapist.

A second part of this strategy is empowerment. Letting boys participate in rule-setting is both empowering and age-appropriate. They have a freedom of expression, which they most frequently associate with adults. This is a rare opportunity to say anything on their minds in any language they choose. Additionally, most of the boys that I see would associate profanity with masculinity, since the male role models in their lives use it extensively. I believe most American males including these boys regard profanity as a "male language". It is discouraged or prohibited in the presence of females and authority, but widely used in male peer and work groups. The boys also classify it as "grown up". In other words, allowing this language, identifies this as a group of "men," something in which the boys take obvious pleasure.

It is important to stress to the boys that the rules outlined here apply only to this group. I do not advocate that they use street language in school or in their homes. This can become a real problem if not addressed with both the boys and, in many cases, with their parents. The knowledge that I allow boys to cuss in group causes frequent concerned inquiry from parents, foster parents, and even social workers and probation officers.

The therapist also has some rules that he must follow in this kind of group. I believe it is important not to touch the boys in view of their victim status. This may sound withholding and unloving. I have never had a problem develop out of this policy. On the other hand, I have heard of therapists who permit male victims to engage in seductive behaviors, including sitting on a male therapist's lap and wriggling around. This kind of thing is most likely very frightening to the child since it will make him feel that limit setting in this sexually charged area is up to him. Any kind of seductive behavior directed toward the therapist should be discouraged. Sometimes it can be analyzed and discussed in group, but this is potentially explosive and should be undertaken with sensitivity to the group's reaction.

Any therapist attempting to run this type of group is going to be provoked, from time to time, to a great deal of anger. I believe it is O.K. to express this as long as you do not express it in a way that is personally rejecting to the child. If you go too far, you can always admit that to the child. In my judgment this is modeling of anger management. If you don't get angry in the face of the kind of provocation you are going to get from some of these children, they are going to regard you as either inhuman or dishonest.

COGNITIVE COMPONENTS OF GROUP THERAPY

In addition to the opportunities for free and spontaneous expression offered by group, the therapist needs to build in a significant cognitive component which is simply taught to the boys as part of the group process. Essentially this is a value agenda which is gone over almost as a lesson from time to time. I periodically ask boys to answer some questions based on this cognitive component and will challenge them if they show behaviors in group which indicate they have not learned or internalized this component.

One of the key elements in this cognitive component is a requirement that they learn the kinds of sexuality that are going to get them in legal trouble: specifically, any sexual act involving force, a sexual act involving younger children, and a sexual act involving close relatives. Also part of this component is the idea that victims are not to blame for what has happened to them, nor could they have fought off the perpetrator. In dealing with this, it needs to be stressed that they may have been talked into consenting, but the blame lies with a more experienced and powerful person who took advantage of them. I teach also that masturbation is harmless as long as it is a private activity. Boys typically come into group with a great deal of shame about this. Boys of this age often associate masturbation with homosexuality, probably because it is often connected with homosexual fantasies. The cognitive component also involves teaching that violence against other human beings is not O.K. in any form, sexual or otherwise. There are some other areas in this cognitive component which may need to be included depending on group composition. With some groups it is necessary to educate in areas of drug abuse or satanism.

This cognitive component is easily integrated into the overall group process. It does not vary, in most cases, from values children are exposed to from other adults. Masturbation being O.K. and a tolerant attitude toward consenting sex would be its main differences from standard cultural values. This material should be presented low key and in a natural manner, most often as a part of the formal discussion time in the group itself.

Group Format

These groups consist of two parts, of which the boys are well aware. The first part is an activity/game time designed to get the boys comfortable and also to allow for the inevitable late arrival. The group is allowed to select a game from a wide variety of choices in the office. The game is played as a pleasurable mutual activity. It is important to choose games which do not last too long. During this period, food and drink are served. Lemonade is constantly available, as are crackers for nibbling as we talk. One is that groups are held after school, and boys are often hungry. The second is to gratify their symbolic hunger and to provide a symbol of nurturance within the context of the group. At the end of the group a donut is available to those who have earned it as part of a behavior control system.

After the initial game session there is an obligatory talk time which varies in its specific nature from week to week. Sometimes this is a point at which the cognitive agenda described above is introduced and discussed. At other times I may have picked up interactions between the boys or comments during the games which merit follow-up discussion in the group. If new boys show a great deal of fear or resentment toward me, I will open up the issue of fear that I might perpetrate against them. This is also a time which any sexually tinged discussions or actions taking place between boys can be discussed.

If there is no obvious agenda for the talk time, I fall back upon group exercises. I have compiled a large collection of cards with questions relating to a wide range of sexual issues typed on them. Many of these cards have actually been contributed by children and typed on the cards for inclusion in the card box. This is a source of pride for boys in the group. The cards are used by asking each boy to select one randomly (they are not allowed to choose their card) and then to answer the question. Some of these cards cause a great deal of anxiety and, particularly, new boys will refuse to answer them. In this case I generally allow them to select a second or third card, although I do require that the card be read out loud to the group so I can get an indication of what key conflict areas are involved. Sometimes the group does not get any further than to have everyone contribute to a discussion of questions selected by one or two boys.

Another group technique is to draw from a pile of pictures that I have selected from a wide range of magazines and mounted on cardboard.

None of these pictures are explicitly sexual. Some of them are somewhat suggestive, and some of them are neutral, relating to non-sexual issues. Boys pick these up without being able to see in advance what the picture is, or in other cases I select the picture to work on some particular theme. The boys then make a group story with each boy contributing until the story is completed. Stories usually acquire a highly sexual nature, and the group can be extremely chaotic at this time. In general, whenever sexual issues are discussed, this kind of group gets extremely active and agitated.

After their group story has been told, I will often make some interpretative comments about it or ask the boys to make some interpretative comments. Examples of this chaotic and violent material is presented in another chapter. There are times when the group is in a mature stage when the boys will produce less violent and sexually chaotic stories. Sometimes this is done self-consciously. The group will start to comment that the story is getting violent, or boys introducing certain ideas unacceptable in the group will come under pressure from peers to amend the story. This technique is essentially part of an uncovering process in which I am hoping to bring out underlying sexual fantasies and feelings so the boys can deal with them as conscious formulations rather than as suppressed fantasies. Over a period of time, a boy's contribution to these stories become less sexually pathological.

Another technique is to encourage use of the stuffed human and animal figures to put together dramas. Usually the boys divide into groups of two, and make up a skit acted out with the figures. These dramas usually deal with sexual themes, sometimes with molestation, sometimes with rape. Themes of child physical abuse also emerge in these stories. All of these are discussed with the group after the various dramas have been produced.

In spite of these techniques permitting a great deal of violent fantasy in group, to my knowledge, none of the boys I have ever worked with has acted out violently against anyone else. I believe, and there is some support in the literature for my belief, that verbalizing these fantasies has a containing and settling effect that keeps them from being translating into acts in the real world. It is important to interpret these fantasies to help the boys identify the trauma and conflict which underlies them. The production of less violent and disturbed fantasy content is a measure of progress in treatment. One of the arts of this process is knowing when to attempt to tone down or channel a fantasy away from violence and when to shut up and encourage free expression. If the therapist intervenes too soon, you simply shut off the flow of fantasy and deprive yourself and the patient of valuable clinical information.

Birthdays

I feel it is important to celebrate boys' birthdays in group. This is for a variety of reasons. It specifically targets the self-esteem cluster of problems, stressing that each boy is important and this important day in his life is a source for special celebration. It can also be an occasion for empowerment. The boy whose birthday is to be celebrated has a choice of having a cake personalized with his name or a pizza with two toppings of his choice. This considerably enhances the boy's status in the group. When the food is actually served, the boy whose birthday is being celebrated gets to select the first piece, and then to select the next boy to get a turn at the food.

Birthdays are celebrated at the end the group as part of a general process of winding down. The discussion and story-telling parts of the group are provocative of anxiety and hyperactivity. It is important to take some steps to get the boys calmed down before they leave the group. At the end of the group a second doughnut is served if there is no birthday celebration. These feeding activities provide a transition from the probing, exploring, and fantasizing phase of the group to a calmer, nurturing part of the group.

Maintaining Order

As anyone who has worked with junior-high age children will be aware, maintaining order with this population is a problem. Many of these boys have conduct disorders as well as sex abuse issues. Others are hyperactive. Some are in puberty. The group discusses sex and victimization which are charged with intense feelings. This gets out of hand very easily.

A calm, firm, no nonsense attitude by the therapist is important. It discourages limit testing and acting out. It must, of course, be mixed with warmth and empathy. It is also necessary to remove boys with irresolvable hostile and negative attitudes toward the group. This attitude contaminates and eventually destroys a positive group climate. There are also some techniques for reducing anxiety and acting out. One is to provide drawing paper, pencils, and markers so boys can draw as the group is discussing things. This reduces tension. It also provides some valuable diagnostic information. Occasionally I will actually introduce one of these drawings as the focus of group discussion. The injunction that the group should be no longer than one hour is also aimed at maintaining order. That is about the maximum time that most boys in this age range with this kind of problem can continue without becoming restless and inattentive.

As an ultimate system of discipline, I use a point system in these groups. This is usually necessary at particularly tense times or when the groups get larger than I would like them to be. It is rarely necessary to use this with a group of four or five. The point system is arbitrary, simply involving subtracting of 10 points at a time for violation of group rules. It is enforced somewhat permissively. If boys lose ten points, they cannot participate in the clean-up activity, for which I pay a small fee. If they lose 30 points, they do not get the final doughnut. At times this technique allows me to salvage a valuable treatment experience from what would have otherwise become sheer bedlam. If the acting out in group involves relationships between boys or between the boys and myself, this is discussed as a clinical issue rather than handled in a disciplinary way.

If none of the above techniques are effective in controlling acting out with certain boys, I will schedule a private discussion with them, inform them that their behavior is unacceptable and they must make a choice to improve their behavior or leave the group. Generally this is resolved in the direction of improved behavior. Very occasionally, perhaps two or three times per year, I do actually have to remove a boy from the group for persistent unresolvable failure to follow the rules. I have never had to remove a child for hitting, although I would not hesitate to do so if necessary.

I have also removed a few children because their placement in the group seemed inappropriate due to their immaturity, neediness, or extremely sexualized behavior. For example, one boy made a point of getting under the card tables, which separate the boys during games, to see if he could see their genitals. In the same session he made a direct sexual advance on another child. The propositioned child promptly announced the matter to the entire group. This turned the offending child into a scapegoat which was beneficial to neither him nor the group.

Since I could not resolve this with discussion, it became necessary to remove the boy from the group.

TREATMENT OF TRAUMA CLUSTERS

Earlier in this work, a series of several trauma clusters, resulting from molestation, were identified. The manner in which this type of group deals therapeutically with each of these clusters will be examined here. Sexualization is targeted in a variety of ways. Among the primary methods are the cognitive elements taught to the boys as part of every group; what is acceptable sexually and what is not acceptable sexually. The boys are also channeled toward a legal, non-assaultive sexual outlet. For their age group, this is often masturbation. As a longer term goal, they are pointed toward consenting sex with peers as an answer to their sexual needs.

Reduction and control of sexualized behavior is shaped by the group process also. Both I and the more mature members of the group will give negative feedback to excessively sexualized behavior. Frequently, new boys enter the group and engage in a lot of erotized behavior toward other boys in the group. No actual touching or propositioning, but their feelings and intentions are obvious. This is rather quickly confronted by group members as inappropriate. On a deeper level, sexualization is targeted by some of the relationship aspects of treatment. The group provides a variety of selfobjects with better degrees of self-control than the new boys in the group.

The sexual identity cluster is approached with a number of techniques. It is dealt with in the purely cognitive content of the group. In the relationship area, I believe these boys' masculine identification is strengthened by a positive sharing experience with other males. The group also provides identification figures. The group culture emphasizes that the boys have permission to be sexual within appropriate limits and to explore their sexual identities without shame or prejudice.

The trust and betrayal cluster is also targeted in group. The very persistence of the group over years is an indicator that human beings can be counted upon in very predictable ways. My own behavior is particularly important, since I am of the same sex and, in some cases, roughly the same age as the perpetrators. This is one reason I do not touch the boys or permit them to engage in any sexually seductive behavior with me. I also attempt to be reliable in terms of attendance at sessions and give abundant advance notice of sessions to be cancelled other than for reasons of illness. I do some work with the boys involving direct discussion of their feelings of distrust. I have spotted anxiety in boys, suggested that it had to do with me, and been told quite bluntly that, yes indeed, they did not trust me. The issue is usually a fear that I will molest them. Reassuring words have little value. I have to tell the boys to check me out over time and see how I behave and make up their mind based on that.

The self-esteem cluster is also a focus of group treatment technique. The celebration of birthdays and the inclusion of cards written by boys in the question box are two symbolic statements of their importance. In general I try to show sensitivity to the needs and feelings of each boy. It is important not to show favorites in group for obvious reasons relating to self-esteem. Individual worth is further insisted upon by a group rule requiring of mutual respect mixed with frankness and honesty. Many of the questions in the card pile deal with the damage to self-esteem done by molestation, and the issue is dealt with directly in such discussions.

Anger and rage are dealt with in a number of ways. The basic strategy is that a more secure sense of identity and self-worth will result in a lower level of rage and anxiety, which I see as largely compensatory for the trauma these boys have experienced. The group also sets formal limits on the acting out of anger and rage. It stresses the development of loving and cooperative relationships between members of the group. Boys who get too far out on limbs of anger and rage come under rather strong peer pressure to tone it down.

The power/powerlessness cluster of problems also is dealt with by a number of procedures taking place within the group. As much authority as possible is given to the boys in the running and management of the group. Obviously this cannot be too much, given their age and problems but, where possible, decisions are made democratically. The more mature boys are encouraged to take a leadership role in the group. I often specifically seek the opinions of certain mature members during discussions and if have to exit the room briefly, I will give these boys authority to run the group in my absence.

Cognitively, power needs and empowerment are targeted by discussion of the inability of victims to prevent sexual assault, but also by helping them to realize that they are no longer small, weak, and helpless. They now are able to say no, set limits, and report people who make inappropriate sexual advances on them. Allowing children to prepare some of the cards in the question box is also an empowerment technique.

Finally, the loss cluster is addressed in a number of ways. The group itself becomes a strong influence in the lives of many of these boys. They look forward to coming and continue to come on a voluntary basis, often for years. As a general rule, I allow the boys to determine their termination. If they tell me they are ready we discuss it, and I will generally accept any well thought out position of a need to terminate. This puts the issue of loss and separation under their control, giving them a powerful analogy for future life situations. Loss is also dealt with by helping boys restore their damaged (lost) sense of self and maleness. Finally, the group itself is a powerful source of restoring their ability to relate to other males which was damaged in the course of their victimization.

GROUPS FOR BOYS FOURTEEN TO EIGHTEEN

These groups have many similarities to the groups for younger boys in terms of what is intended to be accomplished. These groups are also all male and open ended. The basic goal is the repair of damaged masculinity. The dissimilarities lie in how these goals are accomplished and the degree of resistance encountered in groups of older boys. It is much harder to work with boys in this age range about problems of sexual victimization. There is much less spontaneous talk in these groups. In the younger boys' group the issue is getting them to be quiet and to listen to others. In the older boys' groups the issue is often getting them to talk at all.

When meeting with a group of boys who have been sexually molested is first proposed, a high percentage of boys in this age range reject the idea out of hand. In some cases I think their rejection is not inappropriate, and they can work out their issues in individual treatment. In many cases individual therapy is the treatment of choice. On the other hand, some of these boys can benefit from group, and should be encouraged to involve themselves. In such cases, the pre-screening interview is of extreme importance. The group should be honestly described, as well as the possible benefits that a boy might hope to get from participation in the group. If his anxiety is high, he might be invited to start individual therapy and join the group, if he feels more secure after working on his problems individually.

I have two kinds of groups for male victims in this age range. One is for those who are dealing with serious conflicts about homosexuality. The other tends to deal only with issues surrounding the development of heterosexuality and avoiding perpetration. I will describe the general nature of these groups to the boys during the screening interview and allow them to make a decision about the one that might be of most help to them.

The format for these groups is different than for younger boys. It is more traditional. These groups are two hour talking sessions which meet once a week. I feel the once a week interval is optimal. As with the younger boys, I serve food and drink but do not tangle it up in a reward system. The only rule I explicitly state is no hitting. I enforce as necessary rules about respecting other group members, including myself, and no sexualized behavior. In this kind of group, sexualized behavior is not likely to take the form of seductive acting out in group. A risk in this kind of group, however, is the arrangement of liaisons outside of the group which must be dealt with quite firmly. I explain to the boys that it is rule of all group psychotherapy that you may not be sexually involved with other group members while the group is going and that such involvement will result in termination from the group.

I have basically the same cognitive component for these boys as for the younger boys. I do, however, additionally teach them the Kinsey scale of heterosexuality to homosexuality and will, from time to time, ask them to make a placement of themselves along this scale. This is of most benefit in the group that is wrestling with homosexual issues, and they frequently bring up a wish to rate themselves on this scale. One thing they have pointed out to me is that their placement on this scale changes almost from day to day. I do not believe they are being dishonest on this, but are simply reflecting the ebbs and surges of adolescent sexuality.

Among these older adolescents the fear of being deviant in any way is much greater than with the younger boys. Most have an almost phobic fear of pedophilia and homosexuality, at least at the beginning of treatment. The overwhelming majority of boys in this age range want to work only on the development and strengthening of their heterosexuality. The ability to deny and simply to suppress and hide unacceptable sexual feelings is a constant problem with this age group. Getting them to deal with these issues without humiliating and embarrassing them is one of the key skills required of a successful therapist doing groups with this population.

In spite of their extreme resistance, some of these boys, in the long run, will have to come to terms with being gay or bisexual. Many of these boys do seem to be bisexual and describe very strong sexual interest in both males and females, when they are truly honest. This kind of discussion can be facilitated by the therapist. This group, as well as the younger boys, needs an environment in which they feel that they can talk frankly. One of the therapist's key roles is to return the topic to sexual issues when it wanders off into tangential and relatively meaningless concerns. Sex education has some use with this population, and this is included in the cognitive part of the program. This includes condom usage, AIDS, AIDS prevention, venereal diseases, the need for responsible sex, the linking of sex and love, and a number of other age-appropriate issues.

Relating to a male therapist is more difficult for these older boys than for the younger ones. Developmentally they are at a stage where they need to emancipate themselves from the father and mentor figures. In order to do so, they often have to push such figures away from them. If you look carefully, however, the ambivalence and idealization are often concealed underneath the surface. This is more likely to be manifest in individual than in group sessions. To express affection for and attachment to the therapist in group would probably be censured whereas some boys feel safe in discussing this individually. This is one of many reasons boys in this age range should have both individual and group treatment.

A male therapist working with boys in this age range is going to have a great deal of anger, competition, and rebelliousness directed at him. To a certain extent this is age-appropriate emancipation, but beyond that it is probably a frank and honest expression of their rage with males who have molested them and damaged their sexuality. When it is that, it needs to be dealt with in those terms as a transference issue. The whole issue of authority is crucial in dealing with this population. In general, this group is much better behaved than the younger boys. The strong measures needed to maintain order with the younger boys are rarely necessary here.

Nonetheless, the therapist needs to maintain a benign control and keep the group working on appropriate goals. It is also important, as with the younger boys, that group members not be allowed to devalue the therapist. This is a particular problem with new boys who often have an intense level of rage with males and a strong need to control their social environment. A mature group generally will help the therapist to calm this kind of patient. The kind of authority needed in this type of group I would describe as grandfatherly, with the ability to come on very strong when you are under attack.

It is often important to de-emphasize your authority. Since this group is conducted in a circle, I make a point of selecting the same kind of chair that most of the boys sit in. For some time I had sat in my desk chair which was larger and more comfortable than the chairs the boys were in. When I moved out of that I noticed the development of a much more honest and egalitarian relationship with the group. Not surprising, but it underscores the need to pay a lot of attention to the symbolism in some ostensibly trivial matters. Another technique is to allow a boy to lead part of the group. I have done this on numerous occasions and, in general, it can be very successful. If a boy is to lead the group, however, he needs to be one of the boys' natural leaders or he will be ignored and the process will go nowhere.

These groups are not structured as tightly in terms of what happens as are the younger boys' groups. They usually open with an invitation to group members to discuss whatever is on their minds. This again de-emphasizes the authority role of the therapist. In this kind of group it is important to discuss relationships between group members and between members and the therapist. In the group dealing with homosexuality, the issue of who is attracted to whom becomes very important. This issue is sometimes discussed. Even more important is what the attraction is about. Typically sexual attraction flows from a low status group member to a high status group member. This appears to me to be an attempt to get something through selfobject transference that is not available through other means. That something is the power and masculinity which the lower status boy assigns to the boy with higher status to whom he is attracted.

A therapist working with this kind of group needs to pay a lot of attention to the banter which inevitably goes on at the edges of such a group and bring it into the main group discussion. Often, very important group process is buried in the midst of seemingly trivial banter. Sometimes the talk going on in the waiting room, or covertly as others talk, deals with issues more important than the central focus of group discussion. At other times it is resistance and needs to be dealt with as such.

USING DREAMS IN GROUP

Dreams are an extremely valuable tool for boys who have the ego strength to use them. Almost invariable they bring out the key issues with which patients are dealing. The dreams which boys are willing to present in group often allow a focus on issues of concern not just to the dreamer, but to the entire group. When groups will tolerate their use, they are probably the best single mode for cutting through the collective evasion and resistance that characterize all treatment groups at one time or another. Generally, the younger boys are unable to use dreams in group. They seem to generate too much anxiety. The younger boys, typically, will not be quiet and listen to and examine another boy's dream. From time to time, it is possible to get the older boys to do this. I have developed a model of dream interpretation based in Winson (1985), and Hobson (1988) in neurology and Greenberg (1987) within self-psychology. Since I make more use of dream material in individual sessions, more will be said of this approach in the chapter on individual treatment.

It is difficult to get boys to use dreams in group for a variety of reasons. As a general principle, the higher the general level of psychosocial functioning of boys making up the group, the better the use that can be made of dreams in group. The more borderline and antisocial the group members, the less likely they will be to allow access to their dreams. The reasons for this are complex. The more disturbed by definition have weaker egos and are more likely to relay on defense mechanisms such as denial and repression. These boys, typically, do not remember dreams and will make no effort to do so. Even those who do remember dreams are often resistant to discussing them. Sometimes the content involves issues of shame or guilt. Other dreams allude to issues such as repressed death wishes and fear of psychosis that are too frightening to discuss. Some boys are unwilling to experience the loss of control involved in a process that could lead to disclosing something they do not want others to know. Fear of being shamed in group leads some boys to deny in group that they have a dream, and then proceed to tell me the dream in the course of individual treatment.

The manner in which a well functioning group will use a dream is illustrated by the following dream told by a sixteen year old boy molested at age nine by an older male. On the surface this young man had a strong superficial masculinity. He was an athlete involved in several forms of athletic activity and had immense physical strength. He was greatly respected for these attributes by other members of the group. His dream was as follows:

> He goes with a girl to a party. The group of people he is with forms a dance line which is supposed to include him and the girl. He cannot join in. A white boy who is much richer and better looking than he comes along, takes his girlfriend into the room, and has sex with her. The patient is very angry and gets into a fight with the other boy. He notes that he could, in fact, tear this boy to pieces, but in the dream he cannot win. He continues fighting, but his blows have no impact on the other boy. His girlfriend continues to prefer the other youth.

In group, I focus on dance as a symbol of sex and asked the patient if he had a fear of sexual involvement with females. He said that he did and, in spite of his athletic prowess, he had not had sex with a same age female and felt very inept in this area. This boy is of mixed racial ancestry. I asked him about envy of whites or a feeling that whites are sexually more appealing to the girls he wants. He denied a racial content, but acknowledged that he felt strong envy for males who had an easy-going way with females and could attract all the females they wanted. He related the dream figure to a boy with these traits he knew at school. The girl was one on whom he had a strong crush but had never developed the nerve to approach.

The group pointed out to him that he was good-looking and should have no trouble attracting females. The discussion moved from there to things that this young man, as well as other boys in the group, could do to be more appealing to females and what there may be about various group members which caused females to be turned off by them. This dream illustrates an additional clinical fact about this population. Typically, when these boys are referred to me, they have a history of being molested, sometimes of molesting someone else, but almost never do they have any sexual experience with same-age females. In this group, which works predominantly on the development of heterosexuality, the dream provided the take-off point for a long and extended discussion of these issues.

This boy continued to dream of the same girl. Eventually, he approached her and found out she was indeed interested in him. He was able to get her to agree to go to his high school prom with him. All of this was discussed in group. The group was able to see that dreams can serve as plans of action, and that previously shy boys with low self-esteem can develop positive relationships with female peers. This provided the group with an example of the kind of empowerment that is possible with hard work in therapy. It also provided the group with a case study in the step-by-step strengthening of the expression of masculine sexual identity.

Using Question Cards

When dreams are not available, I fall back on the same pile of cards which I use with the younger boys. This gets the group into a wide number of topics involving sexuality, victimization, the risk of perpetration, dealing with unwanted sexual feelings, etc. As with the younger boys, I will use the material generated by these cards to get a wider discussion. When there is a great deal of resistance to discussing interpersonal relationships in the group, I use the technique of asking one or several boys, or sometimes the whole group, to give two ideas regarding each other person in the room. This brings out a great deal of material about selfobject and other relationships going on within the group.

Working with groups of male victims in this age range is not as rewarding and dynamic as working with the younger boys. In my judgment it does, however, frequently provide a useful adjunct to individual treatment where issues can often be worked on more intensely. In spite of the general problems discussed here, there are a number of boys who use this kind of group well and who would make little use of individual treatment. For most cases in both age ranges, the greatest growth will be seen in boys who can be involved in both individual and group treatment and whose families are also involved in the treatment process.

I believe the approach outlined here for group treatment of the older adolescent victims addresses most of the issues of the seven clusters in a manner similar to that already outlined in discussing group treatment for the younger boys. Because of the limitations imposed by the later adolescent developmental stage, it may not be possible to meet all of these needs in a group setting. In designing a treatment program, it is necessary to review the seven trauma clusters to be sure each patient is having those issues addressed. With the older boys, it will often be essential to include individual treatment to be sure the seven basic issues are confronted in the course of treatment.

SUMMARY

In this chapter the kind of group treatment I believe to be most helpful to the young male victim has been presented. The specific needs of each boy will depend upon age and developmental level. Group treatment must address the seven cluster issues identified from the literature as traumatic results of victimization. If the treatment does not address all of these issues, it is not complete and cannot be expected to be fully effective. In such cases, increasing weight must be given to adding individual and family treatment even where this poses a hardship for families, foster families, or placing agencies.

Chapter 11

INDIVIDUAL AND FAMILY TREATMENT

Individual and family treatment are necessary components of a complete treatment plan for the young male who has been sexually molested. A few boys will not use individual treatment. Some families are unwilling to be involved. In the overwhelming majority of cases, the limitations on the treatment plan are imposed by reality and not by the patients. I have tilted slightly toward the provision of group treatment as the sole modality if only one modality can be offered. This is partly because I feel the male peer group is usually the single most valuable reparatory experience the boys in the seven to fourteen year old group can have. This is particularly true in dealing with the issues arising out of the victim feeling that they have been chosen for victimization because they are uniquely defective. Group support and the awareness that many other boys struggle with the same issue are a vital parts of recovery. This issue looms particularly large at the beginning of treatment. No amount of reassurance in individual therapy seems to have the same impact on these feelings as does the group experience. Although group seems less meaningful to the older boys, for most it remains the single most valuable experience.

The realities that make it impossible to offer individual, group, and family therapy to all victims are manifold. Some parents, foster parents, or residential treatment facilities will only bring a child once a week to treatment. In other cases the family's financial resources are so limited that only one modality can be used. Where treatment is publicly funded, agencies may lack the resources and staff to offer a comprehensive program. Where financial considerations loom large, group will most often be the modality of choice. There are a minority of cases where group would not be the first choice of treatment if only one modality can be offered. The bright, highly motivated patient may get more out of individual treatment. Ideally such boys might be exposed to group only briefly in the course of a long treatment, emphasizing individual therapy. A boy with overwhelming shame and anxiety may need long individual treatment before

163

he enters a group. Some families are so dysfunctional that the family chaos will undermine any gains in individual or group treatment. In such cases, if only one modality is to be offered, it should obviously be family therapy. These are all matters for careful individual diagnosis and treatment planning.

It is important to note here that what I am describing is my approach to individual and family treatment. It is an approach designed to incorporate the diagnostic and theoretical material discussed earlier. It is a format in which each of the seven problem clusters identified from the literature can be addressed in a variety of manners. Needless to say, clinicians vary in style. There are other methods of individual and family treatment which would probably also be effective with this population.

Family Treatment

Male victims, except in the most severe cases of parental neglect or abuse, will benefit if their parents are involved in the treatment. Obviously, special parameters must be invoked where the parent himself is a perpetrator hoping to reconcile with the child. The remarks in this chapter do not refer to these situations. They assume that the child has been molested by someone other than one of his biological parents or a step or adoptive parent.

I regard the treatment of parents who have offended against their children as a highly specialized and risky form of treatment. If the treatment has a preordained goal of reconciliation the process is even riskier. In this kind of case there is a need for very special diagnostic skills. Parents who molest their own children have a variety of motivations for seeking treatment with and reconciliation with their children. In some cases it may be a genuine wish to repair the damage they have done and to resume a parental relationship with their child. More common are situations where the offending parent wants to be involved in treatment for reasons having little to do with the child's well being. If divorce is involved, the motive may be to get custody as a symbolic victory over the other parent. Some offending parents get into power struggles with court personnel and want reconciliation with their child to win a power struggle with a social worker, probation officer, or judge. A wish for reconciliation can also be driven by parental pedophilia or a desire to get a welfare check for the child. These are the realities of the street and a reflection of the sad world in which we live, but they are realities that must be faced in many incest cases. If these issues are present, prognosis is so poor that I would not attempt treatment. In the face of such negative parental motivations the child needs to be placed with a less toxic family member or in a residential care facility. The incestuous perpetrator with poor motivation for treatment represents one extreme on a spectrum. At the other end is the protective parent of a child molested by someone outside the home. In between are a variety of situations requiring careful examination and treatment planning. These include cases where boys have been molested by a mother's boyfriend or a stepfather who leaves the home. Before offering home based family treatment in such cases, the mother's ability to be suitably protective in the future needs to be assessed. Too often mothers in such cases will allow the perpetrator to return to the home once the initial flurry of agency concern has passed. Other parents may have ignored the child's protests about what was happening. Some were told but looked the other way when they could have been more protective. This problem exists even when the perpetrator never lived in the home. Many parents ignore seemingly obvious signs that their sons are involved with pedophiles. Issues of guilt and shame loom very large with parents who have not been fully protective. Even parents who have been as protective as possible, may feel shame and guilt about things they did not see or do at the time.

Any parent dealing with a child who has been molested has a number of tricky issues to deal with. One of them is to figure out the appropriate level of protectiveness to exercise with the child. Many parents become overprotective, particularly in sexual areas. Sometimes this becomes pervasive and the child is virtually confined to the home. Parents in this situation can also become almost paranoidly suspicious of older males. They may also be alarmed by any sexual expression in the victim child. Obviously some parental guidance, and sometimes individual treatment for the parent, is necessary in such cases.

These inappropriate parental reactions will be markedly exaggerated where the parent feels guilt and responsibility for their child's victimization. This is almost universal, even where they objectively bear no responsibility. If the clinician approaches the parent in a way which aggravates this guilt, the parents will often remove the child from treatment. Dealing with the parent who feels responsible for what happened is one of the trickiest issues in family therapy. The issue is usually best managed with comments that all parents feel some guilt and responsibility. Parents need to be reassured that it is always easy to look back and see what one could have done with more information. Even where the parent actually was irresponsible, it does not do much good to emphasize guilt and responsibility early in the treatment process. Once a strong treatment alliance is established with the parents, then that issue can be dealt with.

As a general principle, I believe parents with major issues of guilt and responsibility about what happened to their boys should have separate individual therapists to help them work through these issues. Another approach would be to organize a parent group for parents of children who have been molested. I have done this with the parents of adolescent perpetrators and found it very effective. It is, however, difficult to get parents to overcome the issues of shame involved in sharing this kind of material, even with other parents in the same situation.

Another sensitive issue for parents is brought up if they themselves have been victims of molestation as children. This can reactivate all of their dormant conflicts about what happened to them. Parents in this situation also need to be referred for their own treatment. Even if parents are referred to another therapist for their own direct treatment, it is important that the clinician treating the child have some involvement directly with the parents. If the parents are in their own therapy this should take the form of frequent consultations with the parents' therapist. It should often include at least monthly meetings with the parents to help them understand what is going on with the child, and what they can do to facilitate his recovery. The major exceptions would be where the parents have behaved outrageously toward the child, and the child is no longer in their custody or, if the child is a mid-to-late adolescent at the edge of emancipation.

When I speak of family therapy, I do not always mean getting the entire family together in one room and talking about the issues. Sometimes this is indicated. I tend to use this specific approach for crisis situations that do indeed involve the whole family. If a crisis situation involves only the victims and parents, I would not bring in siblings unless I could formulate specific and clear treatment purposes in doing so. An example would be a case in which a sibling might be teasing the child about what had happened.

The nature of family involvement depends very much on the individual situation. The age of the child plays a role. The younger the child, the more essential parental involvement is to successful outcome. It is an unfortunate reality that many parents do not wish to be involved in treatment. Sometimes this is to avoid their own issues about being molested as children themselves. Another common reason for such resistance is to avoid their guilt. These parents will bring you the child but will not be meaningfully involved in the treatment. If that is all the parents will do, it is better to treat the child individually than to offer no treatment at all. Many times, however, with a sensitive approach, these parents can be enticed into treatment, at least if it is specified that the purpose is to discuss how they can understand and help their child, rather than putting any specific focus on them or their issues.

In addition to full family meetings or conjoint meetings with the victim and parents, from time to time I will also meet conjointly with one parent or both parents and the child. This, again, would be to work on specific issues such as issues in the father/son relationship or issues in the mother/son relationship. It might also be for the purpose of dealing with specific conflicts between the victim and one parent or another.

Parent guidance, referral for individual treatment of the parent, family meetings, and dyadic meetings between the parent and child are all modalities that I use at one time or another in the treatment of most children. My treatment is relatively long-term. The specific modalities may shift over a period of time. Treatment may start with regular parent guidance sessions weekly. These may become less frequent as the process proceeds. The critical factor here is to be flexible and willing to change the treatment format according to the unfolding treatment situation. More will be said about working with parents in the sections on dealing with victims of specific age groups.

DREAMS

I make as much use as possible of dream material in working with children of all ages. As a general rule, this population is not one which can make productive use of dreams in therapy. Recurrent nightmares derived from their abuse are common. The modal method of dealing with nightmares and less traumatic dream material among young male victims is either not to share it with the therapist or to repress the memory of the dream. When, however, these children are able to bring dream material into the treatment situation, these can be extremely valuable adjuncts to treatment. My use of dreams is based in recent neurological research on the biological nature and purpose of dreams. A complete review of this material is obviously beyond the scope of this book but, briefly, I have relied heavily on works by J. Allen Hobson (1988), Jonathon Winson (1985), Rosalind Cartwright (1978), and R. Greenberg (1987). These individuals come from surprisingly different backgrounds but arrive at similar conclusions about the nature of dreams. Hobson is a psychiatrist and neuroscientist at Harvard; Winson, a neuroscientist at Rockefeller University; Cartwright is a psychologist working in a sleep laboratory at the University of Chicago; and Greenberg, a self-psychologist.

Grossly oversimplifying, these writers conclude that dreams represent a neural problem solving device in which it is possible to identify the most significant and emotionally charged problems with which the individual is concerned. At the end of his book Hobson summarizes some general conclusions about the neurological nature of dreams. Those most relevant to this undertaking are:

> 4. Building up from the level of reflexes, it is possible to imagine sleep, and especially REM sleep, as providing a means of converting the necessarily limited genetic program into a functional program for the development of fixed action patterns underlying crucial behavior.

> 6. Carrying this notion a step further, it is possible to suggest that the brain is actually creative during sleep. New ideas arise, and new solutions to old problems may be consciously or unconsciously derived during sleep.

> 8. Dreaming, in its relationship to REM sleep, provides us with a remarkable mirror to our inner selves.

Winson (1985) says it more concisely:

> In man, dreams are a window on the neural process whereby, from early childhood on, strategies for behavior are being set down, modified, or consulted.

It is Winson's word "modified" that opens the door for therapy. In working with patients who are frequent dreamers, I find processes similar to that outlined in the research mentioned. Each dream seems to present a crucial problem with which the patient is concerned. There is at least an allusion to a proposed solution to the problem. Typically, in the early part of therapy, the solution is the same old solution that the individual has always used to cope with such a problem. It is also typically dysfunctional. In the course of treatment, those who are able to work with dreams will be able to identify the problem that they are working on as well as their proposed solution. Over a period of time, it is actually possible to see changes in the kinds of solutions proposed within the dream matrix.

As noted, it is difficult to get male victims to share their dreams. Only a minority of this population makes much use of this therapeutic resource. The technique just described in vignette works best with bright, motivated adolescents and adults. Even where the full technique cannot be used dreams do give an idea of the most basic issues with which a child is confronted. Often, rather than attempting to interpret the dream to the child, I will simply make a hypothesis and proceed to explore with the child issues arising out of that hypothesis with no further mention of the dream itself. This works well with both adolescents and children who tend to respond to dream interpretation with an argument that the dream can't possibly mean whatever you have suggested. By simply bypassing the interpretative step, a great deal of productive material can be brought into discussion. This will be illustrated later.

AGE DIVISIONS

Because we are dealing with a wide developmental spectrum in young male victims, no single approach will be effective in individual or family work. The therapeutic techniques used need to be adapted to the mental and chronological age of the child. Obviously, creating age categories is somewhat arbitrary. The maturity level of the child, his actual emotional age, is more important than the chronological ages given here, but for heuristic purposes the following divisions are offered. The first group would consist of children seven years of age and younger. The next grouping would be roughly eight to fourteen. Last is age fourteen through the end of adolescence. The group seven and younger needs to be further broken down into the subgroups of toddlers and children roughly between four and seven years of age. Children in these two groups need a somewhat different approach.

TREATING THE YOUNGEST VICTIMS

We know that even babies are molested. Obviously, individual treatment with an infant is impossible, leading into the axiom that the younger the child, the greater the percentage of the work it will be necessary to do with the parents. Parents of very young children who have been molested are particularly likely to be in crisis and will need reassurance and guidance. Their more irrational fears will need to be calmed. They will need help in understanding the possible ramifications of what has happened and how to correct it. Obviously, emphasis needs to be placed upon eliminating any current risk to the child, such continuing contact with potential perpetrators.

Even at very young ages parents will be confronted with sexualized behaviors, such as masturbation, and sexual advances on children, or even adults. Parents need to be told that this is a response to victimization and given techniques for dealing with it. Parental hysteria and guilt also need to be managed at this and every other age level. Much of what is done at this age actually will be simply to prepare the child for possible later treatment. I am speaking here essentially of children from infancy through about three years of age. With some of the two or three year olds I might observe some play for diagnostic purposes or use play to teach some very simple, concrete ideas to the child. With children in this age range, I sometimes have parents in the room to observe so we can follow up with a discussion of what happened and what it meant.

These very young children are often in the room with the parent and me even if am simply talking to the parent. This is a reflection of the reality that a child this age cannot be in a waiting room unsupervised, and often parents do not have baby-sitting. This has some benefits in allowing direct observation of the child, although the therapist needs to be cautious, as does the parent, about what is said in the presence of children who have some comprehension of language. The kinds of cognitive distortions that might result from this situation could be significant. Usually, I provide children in this situation with some toys in a distant corner of the room. Occasionally something of diagnostic interest can be picked up by observation of this play.

Somewhere in the three to four year age range and continuing through about seven, play techniques become, in my judgment, the individual treatment of choice. A word about selection of toys. The treatment of young children who have been sexually abused needs to focus its greatest energy on repairing the damage done by molestation. For this reasons, I feel that the content of the toy chest needs to be carefully selected. In my judgment, the most useful toys are stuffed animals with which children can play out a variety of scenes. I have a wide selection of these animals, ranging in size from several feet long to a few inches high. Some are anatomically correct. There are parent figures, perpetrator figures, sibling figures, malignant figures, benign figures, and neutral figures onto which most anything can be projected.

It is wise to avoid keeping such things as toy soldiers, cars, legos, pogo sticks, or high tech electronic toys and games in the play room. These kind of toys yield little or no play relating to victimization and can be used to avoid issues rather than confront them. Typically, children who work well with play techniques will arrange dramas with stuffed animals or human figures. They will often involve the therapist in these dramas. Sometimes the therapist needs to take the role of commentator. On other occasions it is better to be a participant in the drama. A great deal of teaching, interpreting, and communication of empathy can be done in this context.

The child can meet his need for empowerment by identifying with powerful figures in play. If it is their emotional need, they can control and punish perpetrators and other figures with whom they feel anger and disappointment. The creative therapist can devise ways of dealing with all of the seven cluster issues faced by male victims. Additionally, the play context itself is effective in cutting down on denial. The toys are highly stimulating to the children, usually leading them into spontaneous play which quickly gets into themes involving their molestation. It is important that this play be allowed to emerge spontaneously. Sexual and molestation themes should not be suggested if they do not emerge spontaneously. Once the material does emerge, it can be commented upon or interpreted in terms of the feelings evoked. If a child balks at interpretations, the therapist can cut back and work exclusively within the metaphor so as not to extinguish the play behavior. Some children tolerate interpretation relatively well. Others will discontinue play if you point out too graphically what is going on.

Toward the upper end of the four to seven age range, other techniques can be introduced. Rarely do children want to spend all of their time in play sessions. I have some simple games and also a kitchen in my office which allows children to cook simple things in a microwave. I will typically suggest in a session that they can pick one activity and I will pick another. Typically, I will pick the play if the child picks an activity such as cooking or a board game. Regarding board games, I would suggest that only those that can be played quickly be offered, otherwise the entire session can be consumed in a board game with relatively little therapeutic content.

The principal reasons for providing these games is to add some variety, to give the child a choice of activities (empowerment), and to build and strengthen my relationship with the child by being involved in a pleasurable activity of the child's selection. The cooking has obvious symbolic value in the form of offering nourishment. There is another empowerment issue here. I teach children to cook the most complex things they are capable of, and in many cases this gives them a great sense of accomplishment. Simply teaching a four or five year old to successfully crack open an egg sends a message that they can be competent and that you want them to grow, mature, and do all that they can for themselves. Cooking also provides an activity which decreases anxiety while offering an opportunity to ask questions, particularly about dreams. Dreams in children this age are usually very abbreviated and of mostly diagnostic value. It is rarely of any value to attempt interpretation of a dream with a child this age. The best use of dreams in this situation is to get clues as to what might profitably be discussed with the child.

It is usually important for the therapist to indicate early in the treatment relationship that he/she knows what has happened to the child and to ask them to tell about it. If this creates anxiety, it is best to back off and attempt it again later. As a general rule, children at this age will talk freely about their victimization unless they have been shamed or intimidated. The latter is often the case, since the perpetrator may have threatened the child. An intense fear of the perpetrator is common in children this age. It is important to deal with this by assuring the child that both you and their parents will protect them. I generally tell them that I have worked with hundreds of kids, that perpetrators are cowards, and that none of my children have ever been hurt by a perpetrator after they told what happened. (Fortunately, this is true.)

One of the greatest difficulties in this age range, particularly in children five, six, and seven, is that this is an age at which their sexualization is often egosyntonic. To the great alarm of parents, teachers, and others who must deal with the child, children this age will often state openly that they don't see what was wrong with what happened. I remember, in particular, a very bright six year old boy who was making sexual advances on most of the males in his home and neighborhood. No amount of pressure from his mother could bring this to a halt. He told me frankly that he liked it and thought it was O.K. On two occasions I have attempted to introduce seven year old boys with this kind of feeling into the boys' group. In both cases they were thoroughly rejected by the group, who perceived them as gay.

I have had little luck toning this down until the child reaches eight or nine. By this age they are usually more amenable to peer and social pressure. This ego syntonic sexualization needs to be dealt with candidly with parents. They are often extremely upset about it. If the behavior is going on in school or involves neighbors, a behavior modification plan may be necessary to bring it under control.

TREATING THE EIGHT TO FOURTEEN YEAR OLD

In the chapter on group psychotherapy the rationale of creating a category of boys from eight to fourteen was discussed. This category does not exist in most child and adolescent psychotherapy. It exists in the treatment of young male victims because they have been prematurely sexualized by victimization. They have therefore been forced to deal early with many of the issues that face older boys as they enter adolescence. There remains an arbitrary quality to this grouping. It will not fit in many instances. Most victims between eight and fourteen will respond to the treatment modalities suggested here. Others will not. An occasional eight year old will be better treated with the techniques outlined in the previous section. At the other pole, many fourteen year olds may be too mature for this approach. They may be better served by the approach outlined for middle and late adolescents in the next section.

Young male victims of molestation are a paradoxical group. On the one hand they are prematurely sexualized and have to deal out of phase with adolescent issues even if they have not yet arrived at puberty. On the other hand as a group they are characterized by a pervasive immaturity in nonsexual areas. When they start treatment, they tend to be fixated at a younger age than their dates of birth would suggest. Premature sexualization and immaturity in other areas of development combine to create a rather homogeneous population of boys between the ages of eight and fourteen who often respond to the same techniques of individual and group treatment despite the totally non-traditional nature of this grouping.

This is the age range in which almost all boys should be in group therapy if at all possible for reasons outlined earlier. A combination of individual and group treatment generally has great advantages over providing just group or just individual therapy. This offers an opportunity to discuss material that is stirred up in the group but cannot really be dealt with there. Some boys, particularly toward the lower end of the age spectrum, will want to continue play techniques, at least occasionally.

Most boys in individual treatment in this age range prefer to meet in the kitchen. In this case, I follow the format of allowing the boys to pick one activity while I pick a second. Lack of a kitchen need not defeat this kind of strategy. When I had no kitchen, I brought a popcorn popper into a very small office and offered preparation of popcorn as an option. An agency coffee room with a microwave could provide a similar opportunity with cooperative fellow workers. Nonculinary options might include offering the boy a brief walk in the neighborhood or throwing frisbies on an agency lawn. The issue is offering choice and defusing issues of who is in charge while ensuring that some kind of therapeutic interchange takes place. Get the patient into some kind of situation where he picks an activity of some sort, and you pick an activity with high therapeutic content.

One of the main differences between this age group and the younger boys is that direct talking and use of a board game to stimulate talk play a much larger role than with younger boys. The talk game I use is a mixture of the commercial "Ungame" known to many therapists with a series of cards that I have assembled for use with the game. Any number of commercially available therapeutic games can be adapted in this manner. The question cards used in individual therapy are not the same cards used in group. The main difference is that these cards are not as sexually explicit as those used in group. The rationale here is that use of such highly sexual cards would probably be threatening in a setting where the patient is alone with a male therapist.

The card box used for individual sessions includes a range of questions dealing with molest and sexual issues, but the material is much lower key than the group cards. Also included in this box are questions regarding family relationships, future plans, fears, angers issues, and a wide range of other topics. The game is played in such a way that the therapist also has to answer questions. This seems to perform an equalizing function between therapist and child which facilitates free discussion. Using these cards, boys will answer questions they would never answer as direct inquiries in a one to one interview.

Examples of some of the cards in the box are: "If you were the judge, how would you punish your molester?" "Why do some men molest children?" "Why do some boys go back more than once to get molested by the same person?" "What would you do if you found yourself getting sexually turned on by a much younger child?" "What was the worst punishment you ever got?" "Why is it important for a boy to have a father in the home?" "Why do some parents get a divorce?" "Tell about something that made you really angry." A period of discussion follows each question. The discussion is continued until the child appears stressed, agitated, or bored. Then we move on to answer other cards.

As with all ages, I attempt to elicit dream material from boys in this age range. I usually ask about dreams during the banter that goes on as we cook. About one in five boys is able to offer me any significant dream material. Frequently they will deny having dreams at all. Sometimes they will produce something that is obviously not a dream. In many cases they may simply not have the self-discipline to remember dreams.

To illustrate the use of dream material, I have one rather elaborate and disorganized dream from a boy in this age range. This is an immature and highly disturbed child who was molested by his mother. This child was also molested in a more minor way by an uncle who was present as a voyeur while mother engaged in some of the sexual acts with this child. Throughout his treatment this victim has tended to blame the uncle and exonerate the mother. For purposes of discussion, this patient will be referred to here as Tommy. This is Tommy's dream:

> There was a troll. It came from yesterday. It turned me into a frog, a little frog. He was cute. I went home, but before that he took me to the devil. The devil said he was going to kill my mother. I told the devil, "Mom likes devils." Mom came to the devil. She was a devil, a friend of the other devil. Devils are afraid of frogs. The troll turned me into a frog. I was with him at the devil's house. I was going to run from the troll, but he held me. Then we got to the devil's house. Mom was there. She wanted me to be a devil. I didn't want to be a devil. Jesus came down. He scared the devils. He hurted them. They never came back. Then Jesus turned me back to myself.

After hearing this dream, I asked Tommy if he thought the troll might be the uncle. With a peculiar and inappropriate affect, the child said, "Yes, yes he was." I felt either the interpretation was wrong, or more likely, this child has limited ability to process such direct interpretation. That was all I did with any attempt at formal dream analysis. The main use of this dream in Tommy's treatment was to provide me a road map as to where he had been injured, how he was proposing to deal with the injury, and the destructive byways he might get into as a result of this unconscious effort at self repair.

My impression about the meaning of the dream was that Tommy feels terribly damaged as a result of molestation (transformed into a frog which is no longer attractive to mother). He is clearly placing his mother among the devils. This dream presents the mother as a devil, a sinister and corrupting figure who will lure him into sex if he is not vigilant.

The uncle actually restrained this child in order to facilitate the mother's molesting him, which would further support the idea that the troll represents the uncle. The patient notes he was going to run, but the troll held him. Again he seems to be dealing with his guilt about being involved in the molest situation. He stresses his unwillingness to be involved and the force necessary to make him become sexually involved with the mother. There is an undercurrent here hat this child's basic sense of self worth has been damaged by molestation.

In terms of dream theory, the basic problem presented is being sexually corrupted and damaged by the mother's actions. Tommy's proposed solution is to be rescued by an idealized, magical father figure presented as Jesus. In the dream metaphor, the idealized father transforms him from the frog back to a full human being. This may be what he hopes to get from therapy. If that is true, it suggests he has developed a powerful idealizing transference to me. This will have to become more realistic if he is to really recover since I cannot possibly meet these magical expectations and may become one more disappointment for Tommy if his reality testing does not improve.

A secondary solution to the terror of corruption and engulfment by the devil-mother, is to render himself unattractive to her, a frog. I suspect in the long run this may manifest itself as making himself unattractive to women. Several courses are possible ways of actualizing this dream solution in his later life. He could become homosexual. He could become isolated in a schizoid manner. Less likely he could become sadistic and abusive to women. This dream clearly focuses Tommy's basic trauma and the basic answers his psyche is proposing to correct the problem. As such it provides important clues at to where treatment needs to focus as well as potential problems which may arise in the future as this patient's unconscious wrestles toward some kind of repair to the terrible damage that has been done to him.

Denial, Guilt, and Responsibility

Porter (1986) has correctly stressed the importance of confronting denial when treating young male victims. This is as much an issue in individual as in group treatment. It is a major issue for boys in the eight to fourteen year age range. Denial manifests itself in many ways. Some boys just forget what happened over time. Others minimize the events or their impact on their life. If the perpetrator is a parent, denial may be a desperate effort to reconcile and regain a lost parent. When denial is challenged, resistance can become intense. Where the treatment alliance is strong, I will ask the boy if we can go over the original reports to see what really happened. This is not recommended without the child's assent. If the child is also in group, this is a great help. When new members join, all boys describe what has happened to them, thus stimulating everyone's memory. Group also helps by constantly reaffirming that the victim is not alone.

Besides denial, other major issues for this age group are guilt and responsibility. In many cases, these boys were seduced by male figures or female figures for whom they had love and respect. Like all victims of sexual assault, they must deal with the body's physiological pleasure responses to sexual stimulation. This is the age range in which the concept of homosexuality first emerges for most boys. They begin to hear deprecatory language about gays at school. If they put these words together with their experience, they may conclude that they are homosexual. In this homophobic culture, the child is likely to panic about this. He can easily move into self-hatred and self blaming. This also opens the door for offending sexually against younger females to prove to himself that he is not gay.

Dealing with guilt about "consenting" to and enjoying the sexual experience is one of the trickiest issues in the treatment of male victims. Glib assurances that it was not their fault do not fully resolve the problem. It is usually necessary to the victim to discuss the body's pleasurable responses to sexual touching and also about how cleverly some child molesters trick children into cooperation. I make it plain to boys that most of the boys that I see did agree to the sexual acts, but they were much too young to know what that meant about their future or the problems it would cause them. Some of the cards in the card box deal with issues in this area. One asks, "What is a pedophile, and how does someone get to be this way?"

This leads readily into a discussion of men who prefer to have sex with children and spend a great deal of energy learning how to trick children into having sex with them. I will also point out that only rarely, if ever, is a human being all bad, and even though the molester has done some very bad things to them, he or she may have had other things about them that were nice. This is helpful in getting the child to understand why he may have positive feelings about someone (a child molester) who is hated by society and reviled in the media. This is particularly important where the perpetrator is a parent.

Another card which I usually reserve for group deals with a seduction situation in which an older man invites in a boy next door, starts showing him pornography and talking about sex. This is intended to illustrate the seductive techniques used by molesters. The discussion leads into the molester's intent to get them sexually stimulated and then to make an advance. Boys will also bring up that they thought it was okay since they saw pictures of other children doing it. This observation needs to be tied to the perpetrator's specific intent to achieve this effect.

I believe it is necessary to deal explicitly with the issue that some boys who are molested do become perpetrators. I suspect a high percentage of young male victims have pedophilic urges. A percentage of even the younger boys have already molested someone. Often this goes undetected. If the issue is not brought up in therapy, the patient will be left to deal with the issue on his own. It needs to be stressed that this is not an inevitable outcome and that it can be stopped by treatment. If the boy is also in group, I can usually point out boys who molested a long time ago, but have now solved the problem. Another area of relevant discussion is that it is possible to feel something or to wish to do something and not actually carry it out as an action. Many analogies can be drawn to feelings and impulses in other areas of life which would cause trouble if acted upon and are therefore not acted upon.

Sometime in the eight to fourteen year age range most boys will enter puberty. It is necessary to address the issues that arise at this time both individually and in group. I spend a lot of time describing the changes involved in puberty. For victims, the most important aspect is the upsurge in sexual feelings. This can reactive deviant fantasies and cause great distress. This needs to be discussed openly. Also needing discussion are the age-appropriate sexual feelings for other boys which often come at this time. If left alone with such feelings, boys can become severely anxious and self-condemning. Generally it is wise to stress that the homoerotic feelings of puberty are usually a passing phenomena. This is reassuring to the boys who are homophobic, but essentially heterosexual or bisexual with female preference.

Because a part of the young male victim population is irreversibly in the early stages of homosexual orientation, it is also wise to add the qualification that some boys do grow up to be gay and that many people think that this is O.K. It is extremely difficult to get male victims in this age range and this culture (including American subcultures) to even consider that it would be desirable to grow up to be gay. I touch on this issue very lightly with these boys at this age, hoping to deal with it as they mature somewhat and their egos become stronger and more able to consider other possibilities.

Working with Parents

Working with the parents of boys in the eight to fourteen year age range has many of the same properties as working with the parents of the younger children. The most important difference is that this is the age at which it is appropriate to open the issue of the child's ultimate sexual orientation. If the boy is clearly prehomosexual and the parents can tolerate this information, I will discuss it with them. I always stress that such things are not fixed at the child's age and the outcome is still in doubt.

Sometimes it is necessary to address the risk of perpetration with the parents. This is particularly true if they describe the child as preferring the company of younger children, or there are younger siblings in the home. Sexualization remains an issue for discussion. At this age, male victims may show a precocious interest in the opposite sex. This can be explained to parents as a masculine overreaction to the passivity implicit in victimization or as compensatory for any homosexual feelings stirred up during molestation. The parents should be encouraged to set limits on sexual behaviors. There is little choice but to take into account the parents value system. Highly religious parents will not accept permissive sexual rules just because they are recommended by a therapist. The therapist's role here is to get the parents to understand that their child has been irreversibly sexualized by victimization and that some modification in their expectations for the child need to be made for this reason.

In other cases, particularly at the younger ages of this spectrum, the boys may be involved in promiscuous sexual activity with other males, same age and/or younger. This sexual activity poses management problems for the parents. It also may challenge the parents' value system. No general guidelines can be given for dealing with these situations. The parents need to be helped to distinguish perpetration from prehomosexual behavior. Parents need to be encouraged to set firm limits on any behavior that is or will lead into molesting younger children. It is more difficult to deal with sexual acting out with same age male peers. In some cases this may be the beginnings of a gay identity. In others it may be reactive to their recent abuse. The parents need to be helped to make this distinction. It is useful to reduce their anxiety by pointing out that often boys pass through a period of homosexual acting out in reaction to their abuse and that they gradually abandon this with treatment. Parents also need to know that there is a brief period of homosexual interest and limited acting out at the beginning of adolescence which often passes with time.

Dealing with the parents of prehomosexual boys is a very difficult therapeutic task. Most parents dread this outcome. If this is the clinical picture, it is best to disclose it gradually and tentatively to the parents and carefully watch their reactions to the growing disclosures. There are cases in which it is best to touch on these issues very lightly. In some situations it is possible to have long and candid discussions with the parents. One of the key factors to keep in mind is what way the parents will use the information you give them about the child. If you are too candid, some parents will attempt drastic measures on their own. If the child feels a confidence is betrayed, you may lose your treatment relationship with him.

TREATING THE MIDDLE AND LATE ADOLESCENT

At this point we move toward a kind of therapy that would be more familiar to the general adult therapist. Here I revert to the standard clinical interview in my regular office without the use of games, food, or other techniques specifically for younger children. The main difference between treating a male victim of molestation and a patient with a different problem will be in the issues which come up. Needless to say, there needs to be a deliberate focus on victimization and sexuality. All male victims need to deal with this. Many of them will not do so very willingly. I hear a surprising number of accounts of boys in long individual therapies where their victimization was never discussed.

This is a very delicate matter. I do not believe that discussing the victimization can be forced upon the adolescent. Certainly a therapist should never resort to reading reports to the patient unless that is requested by the patient. On the other hand, I do advocate periodic sensitive questioning in the area to elicit responses from the adolescent about his victimization and his feelings about it. Where the therapist is able to quickly establish rapport, adolescent patients will usually begin to discuss their victimization within the first few sessions. It is unwise to press for this kind of information until there is a sturdy foundation for the treatment relationship.

Discussing victimization is closely related to the issue of denial in general since what is most often denied is the victimization itself. It helps to be relaxed and matter-of-fact when discussing all sexual issues. It is also useful to tell the boys that you discuss sexuality frequently and are not uncomfortable talking frankly about such things. It is also wise to acknowledge that most boys are very uncomfortable when initially asked about their victimization in particular and sexual feelings in general. If possible, boys in this age range should be in group, but expect resistance to the idea of joining a group.

If a boy will enter group, it makes possible the use of material stirred up by the group in the individual sessions. This is a major help in getting through this populations strong proclivity for denial. As with younger boys, in extreme cases I will ask the boy if he wants me to bring in relevant reports and to go over them with him. This is most useful where the adolescent has truly repressed what happened. It is not advisable where shame prevents frank discussion. It should never be done in the presence of ambivalence about this procedure on the patient's part.

Almost always, individual sessions with adolescent male victims are slow and tedious, requiring a great deal of work from the therapist in the early stages. In spite of the need for a therapeutic experience with a male therapist, this arrangement creates some special problems. As Porter has pointed out (1986), therapy with a male therapist resembles in some ways the situations in which the patient was molested. The boy is in a room alone with an older man talking about sex. The therapist may be in the age range of the perpetrator. Additionally, boys will sometimes bring to the relationship erotic fantasies about the therapist. These may result in seductive behavior toward the therapist. This can be both a hazard or an opportunity in the treatment situation.

One boy, Brian, seemed to need an erotized relationship with me as a father figure who could not be seduced in order to make a recovery. His own father deserted him at birth. He had been molested on three occasions since age eight by males old enough to be his father. At the onset of treatment he was strongly homoerotic and regaled the group with erotized accounts of his victimization. He identified himself on the Kinsey Scale as a three (bisexual), but he seemed to me closer to the homosexual pole of this continuum.

Brian spent the better part of two years in individual treatment with me. At first he seemed to be consciously testing me to see if I was corrupt like the other fathers who had seduced him. He dressed exhibitionistically and posed suggestively in his chair. He repeatedly suggested I take him on trips or become otherwise involved in his personal life. I did visit him when he was hospitalized for a medical problem, but turned down all other offers to see him outside the office. I made a point of sitting across a desk from him.

I chose for a variety of reasons not to discuss his seductiveness directly with him. I ignored it while encouraging his increasing number of forays into relationships with girls his age. His seductiveness with me steadily decreased. He worked on dreams, family problems, and his victimization over many months. Toward the end of his treatment he developed a sexually active and committed dating relationship with a girl he brought to the office to meet me. In group he began to describe himself as a two on the Kinsey Scale (heterosexual preference with some homosexual inclinations). He showed no anxiety about occasional sexual attractions to male peers.

In these latter states of his treatment his seductive behavior toward me vanished. The relationship felt to me like father-son. He increasingly consulted me on his relationship with his girlfriend (mostly its nonsexual aspects), career issues, how to deal with his difficult mother and other similar father-son type issues. He was very aggressive in defending me from verbal attack or devaluation in group.

Brian seems to me to have been molested when he reached out for a father to facilitate his male development. He got himself into a by-way of highly erotized relationships with older men which probably would have resulted in exclusive homosexuality or molesting little girls as a compensatory mechanism. He needed a father who could not be corrupted and found it in me. This adolescent seems to have been fixated at the pre-oedipal stage described by Blos (1985) in which the boy relates in an idealizing, passive, and erotized manner to the father. This is a necessary stage in identification with the father and the development of maleness. It is a time in which boys are vulnerable to molestation by father figures.

Most fathers do not betray this and instinctively do what I did in Brian's case. Brian seemed to instinctively know what he needed and used me to get it.

Brians are the exception rather than the rule with the teen age male victim. More commonly, adolescent male victims enter the treatment relationship, not with seductiveness, but with anxiety and distrust, or even suspicion and hostility bordering on paranoia. I make a number of subtle adjustments to defuse these potentially destructive concerns. They are all rooted in the same fear, that the male therapist will molest them as have other once trusted men.

There are a number of ways to reduce these kinds of fears to manageable proportions. One boy is so paranoid of my intentions I see him only conjointly with his mother. Generally, it is wise to conduct interviews with this kind of victim with a barrier of a desk or table between you and the patient. An office with lots of windows and nearby people is also reassuring.

Within the first few sessions, it is usually possible and desirable to discuss the boy's fear of the therapist. Frankly acknowledging the trust issue is appropriate. The therapist should not expect immediate trust and should communicate this to the patient. He should also clearly state that although he does not expect immediate trust, he will conduct himself in such a way that the patient will eventually see that the therapist will not molest him. Staying on your side of the desk, avoiding touch, and encouraging age appropriate sexual interaction with peers will all send the message that you have no sexual designs on the patient.

There are some victimized boys who cannot work with a man at all and should be referred to a female therapist. In these cases, the patient can work on female and mother issues first. If at all possible the boys should eventually return to finish up with a male therapist for reasons elaborated elsewhere. In some cases this might be facilitated by some conjoint sessions with the female and male therapist prior to transferring the case.

The response of boys that I have treated individually ranges from extremely guarded to outrightly enthusiastic. There are some cases where the boy wants to come, is coming voluntarily, but their therapist must initiate almost all conversation. With these adolescents you have to ask lots of questions, listen carefully to the answers, and follow up clues and hints on what is presented. Very often it is necessary to start with material other than the explicitly sexual. All human beings are complex and have problems in non-sexual parts of their lives. With these difficult patients it is often necessary to spend most of the initial sessions time on non-sexual issues, both because they need to be addressed, *per se,* and because this gives the patient some breathing space while strengthening the therapeutic relationship to deal with some of the more difficult issues inherent in their victimization.

Where the treatment alliance is good and the adolescent has a relatively strong ego, dream material can be used in the treatment. This makes for a much richer individual therapy since dreams cut through defense and evasion and go right to basic issues. Ricky, a fifteen-year-old victim in foster care related this dream to me.

> His foster parents (whom he likes) have rented a new house. He knows that the house has previously been occupied by devil-worshipers. The foster parents do not. Once they enter the house, the foster parents discover the nature of the previous occupants. The foster mother tells the patient that he must pack his bags, as they will be leaving quickly. The lights suddenly go out in the house, and the patient panics, fearing he will not be able to escape.

Ricky had a history of dabbling in satanism* which had not been previously explored. Questioning elicited comments that he had participated briefly in a Satanic cult which sacrificed chickens and had group sex as part of its rituals. He denied participating in the sexual orgies with either males or females. Ricky had also molested his younger sister. I asked him if he felt that there was a connection, between this and his flirtation with satanism. He felt that there was, noting that he had been involved in satanism while he molested his sister. I suggested that watching other people involved in sex had probably over stimulated him, leading to the molest.

In looking at this dream in terms of the theories outlined earlier, the problem grappled with in the dream is his fear of the evil in him which is now repressed in the presence of a benign and supportive environment. This dark side of his personality had previously manifested itself in delinquency, sex offending, and outright identification with a symbol of

---

*The issue of the existence and incidence of "satanism" in the United States is very controversial. I am a conservative on this issue and view adolescent's claims to have been involved in this kind of thing with great skepticism. Because it is hyped by certain very popular Rock Music groups it has become part of teen age culture in the U.S. Ricky is a fan of some of the groups who pretend to be or actually are satanists depending on one's interpretation of their behavior, lyrics, and statements. If Ricky was really involved in "satanism," it was most likely a group of adolescent friends acting out things hyped in the media. If he made up the story, I would handle it like fantasy. It would imply an identification with evil on his part. It also implies the linkage of sex and the devil that seem to me almost archetypal in American thinking. This equation of sex and the devil is particularly common among boys who molest others.

evil, Satan. He fears the reemergence of this evil. In part because it threatens his core self's sense of inner goodness and in part because it would surely cost him the love of the foster parents.

The dream is unsuccessful in that, it proposes no solution other than flight. That does not work; evil takes over in the symbolic form of darkness. This implies that his unconscious choice is some kind of "evil" behavior, either sexual or delinquent. I asked Ricky about this. He told me that the foster parents had just brought in a new boy who shared a room with him. He was aware of an urge to molest this younger boy. I suggested to Ricky that he could make a conscious decision to override this unconscious program for action. He agreed to work on this issue with me. I told Ricky I had to contact the foster parents and make them aware of the danger to the younger child and be sure they were at least placed in separate rooms if not separate homes.

This dream illustrates the richness dreams can bring to treatment. It contains enough issues to fuel months of treatment. Without this dream material, Ricky's treatment would have probably remained at the level of sterile discussions of superficial issues. His willingness to share this dream probably prevented another child from being molested. The very fact that he chose to share it seems to be an effort to enlist help from the outside with a problem that is overwhelming him from within.

Strengthening Preexisting Sexual Orientation

Obviously, with middle to late adolescents, issues of sexual orientation loom very large. If the boy is basically heterosexual, I feel that one of the main treatment needs is to strengthen this heterosexuality, using all of the transference mechanisms described elsewhere. One area in which I am a confirmed behaviorist is in reinforcement of a weak or ambivalent heterosexuality through satisfying sexual contact with females. This will not work unless the boy is essentially heterosexual or bisexual with a preponderance of interest in females. Given this kind of foundation, I have repeatedly seen cases in my practice where boys enter treatment with no sexual experience with same age females and blossom in the course of treatment into active heterosexuality. The peer group has been the major vehicle for this transformation, but the process can be encouraged in individual sessions. In some cases the problem is lack of social skills and the therapeutic task is to help the boy learn how to approach and relate successfully to females. Sometimes the issues are deeper: fear, anger, or hostility that the young male has toward females based on his previous life experience. These need to be the focus of therapeutic exploration and resolution if the young male is to become successfully heterosexual.

If the boy is bisexual or gay, he will probably be more or less aware of it at this stage in life. He may, however, be reluctant to either discuss this or to accept it. He may very much want help for him to change this orientation. In general, I do not believe it is possible to change sexual orientation through psychotherapy, but I do not steamroll the patient with this information. As a general principle, I do not advocate any specific identity choice. The greatest problem with presenting homosexuality as something a young male victim must accept is that you will probably have no luck with such an approach. Some victims know they are homosexual or bisexual and accept it. Others wish to fight this with all their strength. Instead of taking the issue head-on, I will become involved in discussions of what it means to be gay, the pluses and minuses of such a sexual orientation, and to provide any factual information I can in a non-judgmental way. This area is full of potential traps for the male therapist. If you appear to be advocating that the boy become gay, you may invite fantasies about your own motivation, including allowing the boy to infer that you may wish to be sexually involved with him. Benign neutrality and helping the boy explore his own identity issues are, in my judgment, the appropriate course.

My experience with boys who are probably going to be gay or bisexual in adult life is that, in middle and late adolescence, they shift back and forth a great deal. Those who have a genuine attraction to both sexes often try to maximize their activity with females, but occasionally slip into sexual activity with other males, about which they often feel very guilty or ashamed. One boy with whom I am working is following such a course. Over time homosexuality seems to be unfolding as his more basic orientation. This is not without great conflict and sometimes denial. At one point he proclaimed himself cured. He had a girlfriend. All homosexual fantasies were gone and he enjoyed sex with his girlfriend much more than sex with males. He wanted to quit treatment with me at that time. He did not. A few weeks later he returned with strong fantasies about molesting younger boys. He now felt strongly that this was his preference. In careful exploration during this session, he finally told me he had gotten very drunk and had awakened in bed, naked, with a good male friend. It was clear to both of us that he had regressed into pedophilia to avoid homosexuality which he feared more. His treatment will remain a struggle for sometime. I fear that if he cannot accept his homosexuality, he will become a pedophile. Both seem equally strong at this time. His most recent decision is to be gay but to stay in the closet.

Parents and the Older Adolescent

Working with parents of boys at this age is very tricky. In general, such work should be de-emphasized because these young men are so near emancipation. Parents, however, often clamor for information about progress and content of the child's therapy. In some cases they will remove the child if some kind of information is not provided. Where necessary, I will give a bland account to the parents with the teenager present. This should be done only with the patient's permission.

In some cases, where there are high risks of perpetration or suicidal behavior, I think it is necessary to work more closely with the parent. This must be handled delicately. It is necessary to tell the adolescent that you cannot allow him to molest others for his sake as well as the victim's. Similar logic applies to suicide. In these situations it is usually possible to get the patient's permission to bring in the parents.

If there are severe conflicts between the child and one or both parents, conjoint sessions, with the adolescent's permission, can be a good way to resolve them. Another option is to refer the parents elsewhere for treatment, with the understanding that the therapists will consult with each other, and information will be shared through the filter of the two therapists.

A final aspect of individual work with the middle and late adolescent involves efforts to prevent perpetration. This is one of the reasons for focusing on issues of sexual identity. If a child feels that the option of homosexuality is not available or acceptable, an unfortunate number of them do choose pedophilia by default. This is probably the most tragic outcome of being victimized as a male. A high percentage of men who are victimized as children never go on to perpetrate. We need to know more about this population, which will be the subject of the following chapter.

Chapter 12

FROM VICTIM TO PERPETRATOR

The transformation of certain male victims into perpetrators of sexual abuse upon others is one of the most critical issues involving in the field of sexual abuse. The sexual abuse of young males sets the stage for individual and family trauma. When victimization transforms a boy into a perpetrator, society suffers. A kind of epidemic is potentiated in which some molested boys seek other children to molest. From among their male victims more perpetrators arise, multiplying the damage to society as a whole.

These remarks raise the question of incidence. How many molested boys go on to molest others? The direct and honest answer to this question is that we do not know. A study by Kaufman and Zigler concluded that in about thirty percent of cases, abused children become abusive parents. This study has two problems for the question at hand. It treats only abuse by parents, and it treats both physical and sexual abuse. I am unaware of any more precise study of this problem. In my own caseload sample twenty-four percent of the boys under fourteen referred to me for treatment as victims had also molested other younger children. Among the older boys, fully seventy percent had perpetrated by the time of referral. As of this writing, none of the non-perpetrators have become perpetrators once they entered treatment.

If the question is turned into, "What percentage of perpetrators are also victims?" much more data becomes available. Bolton et al (1989) cite a series of studies with incidences ranging from nineteen percent of adolescent perpetrators who had previously been molested to seventy-five percent of incarcerated male sex offenders with victimization in their backgrounds. Fay Honey Knopp found rates of twenty-two to eighty-two percent of previous victimization in adult sex offenders in a 1984 publication. Groth (1979) found forty-six percent of fixated pedophiles to have been molested as children. Gebhardt, et al (1986) found that thirty-four percent of incarcerated offenders who had molested females had been previously molested themselves. Over the years the percentage of my adolescent molester case load that are also victims has averaged fifty percent to sixty percent. Regarding perpetrators, it would seem safe to say that roughly half have been previously molested. My experience is that this figure goes to a much higher level when males who have molested other males are separated from those who have molested females. In those cases the rate of previous victimization has consistently been very close to one hundred percent.

A look at the data on the percentage of the American male population which has been molested allows for further, indirect inferences. The literature search with which this book begins suggests that the best studies indicate a rate of about seventeen percent of the male population in the United States has been molested. Given 121 million men in America, this would suggest the presence of roughly twenty-one million male victims in the country at this time. It is extremely unlikely that there are twenty-one million male perpetrators in the United States. It can be safely inferred from this that the overwhelming majority of victims do not turn into offenders. There is, in all probability, a huge, silent majority of victimized males who do not come into treatment for a variety of reasons discussed elsewhere in this work. Within clinical populations of male victims the incidence of perpetration is likely to be high because logically it will be the more traumatized and sexualized males who will be brought for treatment.

The question of how many males survive abuse without becoming sexually assaultive has recently been raised in the literature. Gilgun (1990) studies a sample of thirty-four men in treatment. Of these men, twenty-three had been sexually molested. The rest had been exposed to other forms of child abuse. Of the sexually abused men, nine had no criminal history, seven were child molesters, five were rapists, and one was an armed robber. Gilgun is particularly interested in the factors differentiating the victims who became perpetrators and those who did not. She concludes:

> What differentiated men who committed violent criminal acts from those who did not was the presence or absence of a confidant, even in the presence of major negative factors.

It is significant in terms of one of the theses of this work that Gilgun found in her study that most of the confidants discussed by her subjects were male. This could be interpreted to suggest that at least some of the help lies in providing an identification figure and otherwise strengthening masculine identification. Gilgun suggests that a person reared in a sexualized environment with an early onset of sexualized behavior, are negative indicators in terms of development into a perpetrator. She notes that troubled interpersonal relationships in childhood and a harsh, negative environment also seem to predispose the child toward victimizing others. She speculates that the transition from victim to perpetrator seems to follow a reinforcement model. The role of sexual behavior as a tension-reducing mechanism is an important factor in this transition. Masturbation, rape, and molestation are seen as ways of coping with high anxiety states and, therefore, an attempt at adaptation. Unfortunately the proposed solution is dangerous and damaging to both the patient and society. Gilgun notes other factors that seem to provide a protective mechanism preventing victims from becoming perpetrators. These factors include such broad background features as secure attachments in infancy and early childhood, and the quality of early relationships.

Gilgun's general conclusion seems to be that victims who were in the best psychological shape when they were victimized are those least likely to become perpetrators of abuse on others. As a remedial measure to prevent the transformation of victims into perpetrators, Gilgun urges the provision of confidants for males who have been exposed to abuse of any kind.

Gerber (1990) deals with the same issue in a less rigorous way. Like Gilgun, he cites a strong sense of self prior to victimization as a positive prognostic indicator. He also notes the presence of positive, loving, and balanced male models in the child's life. He feels this is especially true of boys in the twelve to thirteen year age range. Gerber also notes that male children and adolescents who have been sexually victimized will do better if they are, in his words, "sexually functional with themselves (self-pleasuring)." I would translate this, in terms of my own understanding, to mean that males who develop a successful way of expressing their sexuality which is not harmful to others are at much less risk of perpetrating than those who become repressed, inhibited, and denying in their sexuality. A treatment implication would be that therapists should be permissive of or even encouraging toward masturbation and any form of legal, responsible, and consenting sexual behavior. A caveat on masturbation is that if it is accompanied by deviant fantasies, it may set in motion a reinforcement process that could spill over into acting out. This risk needs to be candidly discussed in the treatment process.

Gerber gives a long list of factors involved in the transformation from victim to perpetrator. Many of these factors are closely related to longer duration or greater severity of the abuse situation. Also important are factors involving dysfunctional families, preexisting personality, a social-learning-theory-like conditioning process, and molest by a family member. Gerber also develops the concept of the abuse-reactive child who may actually perpetrate against younger children, but may not be in the process of developing a true paraphilia.

Martha Erickson (1991) cites ongoing studies on physical abuse which also have some relevance here. The basic question of these studies, summarized in the *Harvard Mental Health Letter,* is. "How do some physical abuse victims escape becoming perpetrators of physical abuse upon their own children?" (A personal communication with Erickson in 1992 indicated that this research remains unpublished). As summarized by Erickson, the developing conclusions of these studies parallel those of Gilgun and of Gerber. The availability of a confidant is cited as an absolutely key factor. She notes that victims who do not perpetrate are characterized by an absence of denial. They do not idealize their parents, and they do not remain preoccupied with the abuse, and are not full of rage and shame about what has happened to them. They are, however, able to admit the pain and the damage that has been done to them.

Frailberg, et al (1975), add an additional significant factor. Again, the authors speak generally of child maltreatment and not specifically of sexual abuse, but the entire complex is, in their judgment, rendered less toxic and less likely to result in the abuse of others if the child victim remains in touch with the memories and pain of the abusive experience.* The parallels between physical and sexual are such that many researchers are not distinguishing them. Yet studies which lump physical and sexual abuse as well as those which study only sexual abuse come to similar conclusions about preventing the victim to perpetrator transition.

---

*In correspondence with Bruinsma, a Dutch expert on sexual abuse, he brought to my attention the probable disassociative nature of what most American therapists call denial. I think it is a valid observation that some of what is called denial in this book and in much of the literature on sexual abuse may be a disassociative process. My suspicion is that denial is too big a category to be useful and it needs to be examined in terms of sub-categories. I believe some or even much of it may turn out to be disassociative in nature. Bruinsma noted that Frailberg's observation about remaining in touch with memories and affects about victimization may indicate the absence of a disassociative process and therefore a better prognosis. This material came to my attention too late in the preparation of this book to be explored or integrated here. Those who are interested in further detail will have to hope Bruinsma publishes something on this in an English language journal.

Older research dealt with the issue of the transformation of victims into perpetrators in a more general sense. Psychoanalysis tended to deal with it as a result of fixation created by trauma or identification with the aggressor. Social learning theory would stress repetitive reinforcement and, therefore, probably look to the frequency and duration of the abuse as important factors in whether the patient continued the abusive pattern with others in the future. The presence of powerful negative examples in the child's life, specifically older men who molested and approved of molesting while being admired by the child, would also encourage the kind of learning by imitation postulated by social learning theory. Freeman-Longo (1986) arrives at similar conclusions to those of social learning theory. He postulates that more than one perpetrator, or repeated abuse over long periods of time, is involved in the transformation to perpetrator. He also notes that being molested by a male, in his judgment, creates a greater risk of perpetration.

CONSENSUS IN THE LITERATURE

The literature suggests that the factors mitigating against the transformation of male victims into perpetrators of sexual abuse are becoming identified and, to some extent, agreed-upon. It is clear that there is a need for social support systems for a male child who has been victimized, and that these systems can play a vital role in preventing the transformation into perpetrators. Of these support systems, the singular most important seems to be a confidant, a person with whom the child can talk intimately about what has happened to him. There is some further suggestion in the literature that this role is most often played by an older male. Confidants can include therapists as well as other mentors.

The literature suggests the victim will do better if his entire environment has been supportive in the past. This would imply an in place support system that can assist the male victim in dealing with trauma after molestation. This would include families who react appropriately. Such families would acknowledge that something serious and potentially damaging had happened, but that the damage can be repaired.

The literature makes several implicit references to dysfunctional family systems. Role models, early object relationships, confidants are all apt to be drawn from the immediate or extended family. If the family is dysfunctional, these supports and many others are likely to be absent or weak. A particularly difficult situation is where one or both of the boy's parents are also molest victims. The molestation of a child in this situation can set off a family crisis. Parents can be overprotective or, by their hysteria, communicate to the child that he may be damaged beyond repair.

Several writers mention a social learning type mechanism whereby deviant fantasies of molesting others are linked with masturbation. This reinforces the deviant fantasies. Eventually the fantasies become so erotized that some victims cannot or do not confine them to fantasy. Fantasy thus becomes behavior and the victim a perpetrator.

The literature is also suggestive that the length and severity of the molest episode may predispose toward perpetration in some cases. Most writers list the preexisting personality, specifically a weak sense of self, or crippling developmental factors in the child's early life, as predisposing to a transformation in the direction of perpetration. Denial is mentioned by both Erickson and Frailberg as a transformational factor. Based on clinical experience, I would agree with Freeman-Longo that molest by a male creates a greater risk of perpetration by a female.

ETIOLOGY OF A PARAPHILIA

Some boys who are molested will become pedophiles largely or partly because of their victimization. Many more will molest no one. There may be something in between: victims who enter a temporary period of obsessive sexual activity some of it with younger children or forced on peers. When molestation of children becomes a preferential or frequent sexual activity it is properly classified as a paraphilia. By what route are some boys channeled into a paraphilia which others are able to escape? Here I intend to offer my own ideas based on my experience and the literature, particularly the psychodynamic literature about how this transformation takes place.

This is an attempt to outline a theory of the origin of the paraphilia of pedophilia. It will not explain all molestation or all sexual assault. There may also several routes by which males become sexually oriented to young children. This hypothesis will apply best to the male victims of molestation who become adult pedophiles. It will not explain the victims who become brief or opportunistic offenders but who are not paraphiliacs.

In my judgment, the development of this specific kind of pedophilia is a matter of the development of intrapsychic structures which facilitate the transition from a victim of sexual assault to a paraphiliac who assaults others. This is a complex process that has multiple rather than singular causation. Translating back to the language of self-psychology, victims will be less likely to become perpetrators if they have positive self-object relationships in their lives. This is simply paraphrasing the research centered around the importance of confidants. Based upon ideas developed earlier in this work, I would suggest that victim boys are less likely to assault others if they have a male self-object to help them repair the damage to the nuclear self and to resume development along the male developmental line. When pedophilia is the outcome, being molested by a male has functioned to create a greater risk of offending by mobilizing homosexual feelings that are incompatible with the boy's ideals in the area of masculinity and sexual identity. This view suggests that much molesting of others is an attempt to restore a previous equilibrium in the psychic state specifically in the area of ideals and ambitions in the area of maleness.

The sexual acting out with children can be seen as an attempt at self-repair, at feeling better, at avoiding fragmentation. At the simplest level, this may be what might be described as a sexually addictive behavior, such as masturbation. In a boy with damaged masculinity, the fantasies connected with masturbation may feature distorted concepts about the nature of masculinity. These can include an obsessive concern with power and control over others and/or their humiliation and degradation. Fantasy alone may not serve the function of reducing anxiety, shoring up maleness, and preventing fragmentation. Then the developing paraphiliac may select a younger victim in order to play out in reality the themes he has tried out in fantasy. The crossover from fantasy into reality is a kind of emotional Rubicon for the developing pedophile. It is an act of desperation because fantasy is no longer an adequate defense. Once he begins to act out in reality, the greater erotic rewards become increasingly self-reinforcing.

At this point, theories regarding the role of control, power, and domination, which are very prominent in the field of treatment of perpetrators, can be plugged in directly to the understanding of the development of pedophilia. A male with a profoundly damaged masculinity will have considerable difficulty approaching a female who is a true peer. For this reason, in order to repair the masculinity which, in this culture, is so often associated with domination, control, and power, the developing perpetrator must select a victim with whom he can feel this kind of power and domination. This would lead to the selection of a younger female victim.

If the victim is male, it may seem at first glance that the above explanation is grossly in error. A similar arguments can be made with a few key modifications of the equation. If the victim's maleness is badly damaged, and he has already been sexualized in the direction of sexual interest in other males, he may select a younger boy in search of an idealized male selfobject with whom he wishes to merge in order to gain masculinity. Boys in treatment have shared with me that their attractions to other boys are based on that boy's possession of traits which they desire. At the deepest level the drive may not be to have sex with that boy, but to become that idealized object.

Some male victims could attempt to repair the damage to their maleness by acting out with males who are true peers. This, however, would lead into a homosexual orientation. It is my suspicion that some boys do arrive at homosexuality by this route. By merging with another male, they acquire a masculinity which they feel they lack. This is not offered as a generic explanation of homosexuality which appears to me to be an orientation arrived at from many points of departure. I have no idea what percentage of homosexual males may have arrived at their preference by this route. Data from Bell, Weinberg, and Hammersmith (1981) suggest it is a small percentage. I am simply suggesting that a homosexual preference is one resolution that male victims can use to cope with the trauma of molestation and restore their damaged masculinity.

Those boys who are both homophobic and homoerotic are in a terrible dilemma. The only choice open to them would be a younger male with whom they could feel a sense of power and domination. This resolution is essentially an emotional compromise. Homoerotic feelings are so strong they cannot be contained. Yet a homosexual relationship in which they are dominated by another male or put in a passive position would be the ultimate feminization. Selection of a much younger sexual partner serves the role of avoiding a passive position in a homosexual relationship while still allowing homosexual object choice.

This process of becoming a pedophile is unlikely to take off with boys who have a strong, preexisting sense of male self and/or those who have a strong conscience structure and an ability to empathize with others. In these cases, the presence of the conscience and the ability to empathize with others will play a major role in preventing perpetration. If nothing else, empathy and conscience can help confine paraphiliac feelings to the realm of fantasy until treatment can take hold and, hopefully, eliminate the fantasy structure.

Multiple psychic structures seem to block the development of pedophilia in most male victims. A strong nuclear self is a critical variable. Where the boy has nuclear goals that proscribe homosexuality and pedophilia, these are unlikely outcomes. This tendency is strengthened if the boys also have adequate mechanisms for meeting these goals. Available masculine self-objects also help to make the development of a paraphilia unlikely. Boys with these psychic resources will be able to adhere to their original nuclear goals in the sexual area. If those goals included traditional American masculinity, molestation is unlikely to derail the boy from pursuit and attainment of that goal. Molestation may set off some conflict and temporarily create some kind of sexual acting out, but the basic structure is unlikely to be changed by external trauma. This at least would be the implication of looking at this from the perspective of self-psychology. Here self-psychology and Winson's neurobiology converge. If this process is looked at from the standpoint of critical period development, the statement can be reformulated into: molestation cannot change an orientation formed in a critical period.

This, then, is the basic hypothesis. No claim is made that it is complete. Like anything in psychoanalysis, it cannot be proven. If it offers a guide to treatment that diverts victims away from pedophilia that will be clinical validation.

WHERE IS THE VICTIM/PERPETRATOR BOUNDARY?

This is a crucial question. The reality is probably that there is no boundary but a gray area in the middle of a continuum. The issue is pivotal because a deep chasm divides those who treat victims from those who treat perpetrators. They are two different worlds with radically different philosophies, one having its roots deeply in the camp of mental health and the other deeply in the camp of corrections. Treatment planning would be radically different for a boy defined as a perpetrator as opposed a boy defined as a victim. The dilemma is that many are both. The stakes involved in making this necessary decision are high, both for the individual and society.

If the boy who is both victim and perpetrator is defined predominantly as a victim, he will most likely receive the kind of treatment outlined by clinicians such as Hewitt, Friedrich, Froning and Mayman. On the other hand, if he is identified as predominantly a perpetrator, he will find himself in the much harsher realm of those who treat criminals. These

remarks are not intended to be a plea that all male victims who perpetrate be treated as victims. A complex assessment must be made in order
to see that someone whose needs are predominantly in the area of
treatment of their victimization receives that treatment. This course of
action is appropriate where treatment of the victimization will result in a
cessation of perpetration. On the other hand, it is equally important to
identify victims whose patterns of perpetration have become full-blown
and who are major dangers to the community in terms of damaging
other children in the same way they have been damaged themselves.

A brief look at the realm of perpetrator treatment is indicated. I think
it is important to note that, as a therapist, I have worked both sides of the
fence, including five years as a therapist with a residential treatment
program for adolescent molesters. I have written a previous book involving the treatment of adolescent molesters. I have also spent considerable
time on the other side of the fence, treating in an outpatient setting boys
who are predominantly victims. I continue to devote part of my practice
to perpetrator-oriented treatment for boys who need that focus. I do,
however, select carefully and treat only adolescent perpetrators who can
safely remain in the community.

Once in the realm of perpetrator treatment, the ground immediately
shifts to protection of society. Ryan and Lane (1991) recently published a
work which well summarizes the attitudes, techniques, and clinical thinking of the majority of people working in the treatment of juvenile sex
offenders. In their chapter on treatment, the authors note that sexual
perpetration is not just a personal problem but a social and legal concern
as well. They place heavy emphasis on victim advocacy and victim
protection. One of the practical results of this perspective is in the
authors' words: "These assumptions require the therapist to consider
the needs and rights of others in priority over the needs and rights of the
client." The general assumption is that most clients will be unmotivated
and uncooperative, at least at the onset.

> In order to motivate change, the offender must be placed in a position where
> he has to change and begin to feel uncomfortable with his offense and behavior
> before he can achieve self-control and a sense of genuine adequacy and respon-
> sibility within himself.

Group treatment is given high priority and is often the only modality
offered. Groups are typically high-pressure with a great deal of confrontation and demand for disclosure. Ryan and Lane do advocate that the

therapist respect the essential dignity of the client and make responsible use of their power over the patient. This caution is particularly important since the majority of this work is done in residential or correctional settings where the therapist wields great authority in the patients' lives. Ryan's cautions are well-advised but, sadly, easily ignored by less sophisticated clinicians.

Most recently published approaches to the treatment of sex offenders barely mention victimization and place no emphasis on treating the perpetrator's own victimization. The theoretical chapters in Ryan and Lane place very little emphasis on victimization in the etiology of sex offending. Victimization also gets scant attention from Abel et al (1984) and Salter (1988), who have produced other recent works on the treatment of perpetrators. A major concern among those who treat perpetrators seems to be a fear that the offender will use victimization as an excuse to avoid accepting full responsibility for his actions against others.

Some of this disinterest in victimization may reflect the fact that the perpetrator population is far from one hundred percent victim. It may be with specific questioning these writers would acknowledge that victims within the perpetrator population also need to address these issues. My point of departure is, however, that victim issues are absent or de-emphasized in much of the available literature on the treatment of sex offenders. With probably half of such offenders also being victims, I believe this is a serious omission. I feel that, at some point in the treatment of perpetrators most men will need to deal with their victimization in order to make a full recovery. Treating the victimization alone of course will not solve the problem. I am arguing for expanding the focus of treatment to include victim issues when and where the perpetrator is a victim and is willing and able to deal with these issues.

In place of victimization as a key dynamic factor, clinicians in the sex offender treatment field stress sexually assaultive behavior as "a control-seeking dysfunction" (Ryan, 1991). Lane feels that the purpose of abusive behavior is to develop a sense of power and control through the association of thrill, risk-taking, excitement, arousal, and accomplishment. This is compensatory for the loss of power and feeling of inadequacy typical of young offenders.

I have no trouble with this formulation, except to feel that it is a derivative from damaged masculinity, rather than the primary purpose of abusive behavior. The items on Lane's list are traditionally associated with maleness by men in American culture. To ignore the victimization of males who are also offenders and to emphasize their need for compensatory power over others in an abusive sexual way can create a climate of hostility rather than empathy toward the offenders who are ethically also patients or clients. This can be managed by skilled administrators of clinical programs, but the underlying theory of offender treatment creates a climate that can lead to a very untherapeutic milieu.

The perpetrator treatment field is permeated with the distrust of traditional mental health. Not only is group seen as the primary and central treatment modality, little role is allowed for individual treatment. Salter (1988) does not even list it as a possible need for perpetrators, specifically mentioning only group, family, and behavioral therapy. Ryan and Lane (1991) view individual sessions as a supplement to the group process. They can be used to draw out the painfully shy client. They might occasionally be used to address "uniquely personal concerns," or to conduct physiological testing, or for other similar secondary purposes, including "confrontation of destructive group dynamics."

The mention of physiological testing brings up another issue. There is a presumption that offenders lie, conceal, and evade. To prevent this, the penile plethesmograph is widely used in the sex offender field. In some treatment programs it is used regularly in combination with a polygraph to be sure therapists are being told the truth. To facilitate therapeutic change, heavy reliance is put upon behavioral and cognitive techniques, principally covert sensitization, masturbatory satiation, and cognitive restructuring. There seems to be no emphasis at all on the patient/therapist relationship or transference.

WHY THE DIFFERENCES?

Anyone familiar with the literature in the fields of treatment of sex abuse victims and treatment of sex abuse perpetrators might think they were written on different planets. What is the root of these differences? It is my feeling that they arise, in part, out of the very different data bases from which the information is drawn. The mental health community is most heavily involved in the treatment of victims.

Most of the writers of the literature in the sex offender field operate either in correctional settings, juvenile residential facilities, or come out of academia. A high percentage of the academic studies are done on incarcerated adult populations. Many of the treatment techniques worked out for these incarcerated adult populations are the ones now being advocated and used with juvenile sex offenders.

In the treatment of victims, clinicians write a higher percentage of the literature, and most of these clinicians are based in outpatient settings. Their patients are voluntary with the option of discontinuing treatment if they or their families find it unsatisfactory. The correctional population is basically involuntary. It has been prescreened by courts, and the perpetrator is ordered into treatment for the protection of the community. Often this treatment is in a closed residential setting. Where offenders are left in the community, they are on probation with a requirement that they participate in treatment.

Although there will, without doubt, be errors in this kind of screening process, it is reasonable to assume that a much more disturbed and intractable population is going to be found participating in involuntary treatment in prisons or residential treatment facilities or under the watchful eyes of probation officers. Those who treat victims have far more purely voluntary patients. In the case of children, only those with supportive families usually stay in treatment. So clinicians who see victims and those who see perpetrators usually have a very different kind of population from which to draw inferences about treatment.

When I wrote my original book on the adolescent molester, I was treating basically outpatient molesters referred to me by a local court and boys in a residential program with high standards of treatability necessary for admission. I had trouble understanding why so many of my colleagues treating perpetrators were so drawn to the kinds of techniques outlined earlier. I had an opportunity to see a video of the sex offenders incarcerated in the California Youth Authority. The reason for our difference perspectives became immediately obvious. There would be no way that I would attempt to apply the techniques suggested in this book, or even those suggested in my original book, to the population I saw incarcerated within the Youth Authority. Those are the clients for whom traditional perpetrator treatment is designed and for whom it may be the only therapy offering any hope.

I suspect that there is agreement that therapy will be most effective if the patient wants to change. The problem for people working with perpetrators is that the courts have sent them a number of people who do not wish to change. These therapists are therefore forced to resort to other techniques to impose change on unwilling clients. I have no quarrel with this, since I suspect that the approach advocated within mental health offers very little to a truly criminal population.

The essential issue behind all of this discussion is to be sure that each patient gets whatever treatment is best designed to meet his needs. I do not think there is much room for the error of using perpetrator techniques on pure victims. Behavioral techniques might be worked into a broader treatment plan to prevent perpetration in at risk boys. Still their cooperation and support of their caretakers would be required. The correctional-perpetrator model simply will not sell to a voluntary population. Theoretically, I believe it is a serious mistake not to use transference, therapeutic alliance, and individual therapy with populations who can use them. Many, if not most, young male victims of perpetration can.

I have earlier offered arguments that real repair of structural damage to personality is possible for many young victims. The development of a cohesive self and a strong, secure masculinity offer a far better opportunity to prevent the young male victim from becoming a perpetrator than do confrontive and/or behavioral-cognitive approaches. The most difficult decision is what kind of treatment to offer the boy who is both a perpetrator and a victim.

How Do We Divide the Terrain?

This is the most difficult question of this chapter. How can clinicians determine who is best served by the kind of outpatient mental health approach advocated here, and who is best served by the classical corrections approach? The answer is most simple in dealing with males who are pure victims and have never offended. At the other extreme are the perpetrators who are not victims and who have committed a serious offense of a sexual nature. These clearly belong to the correctional system. Whether they are placed in an outpatient or an inpatient setting would seem to me to depend on both the severity of the offense and the underlying personality of the offender. Presumably, it is the job of community courts to make these decisions.

Getting rid of the easy cases focuses the dilemma. Where do we make the cutoff for the boy who is both a victim of molestation and a perpetrator in his own right? There is inherently a certain arbitrariness to this. I can only offer my guidelines. I am frequently asked to make assessments for local juvenile courts about the suitability of community treatment for young victims who have become perpetrators. I do recommend that a number of young men be placed in residential facilities and route others into outpatient treatment.

To even be considered for the kind of treatment suggested in this book, the boy must be a victim. Additionally, his offense must be minor and the first documented offense. Diagnostically, I am uncomfortable if there is either a thought disorder or antisocial personality disorder in the perpetrator/victim. Substance abuse is also a negative indicator for the kind of approach advocated here. A supportive family is essential. The patient must have identifiable strengths allowing him to use outpatient treatment. Intelligence, some ability to introspect, motivation, and curiosity are necessary if a boy is to fully use the kind of approach that I advocate.

Both the correctional and the mental health communities must deal with the reality that the courts will ask us to treat people who are probably inappropriate for our setting. In my own community the majority of adolescent sex offenders are not sent to placement, and the majority of them do not see therapists who specialize or have special expertise in sexuality, let alone sex offending or victimology. On the other hand, some relatively light-weight offenders who could probably benefit from an outpatient program will be placed in residential facilities where there is a possibility that the techniques outlined earlier may do more harm than good. All therapist need to be aware of these misplacements and do our best to work with the reality with which we are confronted.

SUMMARY

This chapter has dealt with the most unfortunate of the sequela of victimization: the transformation of some male victims into perpetrators. It is a process facilitated by complex factors which are beginning to be identified by researchers. The ability to work out issues arising from the assault in the context of an intimate relationship seems to be one of the key variables. Psychodynamic ideas developed earlier in this work were applied to the transformation of victim into pedophile. Not all crossing of the boundary leads to pedophilia. Once a boy has molested, serious decisions need to be made regarding his treatment. Some may respond best to a correctional model designed for adult offenders and now extended to juveniles in many residential programs. Others retain the ability for structural repair of the damage caused them by molestation. They should be treated with a model, introducing key concepts from offender treatment, but flexible enough to allow for the transformational processes that occur only in the context of transference and therapeutic alliance.

APPENDIX I

BOYS MOLESTED BY PARENTS

This section is somewhat mislabeled. Most of it will deal with boys molested by their fathers. Some brief comments about boys molested by their mothers will be included at the end. This section is included because of the particular theoretical and clinical interest of this situation. Little is known, clinically or statistically, about the phenomenon. I do not have enough data for a full chapter. Hence the appendix status of this material. Williams (1988) reviews the data available up to that time. He regards it as inadequate and containing little information on long-term outcome.

Williams observes that molestation by father forces the boy to deal, at least in the short term, with a number of critical issues. These include stresses which will jeopardize the development of identity and self-esteem. The boy will also have to deal with social taboos involving incest and homosexuality. He will also have to deal with this culture's homophobia and the poor masculine model offered by the father.

I have had the opportunity, over the years, to treat eight cases at some depth and over a prolonged period of time. These are among the most difficult and disturbed boys I have treated. The only comparably difficult group are those who have been exposed to both severe physical abuse and sexual abuse at the hands of men. All of the eight boys referred to me were fourteen or younger at the time of referral. Seven of the boys had already molested younger children. Six had histories of sex with other males, either same age or younger. Seven were, in my clinical judgment, at very high risk for sexual perpetration in the future.

None of the mothers had been protective while the abuse was ongoing. Abuse in all cases involved multiple incidents. All but one boy had been sodomized and orally copulated by their fathers. The exception had been only orally copulated. Six of the eight boys were in foster or residential care. Five of the eight boys were under considerable family pressure, usually from the parent, to forgive or, in several cases, to recant the allegations so father could return home or avoid prosecution.

Three of these boys made a good response to treatment. Two have not been in treatment long enough to assess their response. One became so hostile to me and to the group that I had to remove him from treatment permanently and refer him elsewhere. A second never involved himself in any meaningful way and was terminated for lack of response. Another boy was removed after repeated disruptive behavior in group and repeatedly picking fights with me in group. He later requested to return to treatment, and is making much better use of it at this time.

Clinically, these boys show the same symptom picture as most boys molested by older males. The focal difference appears to me to be in the area of intense loyalty conflicts about the father which are often aggravated by the mother and other family members. Seven of the eight boys always maintained that they loved their fathers. Two adamantly insisted that they felt that what had happened was not wrong. One of these two was the boy permanently removed from the group.

I cannot say much about the boys' fathers since most have fled or are in jail. Even though most of these boys were in foster care, most continued to maintain contact with their mother. Five of these boys were under strong pressure from their mothers to love their fathers, to reconcile, and to recant allegations. Since court regulations in this state require parental visitation in all but the most extreme cases, ongoing visitation with these non-supportive parents is the rule rather than the exception. It often has a negative effect on the boys' treatment.

The motives of the mothers in these cases seem to vary. Sometimes they are legitimately attached to the father. In other cases, the motive is economic. The father had a good income. His removal from the home and/or incarceration has cost the family considerable revenue. Many are highly litigious usually trying to disprove allegations against the father which have already been established in juvenile court. If they cannot undo the original charges, they are usually seeking to have the child returned to their home. One of the mothers was documented to have been facilitating secret visits between the father and son when he was released to her custody for visitation.

In some cases, the mothers seemed to feel very guilty about not protecting their sons. They, too, have a loyalty conflict. In reality they usually must choose to give up the father if they want to keep the son at home. Since the father often is unrepentant and/or in denial, they really must choose sides. They can collude with the father and remain unprotective, or they can protect the son and lose their husband. A common way out of this dilemma is denial. The mother simply denies the reality that the father has molested the son. A variation is to acknowledge what happened, but to consider the problem resolved by religious conversion or brief therapy, and to urge that the son return to a dangerous situation.

Clinically, boys seem to deal with molest by father with the primitive defense mechanism of splitting. Four of these boys idealized their actual fathers. Three were ambivalent, switching from love to hate, with love generally predominating. The eighth was non-committal and, probably, not attached to anyone. Some of these boys are consciously aware of the dilemma they are in and the pressures they are resisting. The boy I had to permanently remove told me up front that he didn't want to say anything about his father to me or the group for fear the father would go to jail. When other boys discussed being molested by men, this child became extremely uncomfortable.

His way out of the dilemma was to engage in provocative, defiant behavior which was probably a deliberate attempt to get out of the group before it mobilized negative feelings about his father and placed him at jeopardy of never being able to return to the home of his mother. His was the mother who was arranging secret visits and urging the boy to recant.

Where there is no consciously accessible rage with the father. It shows up in displacement and in transference. Frank, who is relatively new to treatment, denies any anger with the father who molested him for years. He says that what happened caused him no harm. When Frank plays with the gorilla, the play involves beating it, having it assault smaller dolls, and other similar behaviors. Frank also seems to direct some of his rage with his father toward me. On one occasion, I had to stop him from hitting me in the face with a rubber band. He will play tricks in group, attempting to make me look foolish. If left unattended in the office, he will steal. It would seem that he is displacing rage with the father onto me.

An older boy, the one who was removed from the group and returned at his own request, manifests the typical ambivalence of an adolescent molested by his father. When he returned to a new group, in the course of introducing himself, he started out by saying that he hated his father and had attempted to fight him off when the father intended to sodomize him. I could see the beginnings of tears in his eyes. I asked him if there had been good things about his father. He broke into tears and told me that there had been. Remember, however, that this was the child who was so provocative that I had had to remove him for a time from treatment because of the disruptions he created in group and the intense personal hostility he aimed at me.

Boys Molested by Mother

On this population I have even more limited information. I currently have four boys in this category, although three of them are siblings responding to the same basic situation. I saw more of these cases when I worked for a residential program for sex offenders. Generally, these perpetrators who had been molested by their mothers were psychotic or borderline. I have no idea of the validity of this as a generalization.

Not surprisingly, the three siblings molested by mother show similar reactions. They are all secretive and reluctant to discuss the incidents. Their degree of shame is high. Although I have had them in treatment for a long time, they will go into denial and not remember what happened if we do not periodically review the matter. In these times of denial it is as if what mother did never happened. They will fantasize about reuniting with her. When they are not in denial or disassociation, these siblings go through episodes of severe aggressive acting-out against their foster mothers. Two of them have acted-out sexually with younger children, in both cases, males. The older two boys appear to be heterosexually-oriented, but with a great deal of rage and potential violence toward females. In periods of acting-out, they openly proclaim that they hate females. I suspect that they will become batterers of women if treatment is not successful.

In periods of denial, these siblings seem to need to protect mother from their rage. They make excuses for their mother and blame the incident on her boyfriend. This may be for the purpose of maintaining a psychically necessary connection to a primary object. If they receive letters from the mother, severe acting out usually follows. One of the boys, after receiving a letter from the mother, acted-out severely against the foster mother to whom he normally has a strong attachment. He told her that he knew that she hated him and had always hated him, and that she belonged in jail. Rather clearly, he was not talking about the foster mother.

The fourth boy, now a young adolescent, was molested by his mother prior to age five. He had intercourse with her, among various other sexual acts. This child is extremely sexually repressed. He has not perpetrated and shows no overt interest in any kind of sexual activity with anyone. He is the boy who produced the material about women roasting penises, as well as material about his penis becoming stuck in either a vagina or a man's rectum. This child is very secretive. His occasional productions suggest a great fear of sexuality in general. I suspect he may develop a lifelong pattern of confining sex to fantasy. I do not expect him to perpetrate. I think it is unlikely that he will be involved in sexual activity with either sex, given the intensity of his anxiety. A more malignant outcome may have been prevented in this case by successful adoption and long term therapy.

It is, of course, risky to generalize from such a small sample, but I would point out that the reactions of these four victims of maternal molestation show patterns predictable by the theory of maleness developed throughout this book. These boys have experienced a *de facto* fusion with mother. They need defensive rage and withdrawal from femaleness to forever close the tempting doors of regression to the infantile symbiosis which was once so vividly acted out in reality.

APPENDIX II

MEASURING SUCCESS

After the publication of my original book, *The Adolescent Molester* (1987), a reviewer suggested that it would have been useful to him for me to offer some comments on the success of my approach. I think the same consideration is relevant here, but harder to deal with than the request for such information on the original book. There are several ways in which the effectiveness of this kind of a program can be measured. They are mostly subjective. The most objective criterion would be perpetration since that would be the most easily measurable datum to follow. Plethysmographs can show the presence of deviant arousal. If such measurement indicated the presence of deviant arousal at the beginning of treatment and its absence at the end, it would be suggestive of a highly successful approach. Unfortunately such measurement would be totally unacceptable to my clients, to my community, and to the agencies that refer to me.

I have treated roughly 135 male victims of sexual abuse since 1984. This does not include victims seen for assessment or who dropped out of treatment after two or three sessions. If one of my patients perpetrates while still an adolescent, I am generally notified by local law enforcement, and a report is requested. Since 1989 only two boys in treatment with me in the age range above eight, were arrested for new offenses. One simply propositioned other boys in his group home and was removed. The other had charges filed against him which he denied, then fled the jurisdiction of the court prior to trial. Both boys came to me as victims and perpetrators at the beginning of treatment.

Between 1984 and 1989 four of the older boys in treatment offended. These were all victims who had histories of perpetration before they began treatment. These were all boys in the twelve and thirteen year age range. Three of them remolested siblings living in the same home. In all cases the new incident involved less substantial sexual contact than the original incident. For example, it might be fondling instead of oral copulation. As a principle of practice, I do not recommend that siblings who molest siblings be left in the same home. In these cases the court decided to leave the children with their families and referred them to me. The forth boy fondled a seven-year-old relative on a family visit.

The real problem group for perpetration are the very young boys, particularly the five, six and seven year olds. Early in treatment, if they are sexualized, they are often making sexual advances on people of a wide age spectrum, including some younger children. As a general rule, I have been able to work with the parents and the child to get this under control, but only after several months. With the exception of these little boys, none of the boys brought to me as victims with no perpetration history at the beginning of treatment have turned into perpetrators once treatment began.

For my own use, I have some subjective ways of measuring success. I am constantly evaluating the boy's ability to form long term intimate and, ultimately, sexual relationships with peers and consider the treatment plan to be effective if this ability is developing. It often shows up in teenagers with the beginning of dating in boys who have never previously dated. Also reassuring to me are improved psychosocial functioning manifested in higher self-esteem and a stronger sense of masculinity. I consider it further evidence that treatment is effective if boys are able to form a strong treatment alliance with me, to talk freely, and to disclose previously undisclosed information about themselves, both to me and in the group. I feel that this happens with eighty percent or ninety percent of the younger boys and probably sixty percent to seventy percent of the older boys in treatment.

I am satisfied with this success rate, considering the number of children I have treated. I must confess, however, that I probably improve my odds by selectivity. I screen cases and will not accept boys for treatment who do not appear to me to have a good prognosis and who show relatively little proclivity for re-offending, in my judgment. Additionally, I will remove boys who pose severe behavior problems in group. Some of these boys whom I remove from treatment have been among the highest risk boys that I have treated in my career. These boys did not offend while in treatment, but I do not know what happened after they left.

It would be unfair to make statements about success without dealing frankly with the issue of undetected offenses. As noted earlier in this work, Abel and Becker found roughly sixty offenses for every one for which the perpetrator was caught. Their population was adult and presumably more skillful at concealing their misdeeds, but it would be reasonable to assume that some percentage of the boys I treat have committed sex offenses for which they have not been caught.

The final issue deals with the future. Obviously, in dealing with such young patients, they have many, many years in which to develop paraphilias and to commit sex offenses. There is no way to measure this, and I cannot possibly give any kind of estimate. I can only express my hope that the techniques outlined here accomplish what I intend them to accomplish. If they do not, what I may be suggesting is in fact a sort of Alcoholics Anonymous model where boys who are involved in continuous group and individual discussion of sexual problems are able to avoid perpetration and other blatant sexual dysfunction. How they will do on their own after many years is an open and unanswerable question.

BIBLIOGRAPHY

Abel, G. C., Becker, J. V., Mittleman, M., Cunningham-Rathner, J., Rouleau, J. L., & Murphy, W. D. (1987). Self reported crimes of non-incarcerated paraphiliacs. *Journal of Interpersonal Violence, 2*(1), 3–23.

Abel, G. C., Becker, J. V., Cunningham-Rathner, J., Rouleau, J. L., Kaplan, M., & Reich, J. (1984). The treatment of child molesters. Unpublished Manual available from the senior author.

Adams, H. E., & Sturgis, E. T. (1977). Status of behavioral reorientation techniques in the modification of homosexuality: A review. *Psychological Bulletin, 84,* 1171–1188.

Allen, M. R., Ritualized homosexuality, male power and political organization in North Vanautu: A comparative analysis. In: Herdt, G. H. (1984). *Ritualized homosexuality in Melanesia.* Berkeley & Los Angeles: University of California Press.

Aramoni, A. (1972, January). Machismo, *Psychology Today,* pp. 69–72.

Bacal, H. A. Optimal responsiveness and the therapeutic process. In: Goldberg, A. (1985). *Progress in Self Psychology, 1.* New York: Guilford Press.

Baker, C. D., Preying on playgrounds: The sexploitation of children in pornography and prostitution. In: Schultz, L. G., (Ed.). (1980). *The sexual victimology of youth.* Springfield, IL: Thomas.

Bandura, A. (1977). *Social learning theory.* Englewood Cliffs, NJ: Prentice-Hall.

Bandura, A., & Walters, R. H. (1963). *Social learning and personality development.* New York: Holt, Rinehart, & Winston.

Barton, B. R., & Marshall, A. S. (1986). Pivotal partings: Forced termination with a sexually abused boy. *Clinical Social Work Journal, 14*(2), 139–149.

Bell, A., & Weinberg, M. (1978). *Homosexualities.* New York: Simon & Schuster.

Bell, A., Weinberg, M., & Hammersmith, S. K. (1981). *Sexual preference: Its development in men and women.* Bloomington, Indiana: University Press.

Blake-White, J., & Kline, C. M. (1985). Treating the dissociative process in adult victims of childhood incest. *Social Casework, 66,* 393–404.

Blanchard, G. (1986). Male victims of child sexual abuse: A portent of things to come. *Journal of Independent Social Work, 1*(1), 19–27.

Blanck, G., & Blanck, R. (1979). Ego psychology II. New York: Columbia University Press.

Blos, P. (1975). The concept of acting out in relation to the adolescent process. In: Esman, A. (Ed.). *The psychology of adolescence.* New York: International Universities Press.

Blos, P. (1985). *Son and father.* New York: Free Press.

Boisso, C. V., et al. (1989). Psychological characteristics of adolescent males who have been sexually abused. Paper presented at the Annual Meeting of the American Psychological Association, New Orleans, LA.

Bolton, F., MacEachron, A. E., & Morris, L. (1989). *Males at risk: The other side of child sexual abuse.* Newbury Park, CA: Sage.

Breer, W. (1987). *The adolescent molester.* Springfield, IL: Thomas.

Briere, J., Evans, D., Runtz, M., & Wall, T. (1988). Symptomatology in men who were molested as children: A comparison study. *American Journal of Orthopsychiatry, 58*(3), 457–461.

Bruckner, D., & Johnson, P. (1987, February). Treatment for adult male victims of childhood sexual abuse. *Social Casework,* 81–87.

Bruinsma, F. (1991). *Differing individual system factors in incest perpetrators and paedophilic child molesters.* Unpublished manuscript.

Burgess, A. W., Groth, A. N., Holmstrom, L. L., & Sgroi, S. M. (1978). *Sexual assault of children and adolescents.* Lexington, MA: D. C. Heath, 1978.

Carmen, E. H., Rieker, P. P., & Mills, T. (1984). Victims of violence and psychiatric illness. *American Journal of Psychiatry, 141*(3), 378–383.

Cartwright, R. D. (1977). *Nightlife.* Englewood Cliffs, NJ: Prentice-Hall.

Clark, A., & Bingham, J. (1984). The play technique: Diagnosing the sexually abused child. *Tarrant County Physician,* pp. 54–57.

Cook, M., & Howells, K. (Eds.). (1981). *Adult sexual interest in children.* New York: Academic Press.

Cupoli, J. M., & Sewell, P. M. (1988). One thousand and fifty-nine children with a chief complaint of sexual abuse. *Child Abuse & Neglect, 12*(2), 151–162.

Daldin, H. (1988). The fate of the sexually abused child. *Clinical Social Work Journal, 16*(1).

Dean, K., & Woods, S. (1988). Implications and findings of the sexual abuse of males research. Workshop presented at Child Welfare League of America. Galinburg, TN. In: Dimock (1988).

DeJong, A. R., Emmett, G. A., and Hervada, A. R. (1982). Sexual abuse of children. Sex, race, and age-dependent variations. *American Journal of Diseases in Children, 136*(2), 129–134.

Detrick, D. (1985). Alterego phenomena and the alterego transferences. In: Goldberg, A. (1985). *Progress in self psychology, 1.* New York: Guilford Press.

DeVine, R. A. (1980). Sexual abuse of children: An overview of the problem. In: MacFarlane, K., Jones, B. M., & Jenstrom, L. L. (Eds.). *Sexual abuse of children: Selected readings.* Washington, DC: National Center on Child Abuse & Neglect.

De Young, M. (1982). *The sexual victimization of children.* Jefferson, NC: McFarland.

Diamond, M. (1965). A critical evaluation of the ontogeny of human sexual behavior. *Quarterly Review of Biology, 40,* 147–175.

Dimock, P. T. (1988). Adult males sexually abused as children: Characteristics and implications for treatment. *Journal of Interpersonal Violence, 3*(2), 203–221.

Dragan, S. M. (1990). The functional dynamics of the narcissistic personality. *American Journal of Psychotherapy, 44*(2), 189–203.

Dube, R., & Hebert, M. (1988). Sexual abuse of children under 12 years of age: A review of 511 cases. *Child Abuse & Neglect, 12*(3), 321–330.

Erickson, M. F. (July, 1991). How often do abused children become child abusers? *Harvard Mental Health Letter,* p. 8.

Faller, K. C. (1989). Characteristics of a clinical sample of sexually abused children: How boy and girl victims differ. *Child Abuse & Neglect, 13*(2), 281–291.

Feldman, M. P., & Mac Culloch, N. J. (1971). *Homosexual behavior: Theory and assessment.* Oxford: Pergamon.

Finkelhor, D. (1979). *Sexually victimized children.* New York: Free Press.

Finkelhor, D. (1984). *Child sexual abuse, new theory and research.* New York: Free Press.

Finkelhor, D., & Araji, S. (1986). Explanations of pedophilia: A four factor model. *Journal of Sex Research, 22*(2).

Finkelhor, D., & Browne, A. (1985). The traumatic impact of child sexual abuse: A conceptualization. *American Journal of Orthopsychiatry, 55*(4).

Fisher, G., & Howell, L. M. (1970). Psychological needs of homosexual pedophiles. *Diseases of the Nervous System, 3* (pp. 623–625).

Fitz, G. S., Stoll, K., & Wagner, N. A. (1981). A comparison of males and females who were sexually molested as children. *Journal of Sex and Marital Therapy, 7,* 54–59.

Ford, S., & Beach, F. A. (1951). *Patterns of sexual behavior.* New York: Perennial Library.

Freeman-Longo, R. E. (1986). The impact of sexual victimization on males. *Child Abuse & Neglect, 10,* 411–414.

Freud, A. (1965). *Normality and pathology in childhood: Assessments of development.* New York: International Universities Press.

Freund, K., Watson, R., & Dickey, R. (1988). *Does sexual abuse in childhood cause pedophilia?* Joint Study of the Department of Behavioral Sexology and the Forensic Division, Clarke Institute of Psychiatry, Toronto, Canada.

Friedrich, W. N. (1990). *Psychotherapy of sexually abused children and their families.* New York: W. W. Norton.

Friedrich, W. N., Beilke, R. L., & Urquiza, A. J. (1988). Behavior problems in young sexually abused boys. *Journal of Interpersonal Violence, 3*(1), 21–28.

Fromuth, M. E., & Burkhart, B. R. (1987). Childhood sexual victimization among college men: Definitional and methodological issues. *Violence and Victims, 2*(4), 241–253.

Froning, M. L. & Mayman, S. B. (1990). Identification and treatment of child and adolescent male victims of sexual abuse. In: Hunter, M. *the sexually abused male, 1.* Lexington, MA: Lexington Books.

Gebhard, P. T., Gagnon, J. H., Pomeroy, W. B., & Christiansen, C. V. (1985). *Sex offenders: An analysis of Types.* New York: Harper & Row.

Geiser, R. L. (1979). *Hidden victims. The sexual abuse of children.* Boston: Beacon Press.

Gerber, P. N. (1990). Victims becoming offenders: A study of ambiguities. In: Hunter, M. *The sexually abused male.* Lexington, MA: Lexington Books.

Gilgun, J. F. (1990). Factors mediating the effects of childhood maltreatment. In: Hunter, L. M. (Ed.). *The sexually abused male.* Lexington, MA: Lexington Books.

Godwin, J. (1985). Post-traumatic symptoms in incest victims. In: Spenser, E. & Pynoos, R. S. (Eds.). *Post-traumatic stress disorder in children.* Washington, D.C.: American Psychiatric Press.

Goldberg, A. (1985). *Progress in self psychology.* New York: Guilford Press.

Goldberg, A. (1985). The definition and role of interpretation. *Progress in Self Psychology 1.* New York: Guilford Press.

Goldman, R. L., & Wheeler, V. R. (1986). *Silent shame: The sexual abuse of children and youth.* Danville, IL: Interstate.

Green, R. G. & Kahn, T. (1989). The malingering adolescent sex offender. *Interchange, January.*

Greenberg, R. (1987). Self-psychology and dreams: The merging of different perspectives. *Psychiatric Journal of the University of Ottawa, 12*(2), 98–102.

Grier, W. H., & Cobbs, P. M. (1968). *Black Rage.* New York: Basic Books.

Groth, A. N. (1979). *Men who rape: The psychology of the offender.* New York: Plenum.

Groth, A. N., Hobson, W. F., & Gary, T. S. (1982). The child molester: Clinical observations. In: Conte, J. & Shore, D. A. (Eds.). *Social work and child sexual abuse* (pp. 129–144). New York: Haworth.

Groth, A. N., & Loredo, C. M. (1981). Juvenile sex offenders: Guidelines for assessment. *International Journal of Offender Therapy and Comparative Criminology, 25*(1), 31–39.

Hall, J. M. (1985). Idealizing transference: Disruptions and repairs. In: Goldberg, A. *Progress in Self Psychology, I.* New York: Guilford Press.

Halpern, J. (1987). Family therapy in father-son incest: A case study. *Social Casework, 68*(2), 88–93.

Harrison, P. A. (1990). Correlates of sexual abuse among boys in treatment for chemical dependency. *Journal of Adolescent Chemical Dependency, 1*(1), 53–67.

Herdt, G. H. (1981). *Guardians of the flutes.* New York: McGraw-Hill.

Herdt, G. H. (Ed.). (1984). Ritualized homosexuality in Melanesia. Berkeley: University of California Press.

Herdt, G. H. (1981). Semen depletion and the sense of maleness. *Ethnopsychiatrica, 3* (pp. 79–116).

Hickey, N. V. (1989). The male sexual abuse victim-offender cycle: An etiological exploration through comparison of case studies (Doctoral dissertation, Rutgers University, 1989). *Dissertation Abstracts International, 51,* 02B.

Hobson, J. A. (1988). *The dreaming brain.* New York: Basic Books.

Howells, K. (1981). Adult sexual interest in children: Considerations relevant to theories of etiology. In: Cook, M. & Howells, K. (Eds.). *Adult Sexual Interest in Children* (pp. 55–94). London: Academic Press.

Hunter, J. A., & Santos, D. R. (1991). The use of specialized cognitive-behavioral therapies in the treatment of adolescent sexual offenders. *International Journal of Offender Therapy and Comparative Criminology, 34*(3), 239–247.

Hunter, M. (Ed.) (1990). *The sexually abused male: Application of treatment strategies* (Vol. 2). Lexington, MA: Lexington Books.

Hunter, R. S. (1985). Sexually abused children: Identifying masked presentations in a medical setting. *Child Abuse & Neglect, 9*(1), 17–25.

Johnson, A. (1975). Sanctions for superego lacunae of adolescents. In: Esman, A. (Ed.). *The psychology of adolescence.* New York: International Universities Press.

Johnson, R. I., & Shrier, D. (1985, September). Sexual Victimization of Boys. *Journal of Adolescent Health Care, 6,* 372–376.

Johnson, R. I., & Shrier, D. (1987). Past sexual victimization by females of male patients in an adolescent medicine clinic population. *American Journal of Psychiatry, 144*(5), 650–652.

Jones, D. P. H. (1986). Individual psychotherapy for the sexually abused child. *Child Abuse & Neglect, 10,* 377–385.

Kallman, F. J. (1952). Comparative twin study on the genetic aspects of male homosexuality. *Journal of Nervous and Mental Diseases, 115,* 283–297.

Kaser-Boyd, N. (1988). Ficticious allegations of sexual abuse in marital dissolutions. *Family Law News, 11,* 50–52.

Katan, A. (1973). Children who are raped. *Psychoanalytic Study of the Child, 28,* 208–224.

Kaufman, J., & Zigler, E. (1987). Do abused children become abusive parents? *American Journal of Orthopsychiatry, 57,* 186–92.

Kelly, R. J. (1982). Behavioral reorientation of pedophiliacs: Can it be done? *Clinical Psychology Review, 2,* 387–408.

Kercher, G., & McShane, M. (1984). Characterizing child sexual abuse on the basis of a multi-agency sample. *Victimology, 9*(3–4), 364–382.

Kernberg, O. F. (1985). *Borderline conditions and pathological narcissism.* New York: Jason Aronson.

Kohut, H. (1984). *How does analysis cure?* Chicago: University of Chicago Press.

Kolko, D. J., & Stauffer, J. (1991). *Child sexual abuse: case studies in family violence.* New York: Plenum.

Knopp, F. H. (1984). *Retraining adult sex offenders: Methods and models.* Orwell, VT: Safer Society Press.

Lambert, R. (1984). *Beloved and God.* New York: Viking.

Langevin, R. (1985). *Erotic preference, gender identity, and aggression in men: new research studies.* Hillsdale, NJ: Lawrence Erlbaum Associates.

Langevin, R., Hucker, S., Handy, L., Purins, J., Russon, A., & Hook, H. (1985). Erotic preference and aggression in pedophilia: A comparison of heterosexual, homosexual, and bisexual types. In: Langevin, R. *Erotic preference, gender identity, and aggression in men: New research studies.* Hillsdale, NJ: Lawrence Erlbaum.

Lanyon, R. I. (1986). Theory and treatment in child molestation. *Journal of Consulting and Clinical Psychology, 54* (2), 176–181.

Le Vay, S. (1991). A difference in hypothalamic structure between heterosexual and homosexual Men. *Science, 253*(5023), 1034–1037.

Lidz, T. & Lidz, R. W. (1989). *Oedipus in the stone age.* Madison, CT: International Universities Press.

Mahler, M. S. (1966). Notes on the development of basic moods: The depressive affect in psychoanalysis. In: *Psychoanalysis — a general psychology: Essays in honor of Heinz Hartmann.* Lowenstein, L. M., Newman, L. M., Schur, M., & Solnit, A. J. (Eds.). New York: International University Press.

Mahler, M. S., Pine, F., & Bergman, A. (1975). *The psychological birth of the human infant.* New York: Basic Books.

Mian, M., Wehrspann, W., Klajner-Diamond, H., LeBaron, D., & Winder, C. (1984). *Review of 125 children 6 years of age and under who were sexually abused.* Toronto: Hospital for Sick Children.

Miller, J. P. (1985). How Kohut actually worked. In: Goldberg, A., *Progress in self psychology* (Vol. 1). New York: Guilford Press.

Money, J. (1965). Psychosexual differentiation. In: *Sex research: new developments.* New York: Holt, Rinehart, & Winston.

Money, J., Hampson, J. C., & Hampson, J. L. (1957). Imprinting and the establishment of gender roles. *Archives of Neurology and Psychiatry, 77,* 333–336.

Murphy, J. E. (1987). *Prevalence of child sexual abuse and consequent victimization in the general population.* Paper presented at the Third National Family Violence Research Conference, University of New Hampshire, Durham.

Murphy, J. E. (1989). *Telephone surveys and family violence: Data from Minnesota.* Paper presented at the Responses to Family Violence Conference, Purdue University, West Lafayette, IN.

Nasjleti, M. (1980). Suffering in silence: The male incest victim. *Child Welfare, 59*(5), 269–275.

Nielsen, T. (1983). Sexual abuse of boys: current perspectives. *Personnel and Guidance Journal, 62*(3), 139–142.

O'Brien, M. J. (1989). *Characteristics of male adolescent sibling incest offenders: preliminary findings.* Orwell, VT: Safer Society Press.

Olson, P. E. (1990). The sexual abuse of boys: A study of the long-term psychological effects. In: Hunter, M. *The sexually abused male* (Vol. 1). Lexington, MA: Lexington Books.

Paz, O. (1961). *The Labyrinth of Solitude.* New York: Grove Press.

Peake, A. (1989). Issues of under-reporting: The sexual abuse of boys. *Educational & Child Psychology, 6*(1), 42–50.

Peters, J. (1976). Children who are victims of sexual assault and the psychology of offenders. *American Journal of Psychotherapy, 30,* 398–421.

Pierce, L. H. (1987). Father-son incest: Using the literature to guide practice. *Social Casework, 68*(2), 67–74.

Pierce, R. & Pierce, L. H. (1985). The sexually abused child: A comparison of male and female victims. *Child Abuse & Neglect, 9,* 191–199.

Porter, E. (1986). *Treating the young male victim of sexual assault: Issues and intervention strategies.* Syracuse, NY: Safer Society Press.

Porter, F. S., Blick, L. C & Sgroi, S. M. (1982). Treatment of the sexually abused child. In: Sgroi, S. M. *Handbook of clinical intervention in child sexual abuse.* Lexington, MA: Lexington Books.

Reinhart, M. A. (1987). Sexually abused boys. *Child Abuse & Neglect, 11,* 229–235.

Risin, L. I., & Koss, M. P. (1987). The sexual abuse of boys. *Journal of Interpersonal Violence, 2*(3), 309–323.

Rogers, C. & Terry, T. (1984). Clinical intervention with boy victims of sexual abuse.

In: Greer, S., & Greer, J. (Eds.). *Victims of sexual aggression* (Vol. I). New York: Van Nostrand Reinhold.

Rogers, C. M., & Thomas, J. N. (1984, May–August). Sexual victimization of children in the U.S.A.: patterns and trends. In: Clinical proceedings of the Children's Hospital National Medical Center, Washington, DC.

Roheim, G. (1974). *Children of the desert.* New York: Basic Books.

Rosenthal, J. A. (1988). Patterns of reported child abuse and neglect. *Child Abuse & Neglect, 12*(2), 263–271.

Rossman, P. (1980). The pederasts. In: Schultz, L. G. (Ed.). *The sexual victimology of youth.* Springfield, IL: Thomas.

Ryan, G. D., & Lane, S. D. (1991). *Juvenile sex offending.* Lexington, MA: Lexington Books.

Salter, A. C. (1988). *Treating child sex offenders and victims.* Newbury Park, CA: Sage.

Schoenfeld, T. (1991). Biology and homosexuality. *Science, 253*(5032), 630.

Sebold, J. (1987, February). Indicators of child sexual abuse in males, *Social Casework, 68*(2), 75–80.

Sgroi, S. M. (1988). *Vulnerable populations: Evaluation & treatment of sexually abused children & adult survivors* (Vol. 1). Lexington, MA: Lexington Books.

Shane, M. (1985). Self psychology's additions to mainstream concepts of defense and resistance. In: Goldberg, A. (Ed.). *Progress in self psychology* (Vol. 1). New York: The Guilford Press.

Shane, M. (1985). Summary of Kohut's The self psychological approach to defense and resistance. In: Goldberg, A. (Ed.). *Progress in self psychology* (Vol. 1). New York: Guilford Press.

Shapiro, S. (1985). Archaic self object transferences in the analysis of a case of male homosexuality. In: Goldberg, A. (Ed.). *Progress in self psychology* (Vol. I). New York: Guilford Press.

Shapiro, S., & Doniniak, G. (1990). Common psychological defenses seen in the treatment of sexually abused adolescents. *American Journal of Psychotherapy, 44*(1).

Shengold, L. (1967). The effects of overstimulation. Rat people. *International Journal of Psychoanalysis, 48,* 403–415.

Showers, J., Farber, E. D., Joseph, J. A., Oshins, L., & Johnson, C. F. (1983). The sexual victimization of boys: A three year survey. *Health Values, 7*(4), 15–18.

Shrier, D. K. (1988). Long-term effects of sexual abuse in boys. *Medical Aspects of Human Sexuality, 22*(9), 34–38.

Skinner, B. F. (1953). *Science and human behavior.* New York: Macmillan.

Spence, J., & Helmreich, R. (1978). *Masculinity and femininity.* Austin: University of Texas Press.

Stoller, R. (1968). *Sex and gender.* New York: Science House.

Stoller, R. (1985). *Observing the erotic imagination.* New Haven: Yale University Press.

Storms, M. D. (1981). A theory of erotic orientation development. *Psychological Review, 88*(3), 40–53.

Strozier, C. B. (1985). Glimpses of a life: Heinz Kohut. In: Goldberg, A. (Ed.). *Progress in self psychology* (Vol. 1). New York: Guilford Press.

Stuart, I. R., & Greer, J. G. (1984). *Victims of sexual aggression: treatment of children, women, and men.* New York: Van Nostrand Reinhold.

Summit, R. (1983). The child sexual abuse accomodation syndrome. *Child Abuse & Neglect, 7,* 177–193.

Swan, R. (1985). The child as an active participant in sexual abuse. *Clinical Social Work Journal, 14*(1), 62–77.

Sykes, D. K., (1987). An approach to working with black youth in cross cultural therapy. *Clinical Social Work Journal, 15*(3), 260–270.

Thio, A. (1978). *Deviant behavior.* Boston: Houghton-Mifflin.

Tolpin, P. (1985). The primacy of the preservation of the self. In: Goldberg, A. (Ed.). *Progress in self psychology* (Vol. 1). New York: Guilford Press.

Troy, M., & Sroufe, L. A. (1987). Victimization among preschoolers: Role of attachment relationship history. *Journal of the American Academy of Child and Adolescent Psychiatry, 26*(2), 166–172.

Tyson, P. A. (1982). Developmental line of gender identity, gender role and choice of love object. *Journal of the American Psychoanalytic Association, 30,* 61–68.

Tyson, P. A. (1986). Male gender identity. Early developmental roots. *Psychoanalytic Review, 73,* 1–21.

Urquiza, A. L. (1988). *The effects of childhood sexual abuse in an adult male population.* Unpublished doctoral dissertation, University of Washington, Seattle.

Urquiza, A. L., & Keating, L. M. (1990). The prevalence of sexual victimization of males. In: Hunter, M. *The sexually abused male* (Vol. 1). Lexington, MA: Lexington Books.

Vander Mey, B. J. (1988). The sexual victimization of male children: A review of previous research. *Child Abuse and Neglect, 123,* 671–672.

Vander Mey, B. J. & Neff, R. L. (1986). *Incest as child abuse: research and applications.* New York: Praeger.

Wallace, W. J. (1978). Southern valley Yokuts. In: Heizer, R. *Handbook of North American indians, California* (Vol. 8). Washington, DC: Smithsonian Institution.

Weisz, J. R., Weiss, B., Alicke, M. D. & Klotz, M. L. (1987). Effectiveness of psychotherapy with children and adolescents: A meta-analysis for clinicians. *Journal of Consulting and Clinical Psychology, 55,* 542–549.

Whitam, F. L., & Mathy, R. M. (1986). *Male homosexuality in four societies.* New York: Praeger.

White, R. L. (1985). *The first three years of life.* New York: Prentice-Hall.

Whittemore, K. D. (1990). Perceptions of Juvenile sexual abuse: Gender issues in diagnosis and treatment. *Dissertation Abstracts International, 51,* 03B. (University Microfilms No. 90-22, 326)

Williams, M. (1988). Father-son incest: A review and analysis of reported incidents. *Clinical Social Work Journal, 16*(2), 165–179.

Winson, J. *Brain and Psyche.* (1985). Garden City, New York: Anchor/Doubleday.

Wolfe, B. (1985). The costs of compliance: A patient's response to the conditions of psychotherapy. In: Goldberg, A. *Progress in self psychology* (Vol. I). New York: Guilford Press.

INDEX